THE MEDIA WAR AGAINST THE JEWS

ANTI-ZIONISM *is* ANTI-SEMITISM

#1 *NEW YORK TIMES* BESTSELLING AUTHOR

MIKE EVANS

P.O. BOX 30000, PHOENIX, AZ 85046

Anti-Zionism Is Antisemitism:
The Media War Against the Jews

Copyright © 2025 by Time Worthy Books
P. O. Box 30000
Phoenix, AZ 85046

Unless otherwise indicated, scripture references are taken from
The Holy Bible, New International Version®, NIV®
Copyright ©1973, 1978, 1984, 2011 by Biblica, Inc.®
Used by permission. All rights reserved worldwide."

Scripture quotations marked ASV are taken from
The Holy Bible, American Standard Version.
Copyright © 1901 by Public Domain

Scripture quotations marked ESV are taken from
The Holy Bible, English Standard Version,
copyright © 2001 by Crossway Bibles, a division of
Good News Publishers. Used by permission. All rights reserved.

Scripture quotations marked KJV are from the
King James Version of the Bible.

Scripture quotations marked NASB are taken from the
New American Standard Bible.
Copyright © 1960, 1962, 1963, 1968, 1971, 1972, 1973, 1975, 1977, 1995
by The Lockman Foundation. Used by permission. www.Lockman.org

Scripture quotations marked NKJV are taken from the
New King James Version, Copyright © 1982
by Thomas Nelson, Inc. Used by permission. All rights reserved.

Scripture quotations marked NLT are taken from the
Holy Bible, New Living Translation.
Copyright © 1996, 2004, 2007. Used by permission of Tyndale House
Publishers Inc., Carol Stream, Illinois 60188. All rights reserved.

Scripture quotations marked RSV are taken from the
Revised Standard Version of the Bible. Copyright © 1946, 1952, and 1971
the Division of Christian Education of the National Council
of the Churches of Christ in the United States of America.
Used by permission. All rights reserved.

Hardcover: 978-1-62961-235-5
Paperback: 978-1-62961-236-2
eBook: 978-1-62961-237-9

All rights reserved. No portion of this book may be reproduced, stored in
a retrieval system, or transmitted in any form or by any means—electronic, mechanical,
photocopy, recording, or any other—except for brief quotations in printed reviews,
without the prior permission of the publisher.

I dedicate this book to
my cherished friend of 45 years,
Prime Minister Benjamin Netanyahu.

The State of Israel was surrounded by a ring of fire.
Through his leadership, Israel has vanquished
its enemies in Syria, in Lebanon, in Gaza, in Yemen,
and even in Iran.

It's a story of biblical proportion.

I first met Benjamin on the 4th of July, 1980,
when he was grieving the death of his brother Jonathan,
who was killed leading the Entebbe Raid to Uganda.

And I prayed this prayer over him:

Jonathan loved David, you loved Jonathan.
Out of the ashes of your despair will come
strength from God, and you will be the
Prime Minister of Israel. The following day,
I told the prophecy to then Prime Minister
Menachem Begin, and told him to give him
a job in the government. He did.

CONTENTS

Foreword: Author's Note 7

1. October 7 Changed Everything 9
2. The Ugliness of Antisemitism 27
3. Antisemitism in the Twentieth Century 39
4. The Struggle Continues 53
5. Israel, God's Dream 67
6. The Blessings and Curses of God 79
7. Jerusalem, the Center of God's Plan 95
8. Jerusalem's Spiritual Significance 109
9. Comfort Israel 123
10. The Example of Corrie ten Boom 139
11. God Has Preserved Israel 153
12. Reviving Ishmael 163
13. Exporting Hate 185
14. Treason 205
15. The Media War Against Israel 229
16. The Battle Lines Are Drawn 241
17. The New Antisemitism 265

A Final Word: 5 Reasons to Stand with Israel 287
Appendix: Prayers and Blessings for Israel 291
Endnotes 299

FOREWORD

AUTHOR'S NOTE

I've been combating anti-Semitism since the age of 11, when my father strangled me after I tried to defend my Jewish mother from his abuse. My father was a professing Christian. He was a racist who used to say almost every day, the Jews are running the country, and the blacks are ruining it.

The current rates of antisemitism and anti-Zionism are the highest I've witnessed in my life.

As I was writing this book, a young couple, both Israeli diplomats from the Washington, D.C. Embassy, were gunned down in cold blood outside the Capitol Jewish Museum in Washington, D.C. Yaron Lashinsky, an Israeli citizen, and Sarah Milgram, I knew both of them.

Second, I'm thinking, the Jew-haters have tried to redefine their Jew-hatred in terms of, under the theme of Zionism. A former president of Iran, Mahmoud Ahmadinejad, told me, I like Jews, but I hate Zionists.

He went on to say that the Zionists live to be 82 and Iranians 62. And the reason why is that the Zionists infect rats with poison, send the rats to our crops, we eat the food, and die 20 years younger. I looked at him and said, "Is this a joke?" He said, "No, I don't joke."

It's true. You should read the Protocols of the Elders of Zion, and you would understand it.

It might sound humorous that a man could say such a thing, but it's not. Because this is a nation that's on the verge of having a nuclear bomb, that believes they can usher in the Mahdi, an Islamic messiah, through an apocalypse against the state of Israel.

Billions of dollars have been invested in university campuses in America by Jew haters to poison the minds of the young generation against the state of Israel.

It's an ideological war that has spread like a plague through social media. But it can't be won only with the truth.

CHAPTER ONE

October 7 Changed Everything

On October 7, 2023, Hamas terrorists killed over 1,200 Israelis on the 50th anniversary of the Yom Kippur War. The attacks marked the single greatest act of violence against Jews since the Holocaust, with Israel immediately declaring war against the terror group.

Over 250 hostages from a dozen nations were taken into Gaza by Hamas. Most were Israeli, including women, children, infants, and elderly. Over 70 have since been killed as of this writing. In the following weeks, some were released in hostage exchanges with terrorists, but more than 139 remained held, with the bodies of some found as Israeli Defense Forces took control of Hamas locations.

Hostages from a dozen nations were taken, including 30 Americans who died in the attacks, with 10 taken hostage.

ANTI-ZIONISM *is* ANTI-SEMITISM

The news of the number of American hostages was not released until the first US hostage was freed in a hostage exchange nearly two months later.

As Israel called up reservists and warned civilians in Gaza to flee to safe areas ahead of ground assaults, pro-Palestinian protests launched worldwide, calling for an immediate cease-fire. Protesters stopped traffic on bridges in New York and San Francisco, while others were arrested storming the Capitol in Washington.

At elite college campuses in the US, academic leaders justified the brutal actions of Hamas, equating rape with resistance. Some were criticized, and at least one university president resigned after calls against her antisemitic rhetoric. College presidents at Harvard, Columbia, and U Penn resigned over anti-Israel rhetoric, while others remain under pressure.

A new distinction also became popular during this time. To avoid the label of antisemitism, those on the left made a distinction between anti-Zionism and antisemitism. Anti-Zionism is the view that opposes Zionism, or the belief that the Jewish people have the right to establish their own nation. While the distinction became popular among many liberals, the view does not escape an antisemitic worldview.

Jewish conservative commentator Dennis Prager rightly critiqued this view by the illustration of another nation:

> Imagine a group of people who work to destroy Italy because, they claim, Italy's origins are illegitimate. Imagine further that these people maintain

that of all the countries in the world, only Italy doesn't deserve to exist. Then imagine that these people vigorously deny that they are anti-Italian. Would you believe them?

Now substitute "Israel" for "Italy," and you'll understand the dishonesty and absurdity of the argument that one can be anti-Zionist—that is, against the existence of a Jewish state—but not be anti-Jew.

Yet, that is precisely what anti-Zionists say. They say that Israel's existence is illegitimate. They don't say this about any other country in the world, no matter how bloody its origins. And then they get offended when they're accused of being anti-Jew.[1]

This is precisely the argument the mainstream media often makes in referring to Israel as an apartheid state, comparing it with the racism of South Africa of the last century. Rather than affirming the right of the Jewish people to live in their historical homeland and establish a nation, the media and political left argue for either a so-called two-state solution or even advocate for removing Israel from the map.

I once spoke with a former chief of staff at the White House and asked him what determines when a war begins and ends. He looked at me and said, "The media does." I saw the power of the media during the Vietnam War turn public opinion to such a degree that soldiers like myself were spit upon and called baby killers. I was a medic. I never shot anyone. I only saved lives, and I wasn't even in Vietnam. I was in Korea.

The founding international chairman of Friends of Zion Heritage Center, the late President of Israel, His Excellency Shimon Peres, told me decades ago that the new wars of the 21st century would be media wars, economic wars, ideological wars, and proxy wars. Israel is fighting all four of these wars. And no, they are not winning the media war. Israel has little media influence. They don't have an Al Jazeera, CNN, or Fox News.

Israel is also fighting an economic war. The war with Hamas will cost Israel 10 percent of its GDP in just the first year. Only God knows how catastrophic the damage could be to the State of Israel if Iran's northern proxy, Hezbollah, engages Israel in full-scale war or Israel has to confront Iran directly.

Israel cannot win an ideological war either. Hamas can be defeated, but the ideology of Hamas, which is fundamentally Jew-hatred, will still be alive. And demons do not clear customs. The terrorist state Iran wreaks havoc upon the world, funding war through terror proxy regimes. It is the only terror regime in the world that gets free media like a Jerry Lewis telethon.

The terrorists post their videos and images on social media, and hundreds of millions of dollars pour in. It makes no difference what the truth is. The media quotes statistics from the Hamas-controlled Gaza Ministry of Health as if they are the truth. This is the same Hamas organization that beheaded women and children and raped and burned teenage girls alive in the worst massacre in Israel's history. Hamas uses Palestinians as human shields, firing missiles from hospitals, schools, the backyards of homes in residential neighborhoods, and in mosques, hoping that Israel will retaliate. Yet, the media won't call them terrorists. Instead, the mainstream media reports virtually everything they say unfiltered and unopposed.

The truth is more accurately presented in the audio transcript released by one Hamas terrorist who called his parents in Gaza on October 7. I listened to the conversation in absolute horror:

> TERRORIST: Hello, dad. Dad I am inside Mefalsim. Open your WhatsApp right now and see all the Jews I killed. Look at how many I killed with my own hands; your son killed Jews.
>
> FATHER: Allahu Akhbar, Allahu Akhbar. May God protect you.
>
> TERRORIST: I am talking to you from the phone of a Jew; I killed her and her husband. I killed ten with my own hands.
>
> FATHER: Allahu Akhbar.
>
> TERRORIST: Open your phone and see how many I killed, father. Open your phone, I am calling you on WhatsApp.
>
> FATHER: Crying (unintelligible).
>
> TERRORIST: I am in Meflasim, father. I killed ten. Ten! Ten with my own bare hands. Their blood is on my hands. Let me talk to Mom.

TERRORIST: *I killed ten all by myself, mother.*

FATHER: *May God bring you home safely.*

TERRORIST: *Father, go back to WhatsApp! I want to call you live from Mefalsim.*

MOTHER: *I wish I was there with you.*

TERRORIST: *Mother, your son is a hero. I was the first to enter under the guidance and with the help of Allah. Father, lift your head, lift your head. (Talking to terrorists on the scene: Kill! Kill! Kill! Kill them! Inside, inside, into the city.)*

BROTHER: *Mahmoud, Mahmoud. Come back [to Gaza], that's enough, return.*

TERRORIST: *Return? There is no return; it is victory or martyrdom. My mother gave birth to me for Islam, Allah. Are you serious? How will I return? Look at WhatsApp, look at your phone, look at all the killed.*

Captured terrorists confess they were promised $10,000 and a new house for every Jewish hostage and for killing Jews. This is the terrifying yet accurate truth about the events of October 7. The attacks were the equivalent of Israel's Pearl Harbor or 9/11. For weeks, every day in Israel consisted of funeral after funeral as families grieved the loss of loved ones at the hands of Hamas terrorists.

Iran directly supports Hamas. Iran has been waging a war against what it calls the "Little Satan," Israel, for decades. Iran has been waging a war against the "Great Satan," America. On October 23, 1983, I preached the gospel to the Marines in Beirut, giving them the Christmas gift of a small Bible. A young soldier, 18, from Worcester, Massachusetts, asked me if I could send a message to his mom. So, I had my camera crew tape it. He said, "Dear Mom, I know you've been praying for me. I won't be coming home for Christmas. But I have a Christmas gift for you. I've just accepted Jesus Christ as my personal Savior. Merry Christmas, Mom."

That Marine and 240 others were dead in the morning. I slept on the beach that night.

Since then, Iran has conducted ongoing attacks on numerous countries in a long-term effort to exert influence in the region. A 2021 State Department report observed that in that year alone, "Iran pursued or supported terrorist attacks against Israeli targets . . . including a thwarted January plot to attack an Israeli embassy in East Africa, a January bomb attack outside the Israeli embassy in New Delhi for which the Indian government said the IRGC-QF was responsible, and a disrupted attempt to attack an Israeli businessman in Cyprus."

The United States presently has the USS Eisenhower Carrier Strike Group in the Red Sea south of Israel, including an array of weapons and 5,000 sailors. The US also has a nuclear-powered Ohio-class submarine in the area, the Ford Carrier Strike Group in the Mediterranean Sea, which includes three ballistic missile defense ships and four additional warships. The Pentagon deployed 1,200 additional troops to the Middle East since October 7 to act as a deterrent and protect 45,000 US service members and contractors throughout the Middle East.

Despite the show of force, Iran has attacked US troops over 40 times since October 7. A reported 56 US military personnel have been injured. The US has responded with airstrikes hitting targets in Syria and over 800 targets in Yemen. Yet God continues to work in powerful ways despite the tragedies of recent days. During one of my many trips to Israel following the October 7 attacks, I spoke with four individuals who told amazing stories of divine intervention.

I heard a story of a woman whose kibbutz was attacked by Hamas terrorists. She lifted her hands and started declaring in the mighty name of the Lord that God would blind their eyes. They were entering her room, another room where her mother was, and a third room where the grandchild was. The terrorists went up to all three doors with their weapons but didn't open any of the doors, nor did they fire through any of them. When the Israeli military came, they saw the deaths of many near her home, and she told the story of lifting her hands and crying out to God.

Another woman in Jerusalem was in a terror attack. As the terrorists were firing in her direction, she shouted out loud in Hebrew Psalm 121. It says, "The Lord will keep you from all harm—he will watch over your life" (v. 7). Not a bullet touched her.

A third soldier told the story that his battalion was in a line late at night, going into a highly explosive area, when suddenly he saw a dove flying towards his face. He thought he was seeing things because he had hardly slept for 36 hours. Suddenly, a dove stopped within a foot of his face in midair. He felt he was imagining the dove, so he stuck his rifle out to poke in the direction of the dove. At that moment, he realized the dove was perched on a tripwire. Had it not been for the dove, he would have hit the tripwire, detonating enough C4 explosives to kill his entire battalion.

Another soldier was eating a can of tuna fish. He struck a match to some oil to warm the tuna fish, and it caught on fire. He threw it down into a nearby tunnel shaft, not realizing it contained explosives. It blew up the explosives, and all the terrorists came out of the tunnel, surrendering over his can of tuna fish!

Another soldier had the book of Psalms in his front pocket by his heart. When terrorists shot at him during the battle, a bullet lodged into the book of Psalms and saved his life.

God continues to protect His people, sometimes in miraculous ways. But the battle is far from over. As I write these words, I've just finished a project in Jerusalem during the eight days of Hanukkah, as Friends of Zion hosted eight nights of hope and healing for the suffering nation. I sensed the Spirit of God say to me, "Thou shalt arise and have compassion on Zion, for it is time to show favor to her; the appointed time has come" (Psalm 102:13, KJV).

Israel is under attack by Iran and its demon-possessed proxies. This battle has continued for 6,000 years since the day Abraham pitched his tent on Mount Sinai and made a covenant with God, but I've never seen the battle as fierce as it is at this present moment.

On October 7, the codename for the attacks by Hamas was the Al-Aqsa Flood after the Al-Aqsa Mosque on the Temple Mount. This is where Satan declared that he would exalt himself above the Most High (Isaiah 14:13). Despite the agony Israel is going through, I can hear the prophet Zechariah crying out, "I will set out to destroy all the nations that attack Jerusalem" (12:9, NIV).

Israel is a tiny country about the size of New Jersey, the fifth smallest state in the US. The survivors of the Holocaust poured into Israel as human skeletons, crying and rejoicing as Israel was reborn in March of 1948. But two months later, on May 14, Israel was attacked. The Jewish people believed that neither they nor their children would ever again experience what they had experienced. But they did on October 7.

The prophet Zechariah warned that whoever touches you touches the apple of God's eye (Zechariah 2:8). Israel was born out of a divine land grant from God Almighty to the descendants of Abraham, Isaac, and Jacob when He made a covenant with them. It was a gift from God. The greatest significance of Israel is its spiritual significance. "The law will go out from Zion, the word of the Lord from Jerusalem" (Isaiah 2:3). Then the Lord said to David and us and Solomon, his son, "In this temple and in Jerusalem, which I have chosen out of all the tribes of Israel, I will put my Name forever" (2 Kings 21:7, NIV).

Israel is God's dream. The title deed belongs to Him. A spirit of antisemitism has swept the globe in a way that I've never seen in my lifetime. You and I cannot be silent.

Shortly after the October 7 attacks, I held a special prayer event at Friends of Zion for the families of the soldiers who had given their lives fighting against Hamas. I held in my arms a grieving mother and father whose 27-year-old son, Ariel, rushed into the massacre to save dozens of lives. He went into a shelter where more than 30 terrified young people were lying on the ground, covering their heads in panic as terrorists were trying to break in. Ariel stood up and said, "It's going to be okay. I'm going to save you." The terrorists threw a grenade into the shelter. Ariel picked it up and threw it back at the terrorists. They threw a second one, and he did the same thing, and a third and a fourth and a fifth and a sixth, but on the seventh, the grenade blew up and killed him. He saved many lives, yet lost his own, leaving behind a grieving family and friends.

Another precious mother and father attended with their 10-year-old daughter and a notebook. In the notebook, their beloved 20-year-old son wrote long letters to each family member, including one to his 10-year-old sister.

The letter began with, "Dear Mom and Dad, I know that family is everything and the most important thing. You're my whole world. I love you so much. I'm willing to go to battle despite the great risk of going into the war, knowing that I might not come back, but I believe wholeheartedly in what I'm doing for the nation of Israel and its people. We have no other country. I must defend it. I must defend the babies, the elderly, and the helpless against this inferno of Hamas."

This young Israeli soldier gave his life in service to his nation. After I read the letter, I held the family member, and we all cried. There have been so many widows and orphans from these attacks. I've never felt such a broken heart, but I know the heart of God is broken, too.

Like Esther, we have come into the kingdom for such a time as this. Satan has tried time and time again to wipe the Jews off the planet. Pharaoh attempted it. Hitler attempted it. Now, Iran is on the brink of going nuclear and is attempting it. You and I, as Israel's last line of defense, must do everything humanly possible to help. There's never been a time in my life when our ministry has done more for the nation of Israel. I can tell you the people of Israel are very grateful, but the battle is not over yet.

For me, the battle against anti-Zionism and antisemitism is personal. I have been the target of an assassination. Richard Snell, a member of The Covenant, The Sword and the Arm of the Lord—a white supremacist—aimed to take me off this Earth.[2] On June 30, 1984, while I was working with Israeli Prime Minister Menachem Begin, Snell attempted to assassinate me because I supported Israel and the Jewish people's right to a state in their historic homeland.

Sadly, Richard Snell was labeled as a Christian extremist, even though he was not a real Christian. Real Christians believe in the promise, the truth that God has given the land of Israel to the Jewish people. Real Christians are friends of Israel and friends of the Jewish people.

Snell believed that the United States was being taken over by the Jewish people and other minorities at the expense of "white Americans." My father was also an anti-Semite who cursed the Jewish people and believed in anti-Jewish conspiracy theories. Their ideology is ignorant and intolerant at best; the Jewish community is one of the biggest success stories in American assimilation. American Jews serve in public service roles nationwide and play an active and positive role in the country's future. The Jewish community, a tiny minority in the United States, has always contributed more to society than is possibly known.

In my experience, I have faced too many Christians who are not educated on the Christian's real role in assisting the Jewish people. That is why I have dedicated my life to defending Israel and the Jewish people. I do this by meeting with world leaders to speak about how they can engage and support Israel. In 2015, I founded the Friends of Zion Heritage Center, a $100 million project that helps educate Christians and pro-Israel supporters worldwide about the Jewish state, its challenges, and achievements. The Friends of Zion has also become one of the central institutions in the state of Israel, influencing the world and strengthening Israel's relations globally while fortifying the pillars of Israeli society.

Yet much work remains. Even near my own home, anti-semitism has been deadly. In January 2022, I woke up Saturday morning to drive down Pleasant Run, near where I live, to my favorite Starbucks.[3] As I drove, I passed Congregation Beth Israel as I do every morning. It was around 11 a.m. I am very familiar with the congregation and have participated in many of their services online through Facebook, but suddenly, I saw police cars rushing in every direction on Pleasant Run.

I asked someone nearby what was happening and was told there was a terrorist on Pleasant Run at the Beth Israel synagogue who was threatening to blow it up. The man, later identified as a 44-year-old UK citizen named Malik Faisal Arkram, reportedly had a bomb and held four Jews as hostages.

More than 200 local, state, and federal law enforcement officers converged on the Beth Israel synagogue. The terrorist had been making statements that were going out live on Facebook from the synagogue that he would be going to Jannah, the Muslim concept of heaven. He was shouting about dying and not liking police officers or Jews.

As this crisis was ongoing, I received several WhatsApp messages from Rabbi Goldstein from California, who was also a victim of terrorism in his Poway synagogue. I provided security for the first year for his synagogue after the attack, and he and I have become great friends.

Why would such a thing happen? The answer is simple: Antisemitism. It's being fueled and fed, and it gets Jews killed. Facebook took down the live stream from the sanctuary after being asked by the federal authorities, but there's also another group that Facebook took down.

I spent $5.5 million and five years recruiting young Muslims to my Facebook page, the Jerusalem Prayer Team, attempting to win their hearts and minds before they were poisoned with Jew hatred. All of the hundreds of ads we purchased were approved by Facebook before Facebook took our money and ran the ads. We grew our Facebook site from over 30 million to 77 million likes, one of the largest Facebook pages in the world.

The goal was only to combat antisemitism, but when antisemites began waging war against the State of Israel during the Gaza conflict in May 2021, telling unspeakable lies, I organized a Facebook event with the Rev. Franklin Graham, former presidential candidate and now US Ambassador to Israel, Mike Huckabee, actors Jon Voight and Pat Boone, pastors Jack Graham and Robert Jeffress, and Christian Broadcasting Network President Gordon Robertson, but Facebook shut our page down.

In 72 hours, more than 2.1 million antisemitic, Jew-hating threats were posted on our page. Some of them included death threats. An individual in Jordan claimed that he did it, bragging about it on Islamic social media and in Islamic newspapers. But instead of Facebook punishing the perpetrator, they punished the victim.

After several months of appeals, Facebook put our page back up but told us they were removing all our followers in certain Muslim countries. They said all the people we recruited were inauthentic, even though they approved every ad. I was later informed that the Pakistani government was complaining to Facebook.

By the way, it was a man originally from Pakistan who was the terrorist who attacked the Colleyville synagogue. Antisemitism doesn't begin with a gun in the hands of a terrorist. It begins with young children being brainwashed to hate Jews. Some of them are not Muslims, like the ones who attacked the Tree of Life synagogue in Pittsburgh and the Chabad of Poway synagogue in California, but the vast majority are Muslims.

We must acknowledge the root of the problem and stop the media terror. The media often fuels antisemitism and lionizes these demon-possessed individuals. Terrorism is the only group in the world that gets free media. Everyone else must pay for it. The founder of Israeli intelligence, Isser Harel, described it this way. "You kill a fly and rejoice. We kill one, and 100 come to the funeral." You can be sure there'll be many more recruited who want to become martyrs and be famous. We must stop media terror by cutting it off at its roots.

The sad and inexplicable truth is this: Antisemitism is alive and well on planet Earth, and the United States is not immune. On Oct. 27, 2018, those who love the Jewish people mourned a massive assault by an antisemite. No, it was not on the streets of Jerusalem, Tel Aviv, or another Israeli city. It was in a quiet neighborhood in Pittsburgh, Pennsylvania, on a cool Shabbat morning. Over the centuries, nothing has assuaged that which erupted the moment God declared a covenant with Abraham and his offspring.

The modern-day perpetrator was Robert Bowers. According to police reports, he armed himself with an AR-15 rifle and three handguns, walked into Pittsburgh's Tree of Life Synagogue, and opened fire on its unsuspecting congregants. Included among the 11 dead were a 97-year-old woman, a husband and wife, and two brothers. Among the wounded were four police officers who had responded to the call of "shots fired" in the neighborhood that housed the synagogue. Bowers has reportedly told police interviewers that he just wanted "to kill Jews."

Did that incident shock the American public into shunning antisemitism and its horrendous effects? Unfortunately, the answer is no. For me, all of this is very personal. My mother named me after her grandfather, Rabbi Mikel Katznelson. In the early 1900s, a rabid and bigoted mob burned him to death inside his synagogue in Belarus, along with 2,000 Jewish men, women, and children.

Many people have asked me why I built the Friends of Zion Heritage Center and Museum in Jerusalem. The answer is quite simple: to combat Jew hatred. My work began when I was 11 years old. My father, an antisemite, beat my Jewish mother, declaring her to be a whore. My father, a Jewish man, insisted I was not his son.

My greatest shame was that I could not protect my mother, and when I tried, my father picked me up by the neck and nearly strangled me. At that early age, I knew that my life's work would be to defend the Jewish people.

Anti-Zionism has been an Ebola virus of antisemitism. The sickness has mutated from the pogroms, the Nazi Party, and Hitler, and now it's being fueled and fed by radical Islam. In this book, we'll consider the history of antisemitism, evaluate this form of Jew-hatred based on Scripture and historical accounts, and look at the inspiring ways God has worked through His Chosen People and many Friends of Zion who have stepped out in faith to support the Jewish people in times of need.

CHAPTER TWO

THE UGLINESS OF ANTISEMITISM

O you who love the LORD, hate evil!
—PSALM 97:10, ESV

In 1922, Hitler declared the Jewish people to be Germany's number one enemy, the race accountable for not some but all the nation's internal problems. He strongly stressed what he saw as "the antisemitism of reason" that must lead "to the systematic combating and elimination of Jewish privileges. Its ultimate goal must implacably be the total removal of the Jews."[4] He was so convinced Germany was near collapse that he joined forces with nationalist leader General Erich Friedrich Wilhelm Ludendorff in an attempted coup.

The ensuing riot that began in a Munich beer hall resulted in: 1) the deaths of sixteen individuals, 2) the Nazi Party being outlawed, and 3) Hitler being tried and sentenced to five years in prison. His sentence was commuted to nine months, but during his incarceration, he dictated a draft of *Mein Kampf* (My Struggle) to Rudolf Hess, a devoted sycophant. The tome—filled with a coarse, ill-conceived jumble of antisemitism, fabrication, and fantasy, evolved into the bible of the emerging Nazi Party. By 1939, this hodgepodge of pretense had sold five million volumes and been translated into eleven languages.

It was also in 1922 that Hitler outlined his plan fully in a conversation with a friend, appropriately named Joseph Hell:

> If I am ever really in power, the destruction of the Jews will be my first and most important job. As soon as I have power, I shall have gallows after gallows erected, for example, in Munich on the Marienplatz—as many of them as traffic allows. Then the Jews will be hanged one after another, and they will stay hanging until they stink. They will stay hanging as long as hygienically possible. As soon as they are untied, then the next group will follow, and that will continue until the last Jew in Munich is exterminated. Exactly the same procedure will be followed in other cities until Germany is cleansed of the last Jew![5]

Philosopher Houston Stewart Chamberlain wrote to encourage Hitler in a letter dated October 7, 1923. He zealously advised the Führer that he was perceived as the "opposite of a politician

... for the essence of all politics is membership of a party, whereas with you, all parties disappear, consumed by the heat of your love for the fatherland."[6] In a later missive to Hitler, Chamberlain asserted:

> One cannot simultaneously embrace Jesus and those who crucified him. This is the splendid thing about Hitler—his courage. In this respect, he reminds one of [Martin] Luther.[7]

It is quite obvious from his writings that Chamberlain also viewed Jewish industrialists as Germany's "public enemy No. 1."

The Germans made a disastrous error in judgment in 1925: They removed the prohibition against the Nazi Party and granted permission for Hitler to address the public. Moreover, when he needed it most to expand the reach of the party, a worldwide economic crisis enveloped Germany. Ironically, the resulting magnitude of unemployment, panic, and anger afforded Hitler the opportunity to step forward and claim the role of savior of the nation. On January 30, 1933, President Paul von Hindenburg persuaded the Weimar Republic of Germany to nominate Hitler as Reich Chancellor. Germany had lost its last chance to avoid a Second World War—and the Holocaust.

Hitler's determination to outfox his opponents and remove conservatives from any role in the government took little time or effort. He abolished free trade unions, removed Communists, Social Democrats, and Jews from any participation in politics, and consigned his rivals to concentration camps. He solidified his hold on Germany in March 1933 using persuasive argument, indoctrination, fear, and coercion. The façade was firmly in place, and the people of Germany were soon intimidated into subjugation.

With the death of von Hindenburg in August of 1934, the Third Reich had a determined dictator who held the reins of Führer and chancellor, as well as all the powers of state accorded to a leader. He abandoned the Treaty of Versailles, conscripted a massive army, supplied it with war materiel, and, in 1938, forced the British and French into signing the Munich Agreement. Soon to follow were laws against Jews, the promotion of concentration camps, the destruction of the state of Czechoslovakia, the invasion of Poland, and a non-aggression pact with the USSR. The only obstacles standing between Hitler and the rest of the world were President Franklin D. Roosevelt, Prime Minister Winston Churchill, and General Secretary of the Central Committee of the Communist Party of the Soviet Union Joseph Stalin, along with the armies of Western civilization.

Just one week after Franklin D. Roosevelt was sworn in for his initial term, German laborers had completed Dachau, the original Nazi concentration camp. Within its confines, some 40,000 individuals would be murdered, most of them Jews. Hitler would follow the opening of the camp by nationalizing the Gestapo and bringing it under his full control. Just three months later, he had successfully combined all commands under the aegis of the Nazi Party.

In 1935, the Nuremberg Laws were instituted, and German Jews lost their citizenship with its rights and privileges. They were then totally under the cruel fist of Hitler and his rabid Jew hatred. Like many of the Jews in the earlier days of Hitler's rule, Roosevelt, too, was deceived by the picture presented to the world at the 1936 Olympics. American historian and author Deborah Lipstadt wrote:

> The sports competition was a massive exercise in propaganda and public relations, and many American reporters were uncritical about all that they saw. . . . Americans, particularly non-German speaking ones who only knew Germany from the Games—departed convinced that the revolutionary upheavals, random beatings, and the murders of political opponents had been greatly exaggerated or were a thing of the past. Those bedazzled included not only the athletes and tourists, but personages such as newspaper publisher Norman Chandler and numerous American businessmen. This period marked the beginning of Charles Lindbergh's love affair with the Reich. One reporter was convinced that as a result of the Games, visitors would be . . . inclined to dismiss all anti-German thought and action abroad as insipid and unjust. [The visitor] sees no Jewish heads being chopped off, or even roundly cudgeled. . . . The people smile, are polite,

and sing with gusto at the beer gardens. Visitors to Berlin described it as a warm, hospitable place and Germany as a country well on its way to solving the economic and unemployment problems which still plagued America.[8]

While Hitler was making plans to wreak havoc in Europe, the Jewish community in 1938 Jerusalem was trying to persuade the British to increase immigration quotas. The British, however, saw increased allotments only as putting a match to the Arab fuse—a short one at that. So we read the agonizing accounts of Jewish refugees struggling to escape Hitler's iron fist, only to perish in the waters of the Mediterranean in unseaworthy ships that could find no safe harbor.

As events of the mid-to-late 1930s led ominously toward a Second World War, the Nazis under Hitler had already been searching for a "final solution" for what they considered the Jewish problem.

On January 20, 1942, Hitler's architects of death met at the beautiful Wannsee Villa located in a serene lakeside suburb of Berlin. Their stated objective was to find a "Final Solution to the Jewish Question."

Presiding over the conference was SS Lieutenant General Reinhard Heydrich, chief of the Security Police and Security Service. As the meeting began, Heydrich was determined that none should doubt his superiority or authority, which was not limited by geographical borders. He briefed those in the room on measures that had already been taken in an attempt to eradicate the Jews from both the German culture and homeland.

Fourteen high-ranking German military and government leaders, including Adolf Eichmann, were in attendance. Over a 90-minute luncheon, fifteen men changed the world forever. After years of this continuous rhetoric, it took a mere ninety minutes for Adolf Hitler's henchmen to determine the fate of six million Jews. During that period, roughly what it would take to drive from Jerusalem to Tel Aviv during peak traffic time, the Holocaust became a heinous reality. January 20, 2012, marked the 70th anniversary of that fateful conference. We dare not let these dubious anniversaries pass without marking how little time it takes to alter the course of history.

Initially, steps had been implemented to allow German Jews to immigrate to whatever countries would accept them, but the move proved to be too slow for the Führer and the Reich. Now, the men gathered to implement Hitler's new solution. Heydrich provided a list of the number of Jews in each country; a total of eleven million Jews were to be involved. In his zeal, he determined:

> In large, single-sex labor columns, Jews fit to work will work their way eastward constructing roads. Doubtless, the large majority will be eliminated by natural causes. Any final remnant that survives will doubtless consist of the most resistant elements. They will have to be dealt with appropriately

because, otherwise, by natural selection, they would form the germ cell of a new Jewish revival.⁹

Translation: All must die.

According to the minutes of the meeting, Jews were to be purged, beginning in Germany, Bohemia, and Moravia. After that, they were to be expunged in Europe from east to west. Many questions arose as to how to identify those considered to be Jews. The issue was not resolved during the Wannsee meeting.

Of course, this was not the beginning of the extermination of the Jewish people. Many of the Nazi elite in attendance had already participated in mass murders since the summer of 1941. Even before the gathering at Wannsee, more than half a million Jews had been executed behind enemy lines. The question was how to attain the goal of total extermination in areas outside the battle zone. A more efficient way to eliminate larger numbers needed to be found. No, the meeting had not been called to determine how to begin the process but rather to spell out how the "final solution" would be achieved. By the end of January, death camps equipped with gas chambers and ovens were under construction.

The ordinary citizenry of Germany did not enter the war determined to annihilate six million of their neighbors. It began with a subversive program of antisemitism aimed at blaming the Jewish people for all the ills that had beset Germany following its losses in World War I. Perhaps even Hitler did not begin with total extermination in mind. That seed probably began to germinate only after Jews were denied entry into other countries. It seemed to him that he had then been given a green light to do whatever he wished with the Jewish population. Ultimately, his "final solution" was the Holocaust—the deaths of six million Jewish men, women, and children murdered in the most horrific of ways.

The preservation of a remnant of Jews through all the suffering, wars, and afflictions over the centuries is further evidence that Israel and the Jewish people are God's miracle. Why have the Jews been hated so? Because Satan's only adversary would come through the Jews: The Messiah. Ultimately, He would destroy the powers of Satan.

Our God keeps His covenants; He remains faithful even when we are faithless (2 Timothy 2:13). He has sovereignly decided to preserve the Jewish people as a separate, identifiable people before Him and restore them to their biblical homeland. These truths are revealed in numerous Scriptures. That they would remain on Earth until the end of time as a distinct people group is foretold in Jeremiah, Chapter 31:

> *Thus says the Lord, Who gives the sun for a light by day, The ordinances of the moon and the stars for a light by night, Who disturbs the sea, And its waves roar (The Lord of hosts is His name): "If those ordinances depart from before Me, says the Lord, then the seed of Israel shall also cease from being a nation before Me forever"* (Jeremiah 31:35-36, NKJV).

The next verse makes crystal clear that the God of Abraham has no intention of ever forsaking His special covenant with Jacob's children, despite their many failures:

> *I will direct their work in truth, and will make with them an everlasting covenant. Their descendants shall be known among the Gentiles, and their offspring among the people. All who see them shall acknowledge them, that they are the posterity whom the Lord has blessed"* (Isaiah 61:8-9, NKJV).

God calls the land of Israel "My Land" (Ezekiel 38:16), and He gave it to Israel by a blood covenant that cannot be annulled. God has assigned the land of Israel to the children of Israel and has never canceled that which He assigned.

God said that Israel would be scattered among the heathen, and they were. But He also said they would be re-gathered, and they have been:

> *He will set up a banner for the nations, and will assemble the outcasts of Israel, and gather together the dispersed of Judah from the four corners of the earth* (Isaiah 11:12, ASV).

> *I will bring back the captives of My people Israel* (Amos 9:14, NKJV).

> *For I will take you from among the nations, gather you out of all countries, and bring you into your own land* (Ezekiel 36:24, NKJV).

I will bring them back to this place, and I will cause them to dwell safely (Jeremiah 32:37, NKJV).

I will plant them in their land, and no longer shall they be pulled up from the land I have given them (Amos 9:15, NKJV).

I will say to the North, "Give them up!" And to the South, "Do not keep them back!" Bring My sons from afar, and My daughters from the ends of the earth (Isaiah 43:6, NIV).

Thus says the Lord God: "Behold, I will lift My hand in an oath to the nations, and set up My standard for the peoples; They shall bring your sons in their arms, and your daughters shall be carried on their shoulders" (Isaiah 49:22, NIV).

Isaiah predicted the people of Israel would fly to their homeland hundreds of years before the invention of the airplane.

Who are these who fly like a cloud, And like doves to their roosts? (Isaiah 60:8, NIV).

He also predicted that they would return by ship:

Surely the isles shall wait for me, and the ships of Tarshish first, to bring thy sons from far, their silver and their gold with them, unto the name of the LORD thy God, and to the Holy One of Israel, because He hath glorified thee (Isaiah 60:9, KJV).

The final restoration of Jews to their homeland comes with a wonderful promise:

> *And I will bring again the captivity of My people of Israel, and they shall build the waste cities, and inhabit them; and they shall plant vineyards, and drink the wine thereof: they shall also make gardens, and eat the fruit of them. And I will plant them upon their land, and they shall no more be pulled out of their land which I have given them, saith the LORD thy God* (Amos 9:14-15, KJV).

CHAPTER THREE

Antisemitism in the Twentieth Century

A prophecy against Damascus:
"See, Damascus will no longer be a city
but will become a heap of ruins.
—ISAIAH 17:1, NIV

The Arab–Israeli conflict grew out of the political tension and military skirmishes between both sides. As we have discussed, however, its more recent roots lie in the rise of Zionism and Arab nationalism in the latter half of the nineteenth century. The underlying reason for the conflict was based on the return of the Jewish people to their biblical homeland—a land claimed by Palestinian Arabs. The culmination came in 1948 when the United Nations recognized the modern State of Israel.

Open strife between the two sides began following the collapse of the Ottoman Empire after World War I, with questions of territorial rights shifting over the years from regional issues to more local Israeli–Palestinian concerns. Open hostilities generally ended with the cease-fire following the 1973 Yom Kippur War, but covert activities have relentlessly continued.

Peace agreements between Israel and Egypt were signed in 1979, then between Israel and Jordan in 1994. The so-called Oslo Accords led to the creation of the Palestinian National Authority in 1993, while precarious cease-fires currently exist between Israel and both Syria and Lebanon. Clashes between Israel and Hamas-ruled Gaza resulted in a 2009 cease-fire (although sporadic fighting continued with periodic missile launches into Israel proper).

Various Muslim groups invoke religious arguments to support their uncompromising hatred for Israel and the Jewish people. The contemporary history of the Arab–Israeli conflict is unquestionably affected by those religious beliefs and the Arab desire to occupy all the territories deeded to Israel from the time of Abraham, Isaac, and Jacob.

The Land of Canaan or *Eretz Yisrael* was, as outlined in both the Hebrew and Christian Bibles, promised by God to the Children of Israel. In his 1896 manifesto, *The Jewish State*, Theodor Herzl repeatedly refers to the biblical Promised Land concept.

Out of 12 political parties extant in Israel, Likud is currently the most prominent to include the biblical claim to the Land of Israel in its platform. Conversely, Muslims revere many sites in Israel, including the Cave of the Patriarchs and the Temple Mount. Over the past 14 centuries, Muslims have constructed Islamic landmarks on these ancient sites, such as the Dome of the Rock and the Al-Aqsa Mosque, a scant distance from the Western Wall, the holiest site in Judaism. This proximity has, as much as anything, brought the two groups into sometimes open conflict over the rightful possession of Jerusalem.

Muslim teaching proclaims that Muhammad passed through Jerusalem on his first journey to heaven. Hamas (the Palestinian Sunni Islamist organization), which governs the Gaza Strip, claims that all of the land of Palestine (the current Israeli and Palestinian territories) is an Islamic *waqf,* or indisputable religious legacy in Islamic law, that should only be governed by Muslims.

The Middle East, including Southern Syria (later Mandatory Palestine), had been under the control of the Ottoman Empire for nearly 400 years. Near the end of the empire, the Ottomans began to exert their Turkish ethnic identity, leading to discrimination against the Arabs. Hopes of liberation from the Ottomans led many Jews and some Arabs to support the Allied Powers during World War I.

In the late nineteenth century, European and Middle Eastern Jews increasingly immigrated to Southern Syria, purchasing land from the local Ottoman landlords. At that time, the city of Jerusalem did not extend beyond its protective walled area and contained a population of only a few tens of thousands. During 1915–16, with World War I underway, the British High Commissioner in Egypt, Sir Henry McMahon, secretly communicated with Husayn ibn 'Ali, patriarch of the Hashemite family, and with the Ottoman governor of Mecca and Medina. McMahon convinced

Husayn to lead an Arab revolt against the Ottoman Empire, which was then aligned with Germany against Britain and France. McMahon assured Husayn that if the Arabs supported Britain in that endeavor, the British government would establish an independent Arab state under Hashemite rule in the Arab provinces of the Ottoman Empire, which included Palestine. That revolt, led by T. E. Lawrence (mentioned earlier as Lawrence of Arabia) and Husayn's son Faysal, successfully defeated the Ottomans, and Britain took control of much of the area.

In 1917, Southern Syria had been conquered, and the British government issued the Balfour Declaration stating that Britain favorably viewed "the establishment in Palestine of a national home for the Jewish people" but that "nothing shall be done which may prejudice the civil and religious rights of existing non-Jewish communities in Palestine." The Declaration was issued due to the belief by Prime Minister David Lloyd George and other key members of the British government that Jewish support was essential to winning the war. As one might imagine, the declaration was not received well in the Arab world.

Following the war, the area remained under British rule and became known as the British Mandate of Palestine. It included what is today Israel, the Palestinian Authority, and the Gaza Strip. Transjordan was eventually designated a separate British protectorate—the Emirate of Transjordan, which gained autonomy in 1928. A major crisis among Arab nationalists had taken place with the failed establishment of the Arab Kingdom of Syria in 1920. With the disastrous outcome of the Franco-Syrian

War, the self-proclaimed Hashemite kingdom with its capital in Damascus was defeated, and Sharif Hussein bin Ali, the Hashemite ruler, took refuge in Mandatory Iraq. The crisis saw the first of many confrontations between nationalist Arab and Jewish forces, the Battle of Tel Hai, which led to the establishment of the local Palestinian version of Arab nationalism, with the return of Hajj Amin al-Husseini from Damascus to Jerusalem in late 1920.

Jewish immigration to Mandatory Palestine continued, but less documented immigration was occurring in the Arab sector, bringing workers from Syria and other neighboring areas. Palestinian Arabs saw this rapid influx of Jewish immigrants as a threat to their land and their identity as a people. Moreover, Jewish practices of purchasing land and prohibiting the employment of Arabs in Jewish-owned industries and farms were not well received in Palestinian Arab communities. Demonstrations protesting what the Arabs felt were unfair preferences for the Jewish immigrants set forth by the British mandate that governed Palestine proliferated. Resentment led to outbreaks of violence later that year. Winston Churchill's 1922 White Paper attempted to reassure the Arab population by stipulating that the creation of a Jewish state was not the intention of the Balfour Declaration.

Political demonstrations at the Western Wall in 1929 resulted in riots that soon expanded throughout Palestine; Arabs murdered 67 Jews in the city of Hebron in what became known as the Hebron Massacre. During that week, at least 116 Arabs and 133 Jews were killed, and 339 were wounded.

By 1931, 17 percent of the population of Mandatory Palestine was Jewish, an increase of six percent since 1922. Immigration would soon peak after the Nazis rose to power in Germany, causing the Jewish population in British Palestine to double.

In the mid-1930s, Izz ad-Din al-Qassam arrived from Syria and established the Black Hand, an anti-Zionist and anti-British militant organization. He recruited and arranged military training for peasants; by 1935, al-Qassam had enlisted several hundred men. The cells were equipped with bombs and firearms used to kill Jewish settlers in the area, as well as engaging in a campaign of vandalism aimed at Jewish settler plantations. By 1936, escalating tensions led to the 1936–1939 Arab revolt in Palestine.

In response to Arab pressure, British authorities greatly reduced the number of Jewish immigrants to Palestine. Those restrictions remained until the end of the Mandate, a period which coincided with the Nazi Holocaust and attempts by Jewish refugees to escape Hitler's Europe. Consequently, the majority of Jewish entrants to Palestine were considered to be illegal, further increasing tension. Following several failed efforts to solve the problem diplomatically, the British petitioned the newly formed United Nations for help. In May of 1947, the General Assembly appointed a United Nations Special Committee on Palestine (UNSCOP), composed of representatives from Australia, Canada, Czechoslovakia, Peru, Sweden, Guatemala, Yugoslavia, India, Iran, Netherlands, and Uruguay.

Christian Zionist John Stanley Grauel is credited in some circles with literally making Israel possible. You might recognize the name of the refugee ship SS Exodus, which was made famous by *Exodus*, the Leon Uris novel released in 1958. Uris had earlier covered the fighting in Israel as a war correspondent. His novel would become an international bestseller—the biggest since Margaret Mitchell's blockbuster, *Gone with the Wind*. Director Otto Preminger turned the book into a movie in 1960, with the lead role going to Paul Newman. Grauel may have inspired one of the book's characters.

Grauel was born in Worcester, Massachusetts, in 1917. In 1941, John bowed to his mother's wishes and entered the Methodist Theological Seminary in Bangor, Maine. She would hold great sway over his education regarding the Jewish people and the path John would take in later life.

During his last year at seminary, John met and married. Sadly, he lost both his wife and son in childbirth and never remarried. Shortly after graduation, John essentially became a circuit-riding preacher, as he was sent to pastor several small towns. However, his heart was soon captured by news of the war raging in Europe, and specifically by the suffering of the Jewish people under Hitler's regime. His friendship with Judge Joseph Goldberg in Worcester, Massachusetts, sparked Grauel's interest in Zionism. The judge, whose background was Russian and Jewish, loaned Grauel books on the subject. It sparked his life-long interest in the return of the Jews to their homeland.

Although he could have claimed an exemption from military service as a conscientious objector due to his pastorate, Grauel could not escape his desire to do something to aid the Jews. He solicited the advice of Judge Goldberg and was sent to meet Dr. Carl Herman Voss, the head of the American Christian Palestine Committee (ACPC). Voss persuaded Grauel to take the position as executive director of the ACPC office in Philadelphia. It would totally change the direction of his life.

In 1944, at his first Zionist conference, John met David Ben-Gurion. From him, he learned of the Haganah, the Jewish underground army in Palestine. After returning home, Grauel soon noticed a steady stream of young men going in and out of an adjoining office. One day, his curiosity got the better of him, and he walked next door to introduce himself to the man in charge, Bucky Karmatz. Over a lunch of sandwiches at Karmatz's desk, John discovered that the office was a recruiting station for Haganah. When the two men parted company, John recorded, "I knew I had found my niche. I would join Haganah ... to become part of that organization to rescue those who could be helped to leave Europe. I liked that affirmation of life after the war."[10]

During Haganah meetings at the Hotel Fourteen in New York City, John rubbed elbows with the men and women who would be totally invested in the future of Israel: David Ben-Gurion, Golda Meir, Teddy Kollek, Nachum Goldman, Meyer Wisgal, and others of note who attended the meetings occasionally. At one session, John was informed that an ocean liner had been secured and would be outfitted to transport Jewish immigrants from Europe to the Holy Land. The ship had been named after the owner of the Baltimore Bay Line, the uncle of Wallace Warfield Simpson, who would become the paramour and later wife of Edward VIII, once king of England.

Grauel arrived at the docks in Baltimore expecting to see the luxurious *SS President Garfield* but was met instead by the derelict and rotting hulk of the *SS President Warfield*. He was horrified at the thought of crossing the Atlantic in the old liner but was determined to fulfill his commitment. He boarded the ship and later said:

> By the grace of God and a touch of insanity, I passed from the world of Reverend John Stanley Grauel to John Grauel, ordinary seaman.... There were thousands of leaks ... it took the crew days of scrubbing, sanding, polishing, and mending just to make some order out of chaos.[11]

On March 29, 1947, after a storm delay had set them back by a month, John and the crew set sail for Marseille aboard the ship renamed *Exodus*. He was there ostensibly as an undercover correspondent for the *Churchman*, an Episcopal journal. With that designation, he secured a visa from the British Consulate in Paris, enabling him to legally enter Palestine. His assignment was to make certain the world knew of the events surrounding the ship. Previous attempts to transport Jewish refugees to Palestine had met with ships being seized and destroyed. One ship, the *Struma*, was sunk by a Russian torpedo after having been towed into the Black Sea by the Turks. It carried 769 men, women, and children.

Once he had arrived in Europe, Grauel's job was to arrange for the transfer of refugees from displaced persons camps to the *Exodus*. His tasks were many and varied—cook, distributor of supplies, administrator, and contact person between the refugees and the crew. The ship steamed toward Palestine with more than 4,550 refugees packed aboard. Just as she neared Haifa on the Mediterranean coast, the ship was rammed by the British Royal Navy cruiser *Ajax*, in a convoy with five destroyers, and was boarded by sailors. This was not an easy task, as the *SS Exodus* had been fortified with barriers and barbed wire to discourage such actions. The British reportedly bombarded the ship with tear gas grenades to subdue the passengers. Captain Ike Aronowicz and his crew challenged the boarding party. One crewmember, First Mate William Bernstein, a sailor from California, and two passengers were bludgeoned to death.[12]

The ship that had brought such hope to so many had been attacked by the British navy a mere seventeen miles offshore, in international waters. It was a wanton act of piracy for which the Royal Navy commanders were never charged. Grauel reported that, as the *Exodus* staggered into the port at Haifa, those still able to stand gathered on the deck of the ship and sang "Hatikvah," the hymn of hope.

Grauel, the only passenger onboard with a valid visa, was arrested but soon escaped with help from none other than the future mayor of Jerusalem, Teddy Kollek, and the Haganah. He was approached by a reporter who was a member of the Jewish organization. The unnamed reporter shepherded

Grauel to the men's room, where he was whisked out a back door into a waiting car displaying American press credentials. The Jews onboard the *SS Exodus* were then forced to disembark in Haifa and were eventually and unwillingly returned to British-controlled camps in Germany. Against this setting, Rabbi Judah Magnes rose to present testimony to the United Nations. Assuming what surely must have been a sadly pious look, he postulated:

> We are here in this country [Palestine] with two peoples; so long as it is inhabited by two peoples, the Jewish people will have to do without a state, as it has done for many hundreds of years.[13]

Grauel was summoned to Kadima House in Jerusalem to give a firsthand account of his experiences during the voyage with the refugees to the United Nations Committee on Palestine. As he stood before that group, he leveled his heartfelt accusations regarding the treatment of the Jewish passengers on the *SS Exodus*. He later said of his testimony:

> There was great gratification for me in knowing that my eyewitness report was now a matter of record. Inherent in the nature of the relationship between Christians and Jews was the fact that, because I was a Christian, in this situation, my testimony would be given greater credence than that of a Jewish crew member.[14]

Grauel's witness proved to be an effective means of gaining compassion and support for the Jewish cause. His eloquent speech to the UNSCOP later earned him the moniker of "the man who helped make Israel possible." Prime Minister Golda Meir believed it was Grauel's recounting of the events surrounding the *SS Exodus* that persuaded the UN to support the creation of a Jewish state.[15]

After five weeks of study in Palestine, the UNSCOP group returned to the General Assembly in September 1947 with a report containing both a majority and a minority plan. The majority proposed a Plan of Partition with Economic Union; the minority proposed an Independent State of Palestine.

With only slight modifications, the Plan of Economic Union was recommended and adopted on November 29, 1947. The Resolution carried by 33 votes to 13 with 10 abstentions. As expected, Arab states, which constituted the Arab League, voted against it. At the time, Arab and Jewish Palestinians fought openly to control strategic positions in the region. In the weeks before the end of the Mandate, the Haganah (the clandestine military wing of the Jewish leadership that became the basis for the Israeli Defense Force) launched several offensives to gain control over all the territory allocated to the Jewish state by the UN, creating a large number of refugees and capturing the towns of Tiberias, Haifa, Safad, Beisan and, in effect, Jaffa.

Early in 1948, the United Kingdom announced it would terminate the Mandate in Palestine on May 14. In response, President Harry S. Truman proposed UN trusteeship rather than partition, stating that "unfortunately, it has become clear that the partition plan cannot be carried out at this time by peaceful means."[16] Further, he commented that ". . .unless emergency action is taken, there will be no public authority in Palestine on that date capable of preserving law and order. Violence and bloodshed will descend upon the Holy Land. Large-scale fighting among the people of that country will be the inevitable result."[17]

On May 14, 1948, the day the British Mandate expired, the Jewish People's Council gathered at the Tel Aviv Museum. It approved a proclamation declaring the establishment of a Jewish state in *Eretz Yisrael*, to be known as the State of Israel. In an official cablegram from the Secretary-General of the League of Arab States to the UN Secretary-General on May 15, 1948, the Arabs stated publicly that various Arab Governments were "compelled to intervene for the sole purpose of restoring peace and security and establishing law and order in Palestine."[18]

That same day, the armies of Egypt, Lebanon, Syria, Jordan, and Iraq invaded what had ceased to be the British Mandate just the day before. It marked the beginning of the Arab-Israeli War. The newly formed Israeli Defense Force repulsed the Arab League nations from part of the occupied territories, thus extending Israel's borders beyond the original UNSCOP partition.

By December 1948, Israel controlled most of that portion of the Mandate, including Palestine west of the Jordan River. The remainder of the Mandate consisted of Jordan, the area that today is called the West Bank (controlled by Jordan), and the Gaza Strip, now controlled by the Palestinian Authority and the terrorist organization Hamas. Prior to and during this conflict, 713,000

Palestinian Arabs fled their original lands to become Palestinian refugees due, in part, to a promise from Arab leaders that they would be able to return when the war had been won. The war came to an end with the signing of the 1949 Armistice Agreements between Israel and each of its Arab neighbors.

CHAPTER FOUR

The Struggle Continues

*Joshua said to them, "Do not be afraid;
do not be discouraged. Be strong and courageous".*
—JOSHUA 10:25, NIV

Before the adoption by the United Nations in November 1947 and the declaration of the State of Israel in May 1948, several Arab countries had begun using discriminatory measures against their local Jewish populations. The status of Jewish citizens in Arab states worsened dramatically during the 1948 Israeli-Arab War. Anti-Jewish riots erupted throughout the Muslim world in December 1947, and Jewish communities were hit particularly hard in Syria and Aden, with hundreds dead and injured. By mid-1948, almost all Jewish communities in Arab states had suffered attacks, and their status rapidly deteriorated.

Jews under Islamic regimes were uprooted from their longtime residences, and many became political hostages. With anti-Jewish violence and persecution escalating, a large number of Jews fled or were forced to emigrate from Arab countries and other Muslim countries as well.

In Libya, Jews were deprived of their citizenship, and in Iraq, their property was seized. Egypt expelled most of its Jewish community in 1956, while Algeria denied its Jews citizenship upon its independence in 1962. The majority fled due to worsening political conditions and rabid antisemitism, although some emigrated for ideological reasons.

As a result of Israel's victory in its 1948 War of Independence, Arabs caught on the wrong side of the ceasefire line were unable to return to their homes in what became Israel. Likewise, any Jews on the West Bank or in Gaza were exiled from their property and homes. Today's Palestinian refugees are the descendants of those who left at the strong suggestion of the Arabs in countries that surround Israel. The responsibility for their exodus continues to be a matter of dispute between the Israelis and the Palestinians. The world at large points a finger at Israel for the disparity while seemingly dismissing any Arab complicity.

In 1956, Egypt closed the Strait of Tiran to Israeli shipping and blockaded the Gulf of Aqaba, contravening the Constantinople Convention of 1888. Many argued that this was also a violation of the 1949 Armistice Agreements. Further, on July 26, 1956, Egypt nationalized the Suez Canal Company and closed the canal to Israeli shipping. Israel responded on October 29, 1956, and with

British and French support, invaded the Sinai Peninsula. During the Suez Canal Crisis, Israel captured the Gaza Strip and the Sinai Peninsula.

The US and the UN soon pressured Israel into a ceasefire. Jewish leaders agreed to withdraw from Egyptian territory, and Egypt acceded to freedom of navigation in the region and the demilitarization of the Sinai. Also, the United Nations Emergency Force (UNEF) was created and deployed to oversee the demilitarization. Notably, the UNEF was only deployed on the Egyptian side of the border. Israel refused to allow UNEF on its own territory.

The Palestinian Liberation Organization (PLO) was established in 1964 under a charter including a commitment to "the liberation of Palestine [which] will destroy the Zionist and imperialist presence. . ."[19] On May 19, 1967, Egypt expelled UNEF observers and deployed 100,000 soldiers to the Sinai Peninsula. It again closed the Strait of Tiran to Israeli shipping, returning the region to its alignment in 1956 when Israel was blockaded.

On May 30, 1967, Jordan signed a mutual defense pact with Egypt. Egypt mobilized Sinai units, crossing UN lines (after having expelled the UN border monitors), and amassed troops and equipment on Israel's southern border.

On June 5, Israel launched a surprise, pre-emptive strike on Egypt and then on Jordanian, Syrian, and Iraqi forces. The results of the war continue today to affect the geopolitics of the region.

At the end of August 1967, Arab leaders, in response to the war, met in Khartoum to discuss the Arab position toward Israel. They reached the consensus that there should be no recognition, no peace, and no negotiations with the State of Israel, the so-called "three no's." In 1969, Egypt initiated the War of Attrition, intending to force Israel into surrendering the Sinai Peninsula. The war ended following Gamal Abdel Nasser's death in 1970.

Also in 1970, following an extended civil war, King Hussein expelled the Palestine Liberation Organization (PLO) from Jordan. September 1970 is known as Black September in Arab history, sometimes called the "era of regrettable events." It was the month when King Hussein of the Hashemite Kingdom of Jordan moved to quash the autonomy of Palestinian organizations and restore his monarchy's rule over the country. The violence resulted in the deaths of tens of thousands of people, the vast majority of them Palestinians.

The armed conflict lasted until July 1971, with the expulsion of the PLO and thousands of Palestinian fighters to Lebanon and mounted raids into Israel.

On October 6, 1973, Syria and Egypt staged a surprise attack on Israel on Yom Kippur, the holiest day of the Jewish calendar. The Israeli military was caught off guard and unprepared, taking about three days to fully mobilize. This led other Arab states to send troops to reinforce the Egyptians and Syrians. These Arab countries also agreed to enforce an oil embargo on industrial nations, including the U.S., Japan, and Western European Countries.

These OPEC countries increased the price of oil fourfold and employed that as a political weapon to gain support against Israel. The Yom Kippur War brought about indirect confrontation between the US and the Soviet Union. When Israel had turned the tide of war, the USSR threatened military intervention. The United States, wary of a possible nuclear war, secured a ceasefire on October 25.

Following the Camp David Accords of the late 1970s, Israel and Egypt signed a peace treaty. Under its terms, the Sinai Peninsula would be returned to Egypt, and the Gaza Strip would remain under Israeli control to be included in a future Palestinian state. The agreement also provided free passage of Israeli ships through the Suez Canal and recognition of the Strait of Tiran and the Gulf of Aqaba as international waterways. In June 1981, Israel attacked and destroyed Iraq's newly-built nuclear facilities in Operation Opera.

In 1981, Syria allied with the PLO and moved missiles into Lebanon. In response, Israel invaded Lebanon in June 1982. Within two months, the PLO agreed to withdraw. In March 1983, Israel and Lebanon signed a ceasefire agreement. However, Syria pressured President Amin Gemayel to nullify the truce. By 1985, Israeli forces withdrew to a 15-kilometer-wide southern strip of Lebanon, following which the conflict continued on a reduced scale, with relatively low casualties on both sides.

During the Gulf War in 1991, Iraq fired 39 Scud missiles into Israel in the hopes of uniting the Arab world against the coalition that sought to liberate Kuwait. At the urging of the United States, Israel did not respond to these attacks to prevent an outbreak of all-out war. In 1993 and 1996, Israel launched major operations against the Shiite militia of Hezbollah, which had become a growing threat. In 2000, as part of a greater plan for a peace agreement with Syria, Israel abandoned its occupation of Southern Lebanon.

In October 1994, Israel and Jordan signed a peace agreement, which stipulated mutual cooperation, an end to hostilities, securing the Israel-Jordan border, and several other issues. The conflict had cost roughly 18.3 billion dollars. The peace agreement was also closely linked with efforts to create peace between Israel and the Palestinian Liberation Organization, representing the Palestinian National Authority (PNA). It was signed on October 26, 1994, making Jordan only the second Arab country (after Egypt) to normalize relations with Israel. Contrarily, Israel and Iraq have been inexorable foes since 1948.

In 2006, as a response to a Hezbollah cross-border raid, Israel launched air strikes on the militant group's strongholds in Southern Lebanon, initiating the Lebanon War. The conflict lasted 34 days and resulted in the creation of a buffer zone in Southern Lebanon along with the deployment of Lebanese troops south of the Litani River for the first time since the 1960s. Hezbollah withdrew its fighters from the border areas, and Israel eventually turned over its occupied areas in Lebanon to UN peacekeepers. Both sides declared victory in the conflict.

The 1970s were marked by a large number of major international terrorist attacks, including the Lod (now Ben-Gurion) Airport Massacre and the Munich Olympics Massacre in 1972, and the Entebbe hostage-taking in 1976, with over 100 Jewish captives of different nationalities kidnapped and held in Uganda.

In December 1987, the First Intifada (or shaking off) began. It was a mass uprising against Israeli rule in the Palestinian Territories. The rebellion began in the Jabalia refugee camp and quickly spread throughout Gaza, the West Bank, and East Jerusalem. Palestinian actions ranged from civil disobedience to violence. In addition to general strikes, boycotts of Israeli products, graffiti, and barricades, Palestinian demonstrations that included stone-throwing by youths against the Israel Defense Forces brought the Intifada international attention. Conversely, the Israeli army's heavy-handed response to the demonstrations, with live ammunition, beatings, and mass arrests, brought international condemnation. The PLO, which until then had never been recognized as the leaders of the Palestinian people by Israel, was invited to peace negotiations the following year after it recognized Israel and formally renounced terrorism.

In mid-1993, Israeli and Palestinian representatives engaged in peace talks in Oslo, Norway. This resulted in Israel and the PLO signing the Oslo Accords, known as the *Declaration of Principles* or Oslo I. In side letters, Israel recognized the PLO as the legitimate representative of the Palestinian people, while the PLO recognized the right of the state of Israel to exist and renounced terrorism, violence, and its desire for the destruction of Israel.

The Oslo II agreement was signed in 1995 and detailed the division of the West Bank into Areas A, B, and C. Area A was land under full Palestinian civilian control, with the Palestinians being responsible for internal security. Area B outlined Palestinian civil control and joint Israeli-Palestinian security control.

That area includes many Palestinian towns, villages, and areas with no Israeli settlements. Area C details full Israeli civil and security control, which, by the year 2011, included 61 percent of the West Bank.

The pact further states: "Areas of the West Bank outside Areas A and B, which, except for the issues that will be negotiated in the permanent status negotiations, will be gradually transferred to Palestinian jurisdiction in accordance with this Agreement."[20]

The Second Intifada forced Israeli leaders to rethink the relationship and policies towards the Palestinians. Following a series of suicide bombings and attacks, the Israeli army launched Operation Defensive Shield. It was the largest military action conducted by Israel since the Six-Day War.

As violence between the Israeli army and Palestinian militants intensified, Israel expanded its security apparatus around the West Bank by re-taking many parts of land in Area A. The nation established a complicated system of roadblocks and checkpoints around major Palestinian areas to deter violence and protect Israeli settlements. However, in 2008, the IDF began slowly transferring authority to Palestinian security forces.

Israeli Prime Minister Ariel Sharon instituted a policy of unilateral withdrawal from the Gaza Strip in 2003. This policy was fully implemented in August 2005. Sharon's announcement to disengage from Gaza came as a tremendous shock to his critics, both on the left and on the right. A year previously, he had commented that the fate of the most far-flung settlements in Gaza,

Netzarim, and Kfar Darom, was regarded in the same light as that of Tel Aviv.

The formal announcements to evacuate seventeen Gaza settlements and another four in the West Bank in February 2004 represented the first reversal for the settler movement since 1968 and divided Sharon's party. Trade and Industry Minister Ehud Olmert and Tzipi Livni, the Minister for Immigration and Absorption, strongly supported the move. Still, Foreign Minister Silvan Shalom and Finance Minister Benjamin Netanyahu strongly condemned it. It was also uncertain whether this was simply the beginning of further evacuation.

In June 2006, Hamas militants infiltrated an army post near the Israeli side of the Gaza Strip and abducted Israeli soldier Gilad Shalit. Two IDF soldiers were killed in the attack, while Shalit was wounded after his tank was hit by a rocket. Three days later, Israel launched Operation Summer Rains to secure the release of Shalit. On October 18, 2011, Gilad was exchanged for 1,027 Palestinian prisoners. It speaks of the value the Israelis place on the life of just one of their own.

In July 2006, Hezbollah fighters crossed the border from Lebanon into Israel, attacking and killing eight Israeli soldiers and abducting two others as hostages, setting off the 2006 Lebanon War, which caused widespread destruction in Lebanon. A UN-sponsored ceasefire went into effect on August 14, 2006, officially ending the conflict. Over a thousand Lebanese and over 150 Israelis were killed, the Lebanese civil infrastructure was severely damaged, and approximately one million Lebanese and

300,000–500,000 Israelis were displaced. However, most were later able to return to their homes. After the ceasefire, some parts of Southern Lebanon remained uninhabitable due to unexploded Israeli cluster bombs.

In the aftermath of the Battle of Gaza, where Hamas seized control of the Gaza Strip in a violent civil war with rival Fatah, Israel placed restrictions on its border with Gaza. It ended economic cooperation with the Palestinian leadership based there. Israel and Egypt have imposed a blockade on the Gaza Strip since 2007. Israel maintains the blockade is necessary to limit Palestinian rocket attacks from Gaza and to prevent Hamas from smuggling advanced rockets and weapons capable of hitting Israeli cities.

On September 6, 2007, in Operation Orchard, Israel bombed an eastern Syrian complex, which was reportedly a nuclear reactor being built with the assistance of North Korea.

In April 2008, Syrian President Bashar Al Assad told a Qatari newspaper that Syria and Israel had been discussing a peace treaty for a year, with Turkey as a go-between. This was confirmed in May 2008 by a spokesman for Prime Minister Ehud Olmert. As well as a peace treaty, the future of the Golan Heights was being discussed. President Assad said there "would be no direct negotiations with Israel until a new US president takes office."

Speaking in Jerusalem on August 26, 2008, then-United States Secretary of State Condoleezza Rice criticized Israel's increased settlement construction in the West Bank as detrimental to the peace process. Rice's comments came amid reports that Israeli construction in the disputed territory had increased significantly over 2007 levels.

A fragile six-month truce between Hamas and Israel expired on December 19, 2008, and attempts at extending the truce have failed amid accusations of breaches from both sides. Following the expiration, Israel launched a raid on a tunnel suspected of being used to kidnap Israeli soldiers, which killed several Hamas fighters. Following this, Hamas resumed rocket and mortar attacks on Israeli cities, most notably firing over 60 rockets on December 24. Three days later, Israel launched Operation Cast Lead against Hamas. Numerous human rights organizations accused Israel and Hamas of committing war crimes.

In 2009, Israel placed a 10-month settlement freeze on the West Bank. Hillary Clinton praised the freeze as an "unprecedented" gesture that could "help revive Middle East talks."

Israeli naval forces carried out a raid on six ships of the *Gaza Freedom Flotilla* in May 2010. The ship's captain refused to dock at Port Ashdod. On the MV *Mavi Marmara*, activists clashed with an Israeli boarding party. During the fighting, nine activists were killed by Israeli Special Forces. Widespread international condemnation followed. Relations between Israel and Turkey were strained, and Israel subsequently eased its blockade on the Gaza Strip. Several dozen other passengers and seven Israeli soldiers were injured.

Following the latest round of peace talks between Israel and the PA, thirteen Palestinian militant movements led by Hamas initiated a terror campaign designed to derail and disrupt the negotiations. Attacks on Israelis have increased since August 2010, after Hamas militants killed four civilians. On August 2, Hamas militants launched seven Katyusha rockets at Eilat and Aqaba, killing one Jordanian civilian and wounding four others.

Intermittent fighting has continued, including 680 rocket attacks on Israel in 2011. On November 14, 2012, Israel killed Ahmed Jabari, a leader of Hamas' military wing, launching Operation Pillar of Cloud. A week later, Hamas and Israel agreed to an Egyptian-mediated ceasefire.

The Palestinian Centre for Human Rights claimed that 158 Palestinians were killed during the operation: 102 civilians, 55 militants, and one policeman; 30 were children, and 13 were women. B'Tselem (The Israeli Information Center for Human Rights in the Occupied Territories) stated that according to its initial findings, which covered only the period between 14 and 19 November, 102 Palestinians were killed in the Gaza Strip, 40 of them civilians.

According to Israeli figures, 120 combatants and 57 civilians were killed. An international outcry ensued, with many criticizing Israel for what much of the global community perceived as a disproportionately violent response. Protests took place on hundreds of college campuses across the US and in front of the Israeli consulate in New York. Additional protests followed throughout the Middle East, Europe, and South America.

However, the governments of the United States, United Kingdom, Canada, Germany, France, Australia, Belgium, Bulgaria, Czech Republic, and the Netherlands have expressed support for Israel's right to defend itself and/or condemned the ongoing Hamas rocket attacks on Israel.

And so, the relentless conflict between two entities and two religions continues, abated only occasionally by short-lived pacts, agreements, and accords that are broken with impunity.

CHAPTER FIVE

Israel, God's Dream

"The LORD said to Abram after Lot had parted from him, 'Look around from where you are, to the north and south, to the east and west. All the land that you see I will give to you and your offspring forever. I will make your offspring like the dust of the earth, so that if anyone could count the dust, then your offspring could be counted. Go, walk through the length and breadth of the land, for I am giving it to you".
— GENESIS 13:14-17, NIV

Israel is a tiny country with a population of [barely/just over] 10 million and a land mass comparable to the state of New Jersey, the fifth smallest state in the US. It is 290 miles in length and only 85 miles wide. Israel's role on the world stage should seemingly be relatively minor, yet hardly a day goes by when events in or concerning Israel do not dominate international headlines. What many today seem to overlook is that Israel didn't just rise from the rocky land of Palestine in 1948; it has been in existence for centuries, although known by different names.

Columnist Charles Krauthammer wrote of the land:

> Israel is the very embodiment of Jewish continuity: It is the only nation on earth that inhabits the same land, bears the same name, speaks the same language, and worships the same God that it did 3,000 years ago. You dig the soil, and you find pottery from Davidic times, coins from Bar Kokhba, and 2,000-year-old scrolls written in a script remarkably like the one that today advertises ice cream at the corner candy store.[21]

Until the days of the Roman conquest, Israel had existed as an independent country. A strong Jewish presence was still evident in the land after the diaspora (dispersion) in 70 AD and 135 AD. The Ottoman Empire gained control over the region seven hundred years ago and remained in power until World War I.

When looking at other nations in close proximity to Israel, it is apparent that Israel has always been surrounded by Johnny-come-lately enemies. The Kingdom of Saudi Arabia rose from the sands of the desert in 1913; Lebanon was formed in 1920; Iraq in 1932; Syria in 1941; the Hashemite Kingdom of Jordan in 1946; and Kuwait in 1961.

Of the claims of a so-called Palestinian State, Journalist Rockwell Lazarus wrote:

> There has never been a civilization or a nation referred to as "Palestine," and the very notion of

a "Palestinian Arab nation" having ancient attachments to the Holy Land going back to time immemorial is one of the biggest hoaxes ever perpetrated upon the world! There is not, nor has there ever been, a distinct "Palestinian" culture or language. Further, there has never been a Palestinian state governed BY Arab Palestinians in history, nor was there ever a serious Arab-Palestinian national movement until 1964. . .three years BEFORE the Arabs of "Palestine" lost the "West Bank" and Gaza as a result of losing the 1967 Six-Day War (which the Arabs started).[22]

During World War I, Ottoman Empire Sultan and Caliph of Islam Mehmed V chose to side with Germany and was conquered by Great Britain. In a stunning yet anti-climactic upset of the Turks, British Field Marshal Edmund Allenby marched into Jerusalem without his troops firing a single shot.

With the Turks and Germans having fled the city, the residents of Jerusalem were left to fend for themselves in the face of what they thought would be Allenby's impending attack. They could not know that Allenby, a religious man, was unwilling to inflict damage on the Holy City. He consulted with the War Office and King George V about how to take Jerusalem. His sovereign counseled him to make it a matter of prayer. Presumably, he did just that and ultimately decided to drop leaflets on the city from an airplane. They addressed the absent Turkish authorities and

ANTI-ZIONISM *is* ANTI-SEMITISM

invited the people to surrender. The Arab who penned Allenby's instructions wrote the general's name incorrectly. The leaflet was therefore signed, not "Allenby," but "Allah Bey," which means son of Allah.

The Turks, having seen few, if any, aircraft, were frightened to see them overhead with leaflets raining from the heavens. According to one account:

> General Allenby gave orders before the victorious advance and gave instructions that "on no account is any risk to be run in bringing the city of Jerusalem or its immediate surroundings within the area of operations." General Allenby was familiar with the Scriptures, and he would therefore see fit to protect a dedicated city. He had taken the Bible with him from England for the campaign. Eventually, when the time came to attack and occupy the city, Allenby sent six bombers over it armed with leaflets. The leaflets were to call on the city to "surrender" and the bombs carried were in case of emergency.[23]

Jerusalem's civilian mayor, Haj Amin Nashashibi, accepted Allenby's offer. He borrowed a white sheet from an American missionary and walked outside the city through the Jaffa Gate toward the southwest. He assumed that was the direction from which the main body of troops would come. To help ensure their safety, he and his associates took the cowardly action of surrounding themselves with a small group of boys before and behind them.

Not far down the road, the entourage encountered two British scouts, Sergeants Hurcomb and Sedgwick of the London Regiment. With hand signals, the mayor made his intentions of surrender clear to the two men. Within hours, British troops marched into the city. The Jews, the largest segment of the population, had heard of the Balfour Declaration. The arrival of these troops signified to them the seriousness of the Declaration to give them a national homeland.

Arabs were cheering, too. They were familiar with the exploits of Lawrence of Arabia[24] and the way in which he represented British support for the Arab desire for national independence. Of course, the Christians cheered with the knowledge that Jerusalem's Holy Sites were no longer under Muslim domination.

The six bombers sent to drop leaflets continued circling outside the city. Sighted below was a battery of Turkish artillery manned by gunners about to target the Holy City. The bombers dropped the remainder of their payload on the emplacement. Panicked, the Turks fled. It was as if the prophet Isaiah had seen it all beforehand when he wrote in Isaiah 31:5, NKJV:

> *"Like birds flying about,*
> *so will the Lord of hosts defend Jerusalem.*
> *Defending, He will also deliver it;*
> *Passing over, He will preserve it."*

The objects passing over could easily have been vultures to destroy, but that was not God's purpose. Yahweh's commitment was to save and preserve Israel and His children.

Two days later, on December 11, Allenby arrived at the Jaffa Gate to mark the beginning of the new regime. A fierce Turkish counterattack on November 25 had slowed progress into the Judean Hills from Jaffa, and his troops had fought hard to reach Jerusalem. Allenby dismounted, reached for the visor of his cap, and removed it. Humbly, he entered the Holy City on foot as the bells of various churches and the clock tower rang out a joyous welcome. The British, under Field Marshall Edmund Allenby, had ended the Ottoman rule over Palestine.

Once inside, Allenby mounted the steps of the Turkish citadel and read a proclamation assuring the city's inhabitants that the rights of the religious communities would be preserved and their various shrines scrupulously protected. He also gave formal greetings to the chief rabbis, the mufti, the Latin and Orthodox patriarchs, and other religious leaders.

An official report revealed that:

> From 2 to 7 that morning the Turks streamed through and out of the city, which echoed for the last time their shuffling tramp. On this same day, 2,082 years before, another race of conquerors, equally detested, were looking their last on the city which they could not hold; and inasmuch as the liberation of Jerusalem in 1917 will probably

ameliorate the lot of the Jews more than that of any other community in Palestine, it was fitting that the flight of the Turks should have coincided with the national festival of the Hanukah.[25]

The "war to end all wars" ended in 1918, but the armistice lasted only until Adolf Hitler rose to power in Germany. In September 1939, Hitler ordered his troops to invade Poland in a land-grab attempt to enlarge Germany. French and British leaders issued an ultimatum to the determined Nazi Fuehrer—withdraw or suffer the consequences. Ignoring the demand, Hitler began his march across Europe while both Great Britain and France declared war against the German Reich. It was not until after the attack on Hawaii's Pearl Harbor in December 1941 that America joined the Allies and entered the war both in the Pacific and in Europe. (It was not until 1959 that Hawaii became a state.) After six long and bloody years of battle that would leave six million Jews dead in Nazi concentration camps, Germany surrendered unconditionally in 1945.

At the end of the conflict, Britain found itself in control of Palestine with a growing dilemma: How to walk the tightrope between world opinion and the Arabs. After the horror of the Holocaust, the world increasingly demanded a return to their homeland in Palestine—thought to be a place of safety for the Jews. Arabs in the region were adamantly opposed to the move. Greatly frustrated by the situation, the British announced in February 1947 that control of Palestine would be ceded to the United Nations.

ANTI-ZIONISM *is* ANTI-SEMITISM

In November 1947, the UN offered a partition plan that would divide the region into an Arab state and a Jewish state, calling for British troops to leave Palestine by August 1948. The Jews welcomed the proposal; the Arabs scorned it. The British were suspicious, and because of their skepticism, little was done to prepare the region for their upcoming departure from Palestine. Some British leaders felt it would be impossible for a Jewish state to flourish in the face of such hostility from the Arabs.

In the interim, Jewish leaders moved forward with plans for statehood. A provisional government was established under David Ben-Gurion in March 1948. Two months later, on May 14, 1948, as Egyptian fighter-bombers soared overhead and British troops readied for departure, Ben-Gurion and his political partners gathered at the museum in Tel Aviv:

> At 16:00 [4:00 PM], Ben-Gurion opened the ceremony by banging his gavel on the table, prompting a spontaneous rendition of Hatikvah, soon to be Israel's national anthem, from the 250 guests.[26]

The very day after Israel's rebirth as an independent nation, she was attacked by her much larger Arab neighbors, who supported the Palestinians. Only through the grace and protection of God was Israel able to survive. Again and again, over the years, this tiny island of freedom has suffered assaults and attacks from evil men dedicated to the annihilation of the Jewish people.

Today, Israel is more isolated than ever. Security is a constant struggle as all of Israel's neighbors either actively oppose her or at least harbor those who do. Since the reuniting of the city of Jerusalem, there have been nearly 10,000 terrorist attacks in the Bible land. There have been more suicide bombings in the city of Jerusalem than in any other city in the world.

As my dear friend Prime Minister Benjamin Netanyahu has repeatedly pointed out, the contention is not about a Palestinian state, the division of Jerusalem, settlements, checkpoints, security fences, or borders. The issue is Israel's very right to exist as a nation. Most of the Arab world still refuses to accept this simple proposition.

Not only do they think Israel has no right to exist as a *state*, but they think the Jewish *people* have no right to survive. The opposition of the Arab countries to Israel's national aspirations has always been tied to the Muslim world's ultimate resistance to the right of the Jewish people to exist at all. Peaceful co-existence has never been the goal of the Arabs. Even having Jews living in other lands is not an option for fanatical Islamics and modern-day Neo-Nazis. The real goal has been the abnegation and, in its worst and most absolute form, the very extermination of the Jewish race itself.

This is why Palestinian children are taught to hate and kill Jews from their first breath and why the Islamic world throws parties in the streets every time Jewish blood is shed. This is why, in radical Islamic theology, the successful homicidal maiming and murder of Jews represents the highest aspiration many Palestinian mothers have for their children.

Anti-Israeli sentiment has become the new antisemitism.

It makes Israel the new "collective Jew," which justifies assault on individual Jews as the extension of the state. This hatred—not any other issue—is the true source of murder and terrorism.

Author George Gilder wrote of today's version of the Hitler youth movement:

> Today, Hitler's rants have morphed into a global program of religious education and military ideology sustained by Arab and Iranian oil money. The hundreds of thousands of Brown Shirts in Germany have become millions of frothing jihadi youths similarly inculcated with anti-Semitic hatred and a lust for violence. Leading politicians in Iran, Egypt, Syria, Malaysia, Venezuela, and other nations, and jihadi imams and mullahs around the globe have declared their resolve to destroy Israel. . . .Anti-Semites have the moral support of much of the UN bureaucracy, including its "human rights" apparatus, which is chiefly devoted to anti-Semitic [agitation propaganda.]. . .The UN Secretary General has called for a global boycott of Israel for its efforts to defend itself against new campaigns of extermination. . . .Scores of nations representing 1.8 billion Muslims have endorsed jihad.[27]

The terror wars that Israel fights in the twenty-first century are not against a particular Arab nation. Rather, the conflict is against an unpredictable and often unidentifiable band of terrorists with the ability and mobility to shift from country to country almost at will. They seem invisible, striking without warning. The attacks are meant to instill fear and trepidation among the Jewish populace. This is one of the many reasons the US alliance with Israel is a necessity. The US learned a harsh lesson on September 11, 2001: If terrorism is not contained in the Middle East, there will be more attacks in the West.

Author David Naggar wrote:

> As for Israel, one either sees or does not see that Israel is on the front line of a war that pits the advancement of humankind against barbarism. One either sees or does not see that the fight in Afghanistan is the same as the fight in Iraq and the same as the fight in Yemen and Somalia. The Jihadists are using the whole global boxing ring. They are not confining the fight to the battlegrounds we dictate. Like the game whack-a-mole, if the seekers of liberty and human advancement seem to be gaining the upper hand in one part of the world, Jihadists will simply fold their tents at night and surface in another part of the world in the morning.[28]

The spiritual door was opened for an attack against the US, primarily *because* the policy of the government has been to make demands and pressure the Israelis not to retaliate in a significant way against terrorist strikes launched against them.

Since its independence in 1948, Israel has fought five wars:

ANTI-ZIONISM *is* ANTI-SEMITISM

The War for Independence (1948-49); the 1956 war—the Sinai campaign; the Six-Day War in 1967; the Yom Kippur War in 1973; and the Lebanon War in 2006. In all five cases, Israel was attacked. It was never the aggressor. It won all five wars against impossible odds. Yet amazingly enough, most of the world views tiny, democratic Israel as the threat to peace rather than the homicidal, terror-producing powers that surround her.

In October 2009, less than six months after assuming office, President Barack Obama flew to Cairo to deliver a major speech (See Appendix A) designed to impress the Muslim world. In his remarks, the president designated Israel as the "second major source of tension" in the Middle East—following fanatical Muslim terrorists. At the same time, he stated unequivocally that the United States would not turn a blind eye to the desire of the Palestinians for statehood. It seems that Mr. Obama was then, and still is, dedicated to the proposition of a fifty-fourth Muslim nation. With the creation of a Palestinian state, Israel would be even further isolated—an island in a sea of fanatical Muslim countries.

The friendship between America and Israel has been of the utmost importance to a succession of presidents since Harry Truman, the first world leader to endorse the new nation. In recent years, governments such as the United States of America, Canada, and Great Britain that have long stood with Israel have moved away from their traditional support. We do so at our own peril because we are standing at a prophetic crossroads—one that will determine the future of our world. We must not fail to do our part to fight and win the battle for Israel's survival.

CHAPTER SIX

THE BLESSINGS AND CURSES OF GOD

"The LORD shall bless thee out of Zion: and thou shalt see the good of Jerusalem all the days of thy life".
—PSALM 128:5, KJV

I n Zechariah 2:8, God warns of the danger of offending Israel:

For thus says the LORD of hosts: "He sent Me after glory, to the nations which plunder you; for he who touches you touches the apple of His eye."

Earlier in Genesis 12:1-3, God had assured Abraham that those who blessed Israel would be blessed, and anyone who cursed Israel would be cursed. These three Scriptures alone should be sufficient warning as to why we are called to support Israel:

The LORD had said to Abram, "Go from your country, your people, and your father's household to the land I will show you. "I will make you into a great nation, and I will bless you; I will make your name great, and you will be a blessing. I will bless those who bless you, and whoever curses you I will curse; and all peoples on earth will be blessed through you" (NIV).

Hebrew writer Israel Matzav wrote about blessing and cursing:

> One need not be a Jew or Christian or even believe in God to appreciate that this verse is as accurate a prediction as humanity has ever been given by the ancient world. The Jewish people have suffered longer and more horribly than any other living people. But they are still around. Its historic enemies are all gone. Those that cursed the Jews were indeed cursed.... Those who curse the Jews still seem to be cursed. The most benighted civilization today is the Arab world. One could make a plausible case that the Arab world's preoccupation with Jew-hatred and destroying Israel is a decisive factor in its failure to progress. The day the Arab world makes peace with the existence of the tiny Jewish state in its midst, the Arab world will begin its ascent. The converse is what worries tens of millions of Americans—the day America abandons Israel; America will begin its descent.[29]

In October 1991, during the Madrid Peace Conference, I stood gazing at the ceiling in the grand Hall of Columns in the Royal Palace in Madrid. It was ornately embellished with the images of false gods: Apollo, Aurora, Zephyrus, Ceres, Bacchus, Diana, Pan, and Galatea. The beautiful interior was all glitter and no substance, a disguise for its actual purpose: the place where even more land-for-peace would be demanded of the Jews. From their lofty perch, these counterfeit gods looked down on the official proceedings to elicit a counterfeit peace. Like the apostle Paul at Mars Hill, I prayed to the One True God while under that canopy of idolatry. How ironic that Israel had been forced there, of all places, for an international peace conference—to Spain, where one-third of the Jewish population of its day had been massacred during the Inquisition. Representatives of nation after nation mounted the podium to insult and accuse Israel and to demand that her leaders relinquish the majority of her land.

I still hear their voices reverberating through the marble halls: "We will accept your land in exchange for peace." What they were really saying was: "This is a stick-up. Give me all your land, and you won't get hurt—much." Muggings usually happen on the streets of major cities, and the Madrid Peace Conference, by any measure, was an international mugging. The world was the silent majority, too intimidated to report the crime to the police. Most of the nations represented pretended not to see the gun pointed at Israel's head.

I looked on as US President George H.W. Bush opened the Conference. Israel had been banned from joining the Desert Storm

ANTI-ZIONISM *is* ANTI-SEMITISM

coalition because anti-Semitic Arab countries were incensed at the thought of Jews fighting alongside Muslims. President Bush had also asked Israel not to retaliate when bombarded by thirty-eight SCUD missile attacks. President Yitzhak Shamir honored his request.

At the end of the Peace Conference, Israel was "rewarded" with the freeze of a $10 billion loan guarantee, money needed to provide housing for Russian Jewish refugees. The US awarded Syria billions of dollars, subsequently spent on the purchase of North Korean missiles to be used against Israel. Many of those missiles filtered into the hands of Hezbollah terrorists in Lebanon and have since been launched into Israeli towns and villages in various attacks on its northern cities.

As President Bush opened the conference at the Royal Palace in Madrid, the Perfect Storm (the one made famous by the movie) swirled in the North Atlantic. It created the largest waves ever recorded in that region. The storm traveled 1,000 miles "east to west" (as opposed to the normal west-to-east pattern) to crash onto the eastern coast of the United States, sending 35-foot waves crashing into the Kennebunkport, Maine, home of the Bush family. This was one of the worst storms in American history and one of the top ten in insurance claims. Thirteen people died as a direct result of the storm, and property damage totaled over $200 million.

Furthermore, when the Madrid Conference was moved to Washington, D.C., for a resumption of the land-for-peace talks, Hurricane Andrew struck Florida. It wreaked havoc, causing an estimated $30 billion in damages, leaving 180,000 Americans homeless, and securing a spot on the top ten list of the largest disasters in American history.

The Prophet Daniel wrote in chapter 11, verse 32:

> *But the people who know their God shall be strong, and carry out great exploits* (Daniel 11:32, NKJV).

The nations that ransacked, burned, leveled, and tried to obliterate the Jewish people are today rife with devastation. We have only to examine history to ascertain that the remnants of those once-great empires are now dust and ashes. Time after time, since the beginning of her existence, nations have come against Israel. Yet, like the Phoenix, she has risen from the ashes each time. Not one ruler who ordered the destruction of Jerusalem long survived. Nebuchadnezzar conquered Jerusalem in 586 BC and was doomed to live as a beast of the field for seven terrifying years. He was restored to sanity when he recognized the God of the Israelites.[30] His kingdom of Babylon was conquered by Cyrus the Great.

In 332 BC, Alexander the Great captured Jerusalem. His empire fragmented after his death. Followers of Ptolemy in Egypt and later the Seleucids of Syria ruled over Jerusalem. The Jews, horrified by the desecration of the Temple under the Seleucid ruler, Antiochus IV, staged a revolt and regained independence under the Hasmonean Dynasty. It lasted one hundred years until Pompey established Roman rule in the city. The Holy Roman Empire collapsed after the Temple was destroyed and Jerusalem was leveled.

ANTI-ZIONISM *is* ANTI-SEMITISM

The British, who ruled over Palestine and Jerusalem following World War I, could once brag that the sun never set on the British Empire. Indeed, one-fifth of the world's population was then under its rule. However, after turning away Jews from both Britain and Palestine when they fled Hitler's gas chambers and after arming Arabs to fight against them in Palestine, the empire quickly began to disintegrate. Great Britain today comprises just fourteen territories, consisting of several islands. Gone are the days when the empire stretched from India to Canada and Australia to Africa.

In 1939, Winston Churchill stood before Parliament in London and countered efforts to renounce support for a Jewish homeland. In his speech, he praised the work of those already in Palestine and then damned those who had come against the Jews already in the land:

> They [the Jews] have made the desert bloom ...started a score of thriving industries...founded a great city on the barren shore...harnessed the Jordan and spread its electricity throughout the land...So far from being persecuted, the Arabs have crowded into the country and multiplied till their population has increased more...We are now asked to submit—and this is what rankles most with me—to an agitation which is fed with foreign money and ceaselessly inflamed by Nazi and Fascist propaganda.[31]

Today, little has changed; there are still many whose only agenda is to force the Jews from Israel—or annihilate them, if at all possible.

Yet, Jerusalem and Israel stand today as a testimony to the determination and courage of the Jewish people. The burning question is: Does America stand with or against Jerusalem and the nation of Israel?

Israel is the key to America's survival. Would September 11th have happened if America had stood with Israel over the years rather than weakening her by rewarding terrorists like Arafat and his successor, Mahmoud Abbas? The English Poet Alfred Lord Tennyson wrote: "More things are wrought by prayer than this world dreams of."[32] What might have been prevented had US support for Israel been unwavering, had the churches in America banded together to pray for the peace of Jerusalem, and had chosen to bless Israel?

Rather than offer support, a signal has been sent to would-be terrorists that crime pays and America is weak. Twenty-two years ago, Israel stood up to the nations of the world by attacking Iraq's *Osirak* nuclear reactor. Many nations, including the US, condemned the action. Ultimately, Israel's courageous act may have saved millions of American lives, not only on September 11th but in the months of the war in Iraq that followed.

In 1980, I interviewed Isser Harel, head of Mossad, Israeli intelligence, from 1952-1963. *The Jerusalem Post,* on September 30, 2001, published an article based on that interview—"America the Target" (See Appendix B). It will help you understand the seriousness of the matter. I was so convinced Harel was right that in 1999, I wrote a novel called *The Jerusalem Scroll* in which Osama bin Laden would obtain a nuclear bomb from the Russian mafia and attempt to blow up New York City and Los Angeles. Bin Laden would attempt both, but thank God, he never gained possession of a nuclear bomb. The United States has been blessed beyond measure, and I believe it is because she has been the world's least anti-Semitic country.

> An amazing Scripture in the Bible is found in Luke 7:5 (KJV): *"For he loveth our Nation, and hath built us a synagogue."* The Jewish Elders appealed to Jesus to come to Capernaum to the house of Cornelius, a Gentile, to heal a servant who was close to death. The Jews told Jesus, "He deserves a blessing because he has been a blessing. He has performed some wonderful deeds of compassion for our people."

A similar story is found in Acts 10. God selected a Gentile in Caesarea to receive the Gospel. Why? The answer is given repeatedly in the book of Acts:

> *A devout man [Cornelius] and one who feared God with all his household, who gave alms generously to the people, and prayed to God always* (Acts 10:2, NKJV).

Who were the people to whom Cornelius gave these alms? They were the Jews!

> ...*Your prayers and your alms have come up for a memorial before God* (Acts 10:4, NKJV).

> ...*your prayer has been heard, and your alms are remembered in the sight of God* (Acts 10:31, NKJV).

Three times in the same chapter, a godly Gentile expressed his unconditional love for the Jewish people in a practical way. Then Cornelius was divinely selected by God to be the first head of a Gentile household to receive the Gospel and the first to receive the outpouring of the Holy Spirit.

Why Christians should wholeheartedly support the Jewish people and their beloved country, Israel, may be considered by some to be a selfish reason in some respects, but a valid one nonetheless. After promising Abraham that He would make his offspring a great nation, the God of Israel pledged to *"bless those who bless you"* (Genesis 12:3, NKJV). We have already seen that God's eternal covenant was passed down through Isaac, Jacob, and the 12 tribes of Israel. This means that the blessing promised by the God of Israel would come to those who particularly bless the Jewish people.

How can we bless the Jews? There are many ways this can be done. One of the most important and obvious ways is to support their God-given right to live in their biblical Promised Land, especially in their eternal capital city, Jerusalem. The sad fact is that many governments, international organizations, Muslim groups, and even some Christians do not acknowledge that divine right. For Christians, this non-biblical stand weakens our testimony, weakens the nation of Israel, weakens the United States, and puts our country in harm's way.

In a conference on Israel, author Joel Rosenberg said:

> There is a danger to our country if we abandon or turn on Israel. We are in enough trouble fiscally, but more importantly, morally and spiritually. This is not a good time to add the abandonment, rejection, and betrayal of Israel to our national sins.[33]

Failure or refusal to support the Jews and their right to reside in their ancient homeland can cause us to miss the blessings of God. It can, however, do much more than that; it also places us in danger of being cursed by our Creator. God Himself warns humanity of this danger.

By contesting the right of Jews to live in their covenant land and thereby going against God's Holy Word, many are opening themselves up to be cursed! Therefore, anyone who seeks the blessings bestowed by our Heavenly Father should obey His command to bless His special covenant people.

The Church must never lose sight of the fact that the Lord and Savior we serve, Jesus Christ, was born a Jew. He is the offspring of Abraham, Isaac, and King David. Christians need only look at the genealogies provided in Matthew and Luke. God included them in the Bible for a reason, not so we could hurry through them or skip over them. Jesus is our King because he is David's heir to the throne. New Testament Scriptures only reaffirm God's promises to Israel throughout the Old Testament.

The Liberal Left media has painted a picture of the Palestinians as the underdogs—deprived of their land. Nothing could be further from the truth. Israel has more rights to the land than any of its Arab neighbors, having received the grant first from God in a covenant with Abraham and regaining the land in 1947 through the United Nations. When one looks deeply into the situation between Israel and the Palestinians, it soon becomes obvious that the goal is not for a state; it is to drive Israel from the land altogether.

A singular truth is that wealthy Arab nations have turned away from the Palestinians, refusing to offer them refuge. Why? Perhaps the refusal is based on Jordan's experience with refugees—insurrection and civil war at the hands of PLO terrorists and threats on the life of King Hussein. Added to that are the questions: What other reason would Arab countries have to blame and target Israel? Would the Palestinians even want the land if not for the Jews?

The great Master of the Universe reveals that our personal, family, and national welfare is closely related to how we treat the Jewish people. God not only promised to reward individuals for blessing His covenant Jewish people, but He also pledged in the same Scripture to bless families and, by extension, entire nations: *"And in you all the families of the earth shall be blessed"*

(Genesis 12:3, NKJV). Should anyone need any other reason to support the contemporary offspring of Abraham, Isaac, and Jacob, especially in their brave endeavors to establish a thriving modern state within their biblically designated ancestral borders?

Bulgarian pastor George Bakalav wrote of God's very special covenant with Abraham:

> Prior to Abraham, God had relationship with a number of other saints, such as Job and Noah. However, God promised Abraham two specific things He never promised anyone else: the land of Canaan would become the land of Israel, and Abraham will have a special heir born of his own flesh and blood. This heir of Abraham would be later recognized also as an heir of David, the promised Messiah, the Savior and the ruler of the world. Thus, Abraham becomes the father of the Jewish people. The land of Israel, which at that time was occupied by the Canaanites, is given to Abraham and his decedents as part of this covenant.[34]

As we have seen, both the Old and New Testaments make abundantly clear that Christians must support Israel in every possible way. This does not mean that the Israeli people and their government are perfect. Far from it: They are fallen human beings like everyone else on Earth, in desperate need of salvation.

(See 2 Chronicles 7:14.) Bible prophets, including the Apostle Paul, foretold that the restored Jewish remnant in the Lord's land would mourn over their sins in the Last Days and be grafted back into their own sacred tree.

While working and praying for all of Israel, we must wholeheartedly support what the Sovereign Lord is doing in returning His covenant people to their God-given land. In doing so, we will be blessed as they are blessed. Best of all, we will please our heavenly Father by obeying His revealed will on a matter that is clearly close to His heart:

> *Thus says the Lord: "Against all My evil neighbors who touch the inheritance which I have caused My people Israel to inherit—behold, I will pluck them out of their land and pluck out the house of Judah from among them"* (Jeremiah 12:14, NKJV).

When we refuse to pray for the Jewish people, we are saying simply, "God, I know better than you. I will not obey Your Word." God's Word says, *"I have written my name there* [in Jerusalem]. . . ." Almighty God has promised to dwell with them in the land (Zechariah 2:10). God will determine blessings or curses on nations depending on how they treat Israel.

When God promised to bless Abraham and his descendants, He meant it! A friend in Israel sent me these amazing facts as an indication of how God has blessed His people:

- Israel has the highest density of tech start-ups in the world.

- Israel's companies attract more venture capital per person than any other nation.

- Israel has more companies listed on NASDAQ than Europe, Japan, Korea, India and China—combined!

- Israel has twice the number of engineers per capita than the US.

- Israel has the world's highest Research and Development spending per GDP.
  God keeps His promises and blesses His people!

Additional Scripture readings:

Now the LORD had said unto Abram, Get thee out of thy country, and from thy kindred, and from thy father's house, unto a land that I will shew thee: And I will make of thee a great nation, and I will bless thee, and make thy name great; and thou shalt be a blessing: And I will bless them that bless thee, and curse him that curseth thee: **and in thee shall all families of the earth be blessed** (**Emphasis** mine, Genesis 12:1-3, KJV).

And the LORD said unto Abram, after that Lot was separated from him, Lift up now thine eyes, and look from the place where thou art northward, and southward, and eastward, and westward: For all the land which thou seest, to thee will I give it, and to thy seed for ever. And I will make thy seed as the dust of the earth: so that if a man can number the dust of the earth, then shall thy seed also be numbered. Arise, walk through the land in the length of it and in the breadth of it; for I will give it unto thee. Then Abram removed his tent, and came and dwelt in the plain of Mamre, which is in Hebron, and built there an altar unto the LORD (Genesis 13:14-18, KJV).

As for me, behold, my covenant is with thee, and thou shalt be a father of many nations. Neither shall thy name any more be called Abram, but thy name shall be Abraham; for a father of many nations have I made thee. And I will make thee exceeding fruitful, and I will make nations of thee, and kings shall come out of thee. And I will establish my covenant between me and thee and thy seed after thee in their generations for an everlasting covenant, to be a God unto thee, and to thy seed after thee. And I will give unto thee, and to thy seed after thee, the land wherein thou art a stranger, all the land of Canaan, for an everlasting possession; and I will be their God (Genesis 17:4-8, KJV).

And the angel of the LORD called unto Abraham out of heaven the second time, And said, By myself have I sworn, saith the LORD, for because thou hast done this thing, and hast not withheld thy son, thine only son: That in blessing I will bless thee, and in multiplying I will multiply thy seed as the stars of the heaven, and as the sand which is upon the sea shore; and thy seed shall possess the gate of his enemies; And in thy seed shall all the nations of the earth be blessed; because thou hast obeyed my voice (Genesis 22:15-18, KJV).

And there was a famine in the land, beside the first famine that was in the days of Abraham. And Isaac went unto Abimelech king of the Philistines unto Gerar. And the LORD appeared unto him, and said, Go not down into Egypt; dwell in the land which I shall tell thee of: Sojourn in this land, and I will be with thee, and will bless thee; for unto thee, and unto thy seed, I will give all these countries, and I will perform the oath which I sware unto Abraham, thy father; And I will make thy seed to multiply as the stars of heaven, and will give unto thy seed all these countries; and in thy seed shall all the nations of the earth be blessed; Because that Abraham obeyed my voice, and kept my charge, my commandments, my statutes, and my laws (Genesis 26:1-5, KJV).

CHAPTER SEVEN

JERUSALEM, THE CENTER OF GOD'S PLAN

"Yet I have chosen Jerusalem, that My name may be there. . .".
—2 CHRONICLES 6:6, NKJV

All expressions of divine love still hold true for Israel today; none have been canceled. Israel—the Promised Land, Holy Land, Land of Canaan—is, and always will be, the apple of God's eye (Zechariah 2:8). She remains God's joy and delight, His royal diadem (Isaiah 62:3), His firstborn, His Chosen One, His beloved (Jeremiah 2:2, Hosea 11:1). Indeed, He says of His people, *"For they shall be like the jewels of a crown,"* (Zechariah 9:16).

Israel is not simply a long, narrow strip of land on the Mediterranean Ocean; it represents part of a Divine land grant—from God to the descendants of Abraham, Isaac, and Jacob.

On that day, the LORD made a covenant with Abram and said, "To your descendants, I give this land, from the Wadi of Egypt to the great river, the Euphrates—the land of the Kenites, Kenizzites, Kadmonites, Hittites, Perizzites, Rephaites, Amorites, Canaanites, Girgashites and Jebusites" (Genesis 15:18, NIV).

It was a gift from Jehovah, and the ownership of Israel's land is non-negotiable. In March 2002, Senator James Inhofe (R-OK) addressed the issue of Israel's right to her land:

> Every new archeological dig supports the fact that the Jews have had a presence in Israel for 3,000 years - coins, cities, pottery, and other cultural artifacts. The Jews' claim predates the claim of any other people in the region. The ancient Philistines are extinct, just like other ancient peoples. They do not have the unbroken line that the Israelis have. Ownership is and will be in the hands of God's Chosen People—forever.[35]

There are a myriad of Scriptures to support the rights of the Jewish people to the land:

- ✦ It is God's land and His prerogative to determine ownership:

    - ✧ *The land shall not be sold permanently, for the land is Mine...* (Leviticus 25:23, NKJV).

- *Rejoice, O Gentiles, with His people. . .He will provide atonement for His land and His people* (Deuteronomy 32:43, NKJV).

- *For a nation has come up against My land. . .* (Joel 1:6, NKJV). *Then the Lord will be zealous for His land. . .* (Joel 2:18, NKJV).

+ God determines the consequences of what happens when people violate His covenant:

  - *. . .I will uproot them from My land which I have given them. . .* (2 Chronicles 7:20, NKJV).

  - *Lord, You have been favorable to Your land; You have brought back the captivity of Jacob. You have forgiven the iniquity of Your people; You have covered all their sins* (Psalm 85:1-2, NKJV).

  - *I brought you into a bountiful country. . . but when you entered, you defiled my land and made my heritage an abomination* (Jeremiah 2:7, NKJV).

  - *I will gather all nations, and bring them down to the Valley of Jehoshaphat; and I will enter into judgment with them there on account of My people, My heritage Israel, Whom they have scattered among the nations; they have also divided up My land* (Joel 3:1, NKJV).

- God speaks of the End Times and those who come against Israel:

  - *You will come up against My people Israel...I will bring you against My land, so that the nations may know Me when I am hallowed in you...* (Ezekiel 38:16, NKJV).

- God will save His people, Israel:

  - *"The Lord their God will save them in that day, as the flock of His people, for they shall be like the jewels of a crown, lifted like a banner over His land..."* (Zechariah 9:16, NKJV).

- God has committed the land to Abraham and his offspring forever:

  - *"I will establish my covenant as an everlasting covenant between me and you and your descendants after you for the generations to come, to be your God and the God of your descendants after you. The whole land of Canaan, where you now reside as a foreigner, I will give as an everlasting possession to you and your descendants after you; and I will be their God,"* (Genesis 17:7-8, NKJV).

  - *"With a little wrath I hid My face from you...but My kindness shall not depart from you, nor shall My covenant of peace be removed. . ."* (Isaiah 54:8-10, NKJV).

The loss of governance by Israel through sin and dispersion has not altered God's commitment to make it theirs forever (read Ezekiel 37:1-28).

When you sign your name on a check, you represent that you possess the amount indicated on that check. God wrote His Name in Jerusalem, and He has the power and authority to possess what His name represents.

On July 30, 1980, the Israeli Knesset voted to affirm a united Jerusalem as the capital of the State of Israel. Shortly afterward, I had the privilege of talking with the man who had become my dear friend, Prime Minister Menachem Begin. We discussed the vastness of the territory held by Israel's enemies. For instance, at that time:

- Arab dictators controlled 13,486,861 square kilometers in the Middle East, and Israel controlled 20,770 (Palestinefacts.org).

- The population of Israel was roughly 7.8 million, compared to the population of 300 million living in the surrounding Arab countries.

- The odds against Israel are decidedly skewed. Twenty-one separate countries represent the Arab nations demanding a Palestinian state.[36]

Several arguments abound as to why the Palestinian Authority continues to reject any and all offers of a Palestinian State, as did Yasser Arafat in 2000 and as Mahmoud Abbas has continued to do. Formal statehood would limit the ability of the PLO and Hamas in Gaza to commit acts of terrorism. The same applies to Hezbollah in Lebanon. The organization continues to play a lesser role in the government of that country. Were the leaders of Hezbollah to gain full control within Lebanon's borders—which they could do at any time—the first rocket launched toward Israel from the confines of Lebanon would result in the immediate demise of that country. Controlling Lebanon would reduce the ability of Hezbollah members to attack the nation of Israel. Playing a lesser role in government gives them a license to terrorize Lebanon's neighbor.

This was a lesson learned when Gaza achieved pseudo-statehood. It became easier for Israel to retaliate when attacked. For the PA to achieve statehood would be a catastrophic move: It would lose the "victim" status that it has enjoyed for decades and would lose sizeable donations from US, EU, and Arab backers. Would that those organizations, including the UN and Russia, come to understand that the Palestinians do not want a state. It would rob them of the cover they now enjoy when it comes to terroristic acts against the Jewish people in Israel. It is obvious when, at some point in each round of negotiations, the Palestinians, in a huff, pick up their marbles and go home.

To this day, the same countries trying to foist a Palestinian state on Israel do not recognize Jerusalem as the capital of Israel.

In my discussion with Prime Minister Begin, I asked, "How can this lack of recognition be possible when so many people in America and the world believe the Bible?" Mr. Begin smiled that enigmatic smile of his but offered no answer. As we talked, I told him about a publication that had come into my possession from the Egyptian state information service, "Jerusalem, an Arab City." It had been printed by *al-Ahram Press* in Cairo. The book states on page eight, "Jerusalem was invaded by Christian Arabs in the year 90 BC and remained under their domination until it was occupied by the Romans in the first century AD."[37]

Of course, both of us were well aware that the Arab world's claim to Jerusalem is based on misinformation. How could a state publication declare a right to Jerusalem based on the presumption that Christian Arabs had invaded Jerusalem 90 years *before* the birth of Christ? It is this type of propaganda that floods the Arab world, feeding and fueling hatred for the Jewish people.

The prime minister answered my question before I had time to formulate another:

> Being a student of the Bible, you know that almost 3,000 years ago, King David united the Kingdoms of Judea and Israel. He transferred the seat of power from Hebron to Jerusalem, where he ruled for 33 years. He wanted to build the Temple on Mount Moriah, where Abraham was to offer his son, Isaac, as a sacrifice.

> David petitioned God to be allowed to build a home for Him in Jerusalem. God answered, *"You have shed much blood and have made great wars; you shall not build a house for My name, because you have shed much blood on the earth in My sight"* (1 Chronicles 22:08).
>
> God promised David a son who would follow after him as king and would build the Temple. Since then, Jerusalem has been the capital of the Jewish state...one of the oldest capital cities in the world.

The Prime Minister was aware some detractors refuse to recognize Israel, much less Jerusalem as its capital city:

> We came to Camp David to make peace with Egypt, and one of your statesmen told me that the government of the United States did not recognize Jerusalem as the capital of Israel. I answered, "Whether you recognize or don't recognize it, Jerusalem is the capital of the State of Israel."
>
> After the Six-Day War, the eastern part of Jerusalem was liberated from Jordanian occupation. For 19 years, we couldn't go to the Western Wall to pray. That was the only time since the [second] Temple had been destroyed by the Romans. Under all other regimes, we were free to go to the Western Wall to pray, but the Jordanians didn't allow us passage, in breach of the arms agreement.

> The Olive Mountain Cemetery, in which our greatest sages have been buried for centuries, was completely desecrated. Monuments were destroyed and turned into floors of places which are unmentionable. I will not even use the names [latrines]. All of our synagogues were destroyed...the Jewish Quarter, which was centuries old, was leveled.
>
> Under our jurisdiction, we reconsecrated the Olive Mountain Cemetery, and everyone has access to the Holy Shrines—the Holy Sepulcher, the Church of the Nativity. A Muslim goes to the mosque to pray in absolute safety.
>
> Here in Jerusalem is the government, the Parliament, the President, the Supreme Court. Whoever says, either on behalf of a great power or of a small country, "We can't recognize Jerusalem as the capital of Israel," my reply is always the same: "Excuse me, sir, but we don't recognize your non-recognition."

The prime minister's comments brought to mind something Moshe Dayan said during his address to the 34th General Assembly of the United Nations in September 1979:

> Jerusalem has known many foreign rulers during the course of its long history, but none of them regarded it as their capital. Only the Jewish people have always maintained it as the sole center of its

national and spiritual life. For thousands of years, Jews have prayed daily for their return to Jerusalem, and for the past century and a half, Jerusalem has had a continuous and uninterrupted Jewish majority. [38]

Jerusalem is the symbol of all that Israel represents in our world. Teddy Kollek, Jerusalem's first mayor, wrote:

> Jerusalem, this beautiful, golden city, is the heart and soul of the Jewish people. One cannot live without a heart and soul. If you want one single word to symbolize all of Jewish history, that word is Jerusalem. [39]

Out of the long negotiations to establish a Jewish homeland, a friendship grew between Dr. Chaim Weizmann, a Jewish statesman, and Lord Balfour, the British foreign secretary. Balfour was unable to understand why the Jews were insisting they would only accept Palestine as their permanent homeland. One day, Lord Balfour asked Dr. Weizmann for an explanation. "Mr. Balfour, let's suppose I propose that you replace London with Paris. Would you accept?"

A surprised Balfour responded, "But London is ours!"

Replied Weizmann, "Jerusalem was ours when London was still a swampland."[40]

The very name of the Holy City evokes a stirring in the heart and soul. It has been called by many names: City of God, City of David, Zion, the City of the Great King, Ariel (Lion of God), and Moriah (chosen of the Lord). But only one name resonates down through the centuries—Jerusalem! David's city!

A world map drawn in 1581 has Jerusalem at its very center, with the then-known continents of the world surrounding it. It resembles a ship's propeller, with the shaft in the center being Jerusalem. Another analogy is of Jerusalem as the navel of the earth. Its history can be summed up in one word: troubled! Lying as it does between the rival empires of Egypt to the south and Syria to the north, both striving for dominance in the region, Israel has constantly been trampled by the opposing armies. She has been conquered at various times by the Canaanites, Jebusites, Babylonians, Assyrians, Persians, Romans, Byzantines, Arabs, Crusaders, Ottomans, and the British. While her origins are lost in the hazy mists of antiquity, archaeological evidence of human habitation goes back some 4,000 years. Jerusalem is first mentioned in Joshua 10:1.

We read there that Adoni-Zedek was the king of Jerusalem and fought unsuccessfully against Joshua. The Israelites first occupied Jerusalem during the days of the Judges (1:21) but did not completely inhabit the city until 1049 BC, when David wrested it from the Jebusites and declared it the capital city of the Jewish people.

In *Jerusalem, Sacred City of Mankind*, Teddy Kollek and Moshe Pearlman wrote:

The history of Jerusalem from earliest times is the history of man, a history of war and peace, of greatness and misery, of splendor and squalor, of lofty wisdom, and of blood flowing in the gutters. But the golden thread, the consistent theme running through that history, is the unshakeable association of the Jewish people with the city.

The story of this association is repeatedly interrupted by a succession of conquerors—Egyptians, Assyrians, Babylonians, Persians, Seleucids, Romans, Moslem Arabs, Seljuks, Crusaders, Saracens, Mamelukes, and Ottomans. Yet throughout the three thousand years since David made it the seat of Israel's authority, the spiritual attachment of the Jews to Jerusalem has remained unbroken. It is a unique attachment.[41]

When the Jews were driven from their land at various times, wherever they found themselves in exile, they faced toward Jerusalem when praying. After Nebuchadnezzar signed a decree making it illegal to pray to anyone except him, Daniel 6:10 says:

> *Now, when Daniel knew that the writing was signed, he went home. And in his upper room, with his windows open toward Jerusalem, he knelt down on his knees three times that day, and prayed and gave thanks before his God, as was his custom since early days* (NKJV).

Jewish synagogues faced Jerusalem. When a Jew built a house, part of a wall was left unfinished to symbolize that it was only a temporary dwelling—until he could return to his permanent home, Jerusalem. Even today, the traditional smashing of a glass during a wedding ceremony has its roots in the Temple in Jerusalem. This act of remembering the loss of the center of Jewish festivities during the marriage feast sets *"Jerusalem above [their] highest joy"* (Psalm 137:6, KJV).

CHAPTER EIGHT

Jerusalem's Spiritual Significance

*Break forth together into singing,
you waste places of Jerusalem; for the LORD has
comforted his people, he has redeemed Jerusalem.*
—ISAIAH 52:9, RSV

Compared with the world's great capital cities, Jerusalem is small in size and population, with fewer than a million citizens. It lies alongside no great rivers like London, Paris, and Rome have. It boasts no port, key industries, mineral wealth, or even an adequate water supply. The city doesn't stand on a major thoroughfare connected to the rest of the world. Why, then, is Jerusalem the navel of the earth, the shaft that propels the world ever forward?

The answer can only be found in its spiritual significance. Jerusalem is the home of two of the world's monotheistic faiths—Judaism and Christianity, and is claimed by a third—Islam. Biblical prophets proclaimed that from Jerusalem, the Word of the Lord would go out to the world—a Word that would change the moral standards of all mankind:

> *For out of Zion shall go the law, and the word of the LORD from Jerusalem* (Isaiah 2:3, ESV).

The spiritual stature of Jerusalem is echoed in its physical situation; it sits atop the Judean hills high above the surrounding countryside. Traveling to Jerusalem is always spoken of as "going up to Jerusalem." Those who leave the City of God are said to go *down*—perhaps more than just in the physical sense.

When viewing the history of Jerusalem as a whole, one can see that no other city has suffered as has David's City. At times, the city has been overrun by violent assailants. It is recorded in Jeremiah that the city would surrender after suffering the horrors of starvation—and be reduced to cannibalism (Jeremiah 19).

While Christian and Muslim claims to Jerusalem came much later, the story of the Jews in Jerusalem began three millennia ago and has never ceased. The link of the Jewish people has been historical, religious, cultural, physical, and fundamental. It has never been voluntarily broken; any absence of the Jews from their beloved city has been the result of foreign persecution and expulsion. To the Jews alone belongs David's City, the City of God.

For the Jewish people whose cry for centuries has been, "Next year Jerusalem," it is more than a location on the map; it is not just a tourist Mecca where one can visit various holy sites; Jerusalem *is* holy. It is the essence of that for which Jews have hoped and prayed and cried and died. It is their God-given land.

The God who cannot lie made a vow to His people:

> *The LORD had said to David and to Solomon, his son, "In this house and in Jerusalem, which I have chosen out of all the tribes of Israel, I will put My name forever"* (2 Kings 21:7).

Israel is *God's* Dream; the title deed belongs to Him. It is His to bestow on whomever He will—and He has given the right of occupation to the Jewish people. When God made His eternal promises to Israel, there was no United Nations, no United States, no Russia, no European Union, and no Arab League; there were only pagan nations to challenge this dream, to challenge God and His Word. Today, those same pagan voices are challenging the right of the Jews to occupy a unified Jerusalem.

When you and I, as Christians, are apathetic toward God's divine plan or His eternal purpose, it means that we are rejecting our Lord's divine assignment to the Church. God's prophetic time clock has been set on Jerusalem time throughout history, and the spotlight of heaven remains shining upon the Jews as His Chosen People. It began with them, and it will end with them.

We embrace the name of Christ and serve the God of Abraham, Isaac, and Jacob, and find strength. We heed the warnings of the prophets Isaiah, Jeremiah, Ezekiel, Daniel, Hosea, and Joel and find direction. We sing the Psalms of King David and find hope. The mention of Jerusalem quickens our hearts, for it is our spiritual city. We join our Jewish brothers and sisters in their fight against antisemitism and the threat of terrorism and reap the blessings of God.

God's plan is an eternal one! As Christians, we cannot afford to neglect our responsibility to stand with the House of Israel. It is as important as it is to believe the promises of God. As Christians, we are the engrafted vine; we bow before a Jewish Messiah, and what we do matters in the light of eternity.

Jerusalem is the only city for which God commands us to pray. When you pray for Jerusalem as instructed in Psalm 122:6, you are not praying for stones or dirt but for revival (2 Chronicles 7:14) and the Lord's return. Also, you are joining our Lord, the Good Samaritan, in His ministry of love and comfort to the suffering House of Israel:

> *"Inasmuch as you did it to one of the least of these, My brethren, you did it to Me"* (Matthew 25:40, NKJV).

This is our divine commission.

King David explained precisely why God Almighty has commanded us to pray for the peace of Jerusalem and has commanded a blessing upon us for doing so. The revelation is found in Psalm 122:8: *"For the sake of my brethren and companions, I will now say, 'Peace be within you.'"* God is telling us to pray for the peace of the inhabitants of Jerusalem. David felt that prayer needed to be offered up for all of his brothers and friends who lived there. Prayer needs to be offered today for the Children of Israel and for peace for those who reside there from the over 120 nations of the world. It is the city most targeted by terrorists simply because of hatred for the Jewish people and the significance of Jerusalem to them. It has drawn the Jewish people of the world like a prophetic magnet—those who have prayed, "Next year in Jerusalem."

In Psalm 122:9, David's revelation says, *"Because of the house of the LORD our God, I will seek your good."* When we pray for the peace of Jerusalem, we are ultimately praying for Satan to be bound. In Isaiah 14, Satan said he would battle God from the Temple of the Lord on the sides of the north:

> *For you have said in your heart: 'I will ascend into heaven, I will exalt my throne above the stars of God; I will also sit on the mount of the congregation, on the farthest sides of the north* (Isaiah 14:13).

When we pray for the peace of Jerusalem, we are praying for those who live there and for the Messiah to come. The prophecies of the Bible point to the Temple of the Lord as the key flashpoint that will bring the nations of the world to Jerusalem and result in the battle that will end Satan's reign over the earth for all eternity. It will spell his final defeat!

In 691 A.D., Islamic adherents of the Umayyad dynasty began a campaign to "exalt and glorify"[42] the city of Jerusalem. Umayyad Caliph Abd al-Malik built the Dome of the Rock over the Foundation Stone, the Holy of Holies. It was thought to have been erected in direct competition with Christianity. The edifice still stands today. Islam later attributed another event to the Foundation

Stone: the binding of the son of Abraham, the "Hanif," the first Monotheist. As the Qur'an does not explicitly mention the name Isaac, commentators on the Qur'an have erroneously identified the son bound by Abraham as Ishmael. Thus, Islam teaches that the title deed to Jerusalem and the Temple Mount and all of Israel belongs to the Arabs—not the Jews.

In fact, Muhammad never set foot in Jerusalem, nor is the city mentioned by name in the Qur'an. His only connection to Jerusalem is through his dream or vision, where he finds himself in a "temple that is most remote" (Qur'an, Sura). It was not until the 7th Century that Muslim adherents identified the "temple most remote" as a mosque in Jerusalem (perhaps for political reasons). The truth remains that this site, on which now stands the Dome of the Rock and is sacred to Jews as the Temple site, will be the basis for the battle of the ages that will one day be fought.

There is a divine reason the Church was born in Zion. All roads lead to Jerusalem, Judea, and Samaria. The world is hopeless, and we do not know what to do. Heaven and Earth met in Jerusalem and will, when Messiah returns, meet there again. The destiny of America and the world is linked to Jerusalem. It is the epicenter of spiritual warfare and affects the entire world.

Jerusalem, Judea, and Samaria are the battle zones. It is no accident that the Great Commission is directed toward these prophetic areas:

> *But ye shall receive power, after that the Holy Ghost is come upon you: and ye shall be witnesses unto*

me both in Jerusalem, and in all Judaea, and in Samaria, and unto the uttermost part of the earth (Acts 1:8, KJV).

If Christians are not salt and light, the Great Commission will become the Great Omission!

If our Lord and Savior reached out in compassion to Israel and made prayer for her His highest priority, would we dare make it our lowest? There is a direct correlation between the power Heaven promised for the Church at its birth in Jerusalem and the Church's obedience to be a witness in Jerusalem, Judea, and Samaria. The Church cannot, and must not, ignore Christ's eternal mission for her and, at the same time, expect power from on high. His disciples' obedience was directly related to a power surge from Heaven and the birth of the Church. Can disobedience empower the Church and lift her heavenward to fulfill her final mission?

Another significant reason Christians should rejoice in Israel's physical restoration and strongly support her continued existence in the Middle East is the prophesied future of her ancient and modern capital city, Jerusalem. Scripture reveals that Zion is to be the very seat of the Messiah's earthly reign. The nations on earth will come up to visit Jerusalem when Jesus rules from the Holy City as King of Kings and Lord of Lords!

It is evident from Scripture that the Sovereign Lord of Creation has chosen the city of Jerusalem as His earthly capital. This decision was made by the very same God who promised to restore His covenanted Jewish people to the sacred city and surrounding land in the last days before the Second Coming. How can Christians look for and welcome Jesus' prophesied return and not rejoice in and actively defend the Jewish return that was foretold to at least partially precede it?

God described the details and boundaries of the land in Genesis 15:18-21:

> *On the same day, the Lord made a covenant with Abram, saying: 'To your descendants I have given this land, from the river of Egypt to the great river, the River Euphrates."*

This was a royal land grant, perpetual and unconditional:

> *Also, I give to you and your descendants after you the land in which you are a stranger, all the land of Canaan, as an everlasting possession; and I will be their God* (Genesis 17:8, NKJV).

> *...the land on which you lie I will give to you and your descendants* (Genesis 28:13, NKJV).

God has never revoked Abraham's title deed to the land or given it to anyone else. The spot where God confirmed His covenant is north of Jerusalem between Bethel and Ai. It is in the heart of what is called the West Bank, biblical Judea and Samaria. (The United Nations refers to this as "occupied territory" and demands that Israel relinquish it.) An inalienable right is one that cannot be given away. The Bible declares this so in Genesis 25:23. The people were forbidden to sell the land because *"The land must not be sold permanently, because the land is mine and you are but aliens and my tenants"* (NKJV).

Jerusalem is the only city God claims as His own; it is called the City of God and the Holy City in Scripture. He declared to Solomon in 2 Chronicles 33:7:

> *In this house and in Jerusalem, which I have chosen out of all the tribes of Israel, I will put my Name forever* (NKJV).

At the Middle East peace conference convened at the Royal Palace in Madrid, I was the first person to speak after Secretary of State James Baker concluded his remarks. I asked two questions: Why can't America recognize Jerusalem as Israel's capital? Secondly, we are moving a military presence into the Arab world for security. Why can't we have a military presence in Israel to help its security? It suffered greatly and paid a dear price during the Persian Gulf War. Baker was incensed by my remarks and said he refused to be entangled in a fruitless debate and that the status of Jerusalem should be determined by negotiations.

Until December 2017, when President Trump made the declaration and moved the embassy to Jerusalem, America had failed to recognize Jerusalem as Israel's capital. This was a grave mistake finally corrected. For many years, I had shouted the words of Prime Minister Menachem Begin as a warning from the White House in Washington to the Royal Palace in Madrid. I rebuked world leaders with his words, "God does not recognize your non-recognition position!" At least one heard the message. Additional Scripture Readings:

> *Arise, shine; for thy light is come, and the glory of the LORD is risen upon thee. For, behold, the darkness shall cover the earth, and gross darkness the people: but the LORD shall arise upon thee, and His glory shall be seen upon thee. And the Gentiles shall come to thy light, and kings to the brightness of thy rising* (Isaiah 60:1-3, KJV).

> *And many nations shall come and say, 'Come, and let us go up to the mountain of the Lord, To the house of the God of Jacob; He will teach us His ways, And we shall walk in His paths.' For out of Zion shall go forth the law, And the word of the Lord from Jerusalem* (Isaiah 2:3, NKJV).

> *Look upon Zion, the city of our appointed feasts; Your eyes will see Jerusalem, a quiet home, A tabernacle that will not be taken down; Not one of its stakes will ever be removed, Nor will any of its cords be broken* (Isaiah 33:20, NKJV).

> *Thus says the Lord, "I will return to Zion, And will dwell in the midst of Jerusalem. Jerusalem shall be called the City of Truth, The Mountain of the Lord of hosts, The Holy Mountain"* (Zechariah 8:3, NKJV).

I will not give sleep to mine eyes, Or slumber to mine eyelids, until I find out a place for the LORD, an habitation for the Mighty One of Jacob...For Your servant David's sake, Do not turn away the face of Your Anointed...For the LORD has chosen Zion; He has desired it for His dwelling place. "This is my resting place forever; Here I will dwell, for I have desired it" (Psalm 132:4-5, 10, 13-14, NKJV).

Moreover, I will appoint a place for My people Israel, and will plant them, that they may dwell in a place of their own, and move no more; nor shall the children of wickedness oppress them anymore, as previously (2 Samuel 7:10, NKJV).

He will set up a banner for the nations, And will assemble the outcasts of Israel, And gather together the dispersed of Judah From the four corners of the earth (Isaiah 11:12, NKJV).

The Lord also will roar from Zion, And utter His voice from Jerusalem; The heavens and earth will shake; But the Lord will be a shelter for His people, And the strength of the children of Israel (Joel 3:16, NKJV).

Those who trust in the Lord Are like Mount Zion, Which cannot be moved, but abides forever. As the mountains surround Jerusalem, So the Lord surrounds His people From this time forth and forever (Psalm 125:1-2, NKJV).

Then I, John, saw the holy city, New Jerusalem, coming down out of heaven from God, prepared as a bride adorned for her husband (Revelation 21:2, NKJV).

For thus says the Lord of hosts: "He sent Me after glory, to the nations which plunder you; for he who touches you touches the apple of His eye (Zechariah 2:8, NKJV).

"For I," says the Lord, "will be a wall of fire all around her, and I will be the glory in her midst" (Zechariah 2:5, NIV).

This is the word of the LORD concerning Israel. The LORD, who stretches out the heavens, who lays the foundation of the earth, and who forms the spirit of man within him, declares: "I am going to make Jerusalem a cup that sends all the surrounding peoples reeling. Judah will be besieged, as well as Jerusalem. On that day, when all the nations of the earth are gathered against her, I will make Jerusalem an immovable rock for all the nations. All who try to move it will injure themselves. On that day, I will strike every horse with panic and its rider with madness," declares the LORD. "I will keep a watchful eye over the house of Judah, but I will blind all the horses of the nations. Then the leaders of Judah will say in their hearts, 'The people of Jerusalem are strong because the LORD Almighty is their God.' "On that day, I will make the leaders of Judah like a firepot in a woodpile, like a flaming torch among sheaves. They will consume right and left all the surrounding peoples, but Jerusalem will remain intact in her place" (Zechariah 12:1-6, NIV).

In the last days, the mountain of the LORD's temple will be established as chief among the mountains; it will be raised above the hills, and all nations will stream to it. Many peoples will come and say, "Come, let us go up to the mountain of the LORD, to the house of the God of Jacob. He will teach us his ways so that we may walk in his paths." The law will go out from Zion, the word of the LORD from Jerusalem. He will judge between the nations and will settle disputes for many peoples. They will beat their swords into plowshares and their spears into pruning hooks. Nation will not take up sword against nation, nor will they train for war anymore (Isaiah 2:2-4, NIV).

CHAPTER NINE

COMFORT ISRAEL

*"Comfort ye, comfort ye my people saith your God.
Speak ye comfortably to Jerusalem".*
—ISAIAH 40:1-2, KJV

The setting of Isaiah 40 follows the dispersion of the Jewish people to Babylon. The Children of Israel had been captives, distraught by the circumstances in which they found themselves. Those left behind in Jerusalem, ruled by the Babylonians, were equally distressed. The Book of Lamentations was written as a release for their grief and agitation. In Lamentations 1:17, NLT, the writer records:

Jerusalem reaches out for help, but no one comforts her.

Now, in Isaiah 40, change has come. The Hebrew people have paid the price for their sin, and the time for comfort has come. As the author of one Bible commentary wrote, "God is now comforting you who have been punished." It is time for comfort for people who have long been held captive. God cries out:

> *Comfort, oh comfort my people. . . .Speak kindly to Jerusalem* (Isaiah 40:1-2, NASB).

The price has been paid, and comfort has come as a result of Israel's repentance, of their sighing and lamenting over the cause of their captivity. Jehovah, merciful and gracious, has now sent His spokesman to offer comfort and consolation. He has sent a servant to offer tenderness, the balm of Gilead to bind up their wounded spirits and broken hearts. God's response to their repentance is, "I am with you. I have neither forgotten nor forsaken you." That theme is repeated again and again through the remainder of the Book of Isaiah.

The children of Israel had suffered through a terrible calamity. They needed the comfort of being assured that their time of catastrophe was ending. It was time for encouragement, for knowing that God had not forsaken them. Darkness had covered the land, but Yahweh had not cast Israel aside. The time for restoration was at hand; the time for comfort had come. The God of all comfort had declared it was time for consolation.

In his commentary on Isaiah, Walter Brueggemann writes:

> Enough! Enough sentence, enough penalty, enough payment, enough exile, enough displacement! This is an assertion of forgiveness, but it is not cheap, soft, or easy forgiveness. There is, in any case, a

limit to the sentence. It can be satisfied and served out. And now it is ended!⁴³

The prophetic word given by Isaiah was not just for that time; it is a God-given mandate for Christians to offer comfort, encouragement, and emotional and financial support to the suffering House of Israel. If this Scripture is not for Christians, then for whom is it? Nation after nation has turned its back on the Jewish people. God will not forget those who abandon Israel, just as He will not forget those who reach out in love and assistance. This assignment is echoed in Paul's second letter to the Corinthians:

> *Praise be to the God and Father of our Lord Jesus Christ, the Father of compassion and the God of all comfort, who comforts us in all our troubles, so that we can comfort those in any trouble with the comfort we ourselves receive from God,* (2 Corinthians 1:3-4, NIV).

If you and I are to be godly, our major focus is to become more like Christ; we must offer comfort and consolation to God's chosen people. In Isaiah 6:8, NKJV, God called out, *"Whom shall I send, and who will go for us?"* Isaiah cried, *"Here am I; send me."* The Lord is saying that praying Christians can win the war being fought right now in the land of the Bible. Wake up, mighty men; wake up, mighty women! Wake up, Esthers and Nehemiahs! As Daniel so confidently stated:

> *But the people that do know their God shall be strong and do exploits* (Daniel 11:32, KJV).

As Christians, we are called to show God's love to the suffering House of Israel, as did Corrie ten Boom and her family. Almost four decades ago, in September of 1986, I traveled to Haarlem, Holland, determined to purchase and restore the ten Boom clock shop. On April 15, 1986, I met with the owner, Mr. Cor Van Der Noll, and asked him if he would sell the clock shop so we could restore it to its original condition, as it was when Corrie was alive. As I prayed and waited for his answer, the clocks in the shop began to chime the noon hour. Mr. Van Der Noll looked at me and said, "Yes, I will sell. Do you know why? Today is April 15, Corrie's birthday."

On January 1, 1987, the 150th anniversary of the clock shop, the project was completed. The ten Boom clock shop has been open at no charge to the public since that time as a witness of the love Christians have for the Jewish people.

The lives and deaths of the ten Boom family—Corrie's father Casper and her sister Betsie—their love for the Jewish people, and the sacrifices they made to save some eight hundred Jews during the Holocaust were the inspiration for the Jerusalem Prayer Team. Their story of courage, faith, and determination began on May 10, 1940, when the people of Holland came face-to-face with the reality of war. Germany was poised to invade their country, which had hoped to remain neutral. Earlier in the evening, the ten Boom family had gathered around Casper's prized radio to hear the Dutch prime minister address the country. He assured the people that there was nothing to fear. Casper was incensed by his comments. "It is wrong to give people hope when there is no hope. It is wrong to base faith upon wishes. There will be war. The Germans will attack, and we will fall."[44]

Corrie was in bed asleep when the jarring sound of explosions rent the night. She bolted upright and grabbed her robe. Slipping her arms into the sleeves, she raced downstairs, paused outside her father's room, and hearing only the sounds of his whiffling snores, moved on to her older sister Betsie's room. Corrie felt her way across the bedroom to find Betsie, who was sitting upright in the darkness. The two sisters embraced and said in unison, "War."

They curled up in Betsie's bed and drifted back to sleep. That was when Corrie dreamed that she, Betsie, their father, brother Willem, and nephew Peter were being driven through the square in Haarlem in the back of a wagon. To her horror, they could not climb down from the dray, carrying them farther and farther from their home. She jerked awake and told Betsie about the dream. Betsie reassured Corrie, "If God has shown us bad times ahead, it's enough for me that He knows about them. That's why He sometimes shows us things, you know—to tell us that this too is in His hands."[45]

Five days later, the news came that Holland had surrendered, and Queen Wilhelmina had fled to England. Over the next months, the Dutch people gradually became aware of the horrors of antisemitism. At first, it was negligible—a rock through a window or slurs painted like ugly slashes across synagogue walls and on the front doors of Jewish homes. Jews were denied service in restaurants, libraries, theaters, and other gathering places. Finally, six-pointed yellow cloth stars were handed out that had to be worn prominently on clothing, each bearing the word *Jood* (Jew). Then, Jews began silently disappearing as if they had never existed.

On one of their walks, Corrie and her father saw Jews in the public square being loaded like so many cattle into the back of a truck—men, women, and children—all bearing the ignominious yellow star. Corrie wept for the people; Casper pitied the Germans, for, he said, they were "touching the apple of God's eye."

It was Corrie's nephew Kik, Willem's son, who was responsible for helping the Weils, the ten Booms' neighbors across the street, escape the Nazi threat and who first planted the thought in her mind of working with the Underground. Once the seed was planted, God began to water it and cultivate it until, on May 10, 1942, the seedling burst forth into the light, and the lives of the ten Boom family were forever changed. (Kik died in Bergen-Belsen. He was incarcerated for aiding a downed American pilot.)

The edict had been handed down from Nazi headquarters that the singing of the Dutch national anthem, "Wilhelmus," was *verboten* (forbidden). Corrie, Betsie, and Casper were on their way to Sunday services at the Dutch Reformed Church in Velsen, a small town nearby. The German occupation had been responsible for one good thing in Holland: Churches overflowing with worshippers. Peter, another nephew, had been selected as church organist in a competition of forty entrants. He was in the organ loft, hidden from the crowd below. As the service concluded, the crowd emitted a unified gasp; Peter had pulled out all the stops on the huge organ and was playing the "Wilhelmus" at full volume.

Peter was clearly a hero to the burdened Dutch people, but Corrie worried he might be arrested for his victorious organ recital. For several days his safety seemed secure, but then his little sister, Cocky, burst into the clock shop to inform everyone that Peter had been arrested and taken away to the federal prison in Amsterdam. For two months, he would languish in a cold, dark, concrete cell before being released.

Two weeks later, the ten Boom family home became a way station on the Underground Railroad, which aided Jews in escaping the Nazis. Just before evening curfew, a knock summoned Corrie to the alley door. There stood a heavily veiled woman. When the door opened, she stepped inside and identified herself as a Jew seeking asylum. Casper ten Boom welcomed her and explained that all of God's children were welcome in his home. Two nights later, another furtive knock sounded at the side door. An elderly couple stood there, also seeking asylum.

The following day, Corrie traveled to seek Willem's advice. As he talked with Corrie about procuring ration cards, she thought of a friend who worked in the Food Office. With the help of Fred Koornstra, Corrie was able to secure enough ration cards to feed the Jewish refugees who passed through the ten Boom home.

The secret room, or "The Hiding Place," as it would become known, was the brainchild of one of Europe's most respected architects, whom they knew only as Mr. Smit. (Many of the underground workers were labeled "Smit." This made it difficult for other workers to identify these brave volunteers.) This elderly wisp of a man freely gave his time and energy to design and direct the workmen, who built a room so secure that the Gestapo failed ever to find it. A signal was devised to show that it was safe to enter the ten Boom home. This was an Alpina Watches sign hung in the dining room window.

Once the room was completed, "guests" rehearsed quickly getting into the hiding place until they could vacate the lower floors and be safely inside the compartment in less than two minutes. Corrie practiced stalling techniques to delay anyone who might come in search of the hidden Jews. One of their guests, Leendert, a schoolteacher, even installed an alarm system that would sound an early warning if unwanted visitors threatened.

Since the ten Boom home was in the center of Haarlem, Corrie worked diligently to secure other hiding places for those who came for help. She enlisted farmers, owners of large homes, and others who wanted to give aid to the tormented Jewish population. She amassed a group of about eighty people, some of whom were teenagers, willing to risk their lives to carry coded messages between Corrie and her contacts. One coded message read:

> We have a man's watch here that's giving us trouble. We can't find anyone to repair it. For one thing, the face is very old-fashioned.[46]

That was translated as "an elderly Jew whose facial features would give him away." This was a most difficult individual to place in a safe house. The ten Boom family took him in and provided a haven for him.

Rolf, a local policeman who aided the ten Boom family, stopped at the clock shop one afternoon. He had information that the Gestapo was going to raid a local safe house that night. Corrie summoned Jop, a seventeen-year-old volunteer, and asked him to deliver a message about the planned raid. Unfortunately for Jop, the Gestapo had already swooped down on the home and was lying in wait for the unsuspecting young man. He was quickly arrested and transported to the prison in Amsterdam. When Rolf returned with the news of Jop's arrest, members of the ten Boom family were convinced they should stop their underground activities, but they refused to abandon their Jewish friends. The work had to continue.

Corrie had been in bed for two days with influenza when, on February 28, 1944, a man claiming to need help to rescue his wife from prison came to the clock shop and demanded to speak only to her. Corrie painfully rose from her bed, dressed, and went downstairs. The visitor pleaded for 600 guilders to bribe a policeman and secure his wife's release. She arranged for the money, sent the man on his way, and slowly climbed back up the stairs to her sickbed. Sometime later, she heard the incessant buzzing of the alarm system.

Corrie supposed a drill was in progress—but that was soon followed by the realization that it was no drill. She heard the sound of boots tromping through the downstairs and heavy footfalls on the stairs below her room. She secured the trapdoor to the hiding place, set her "prison bag" in front of the panel, and dove back into her bed, feigning sleep.

The door to her room burst open, and a tall, heavyset man entered, demanding her name. "Cornelia ten Boom," she replied sleepily. The Gestapo leader, Kapteyn, commanded her to arise and dress. He casually asked, "So, where are you hiding the Jews?" Corrie denied any knowledge of Jews or an underground ring. He watched as Corrie pulled her clothes on over her pajamas and, with a regretful glance at her bag, which she had stuffed with necessities in case of capture, turned and walked out of the bedroom. She was prodded down the stairs into the kitchen, only to see a uniformed soldier standing there. Corrie was pleased to see the Alpina Watches sign lying smashed on the floor in the front room. Anyone walking past the shop would know it was not safe to enter.

Another of the Gestapo led Corrie into a separate room to be interrogated. Again and again, she was asked to reveal the secret room. Each time she refused, she was hit repeatedly, but she still refused to answer, although she could taste the metallic tang of blood in her mouth. She cried, "Lord Jesus, help me." Her captor threatened to kill her if she spoke that name again, but he did stop the beating and eventually led her back to the room where other family members were being held.

Corrie was shoved inside, and Betsie was led from the room. Corrie dropped into a chair and heard sounds of wood splintering as cupboard doors were smashed in search of the suspected hiding place. One German was sifting through the treasures that had been secreted in a corner cupboard on a lower floor. As the architect of the hidden room had predicted, it was the first place the Gestapo looked in their search for Jews. The destruction continued for another half hour, yet no one was found. When Betsie returned to the room, she was bleeding and bruised but had kept silent during the interrogation.

As they were escorted from their home, their sanctuary, Corrie realized her earlier vision was about to become reality: She and her family were being arrested, and they would eventually be transported to an undetermined place from which they could not escape. They were taken first to the local police station and placed in the care of their friend Rolf. For the remainder of the day, they were forced to sit on the cold, hard floor of a large room with thirty-five members of the underground family.

Rolf entered the room, spoke briefly to Willem, and then bellowed that toilets could be used only under escort. After he left the room, Willem whispered to Corrie that this would be an opportunity for those inside to dispose of any papers they did not want to fall into the hands of the Gestapo.

Later, as evening fell and darkness settled over Haarlem, Casper gathered the group around him and began to recite Psalm 119:114, KJV: *"Thou art my hiding place and my shield: I hope in thy word."* As he quoted his beloved Scriptures from memory, the group was comforted by their elder, who would shepherd them through many dark days. His unwavering faith gave them renewed strength.

The following morning, the prisoners were loaded onto buses and taken to Scheveningen Prison in The Hague, about twenty-four miles south of Haarlem. When they disembarked, one of the guards pointed at Corrie's father and yelled, "Did you have to arrest that old man?" Willem led his father up to the check-in desk. The head of the prison peered into Casper's eyes and said, "I'd like to send you home. I'll take your word that you won't cause any more trouble."

Those standing nearby clearly heard his reply, "If I go home today, tomorrow I will open my door again to any man in need who knocks." As the group was led to their individual cells, none knew it would be the last time they would see Casper ten Boom. He died ten days later.

Casper's dedication and determination to assist God's Chosen People came as the result of his father, Willem, having taken up the banner passed to him by his great-grandfather, a Christian Zionist, who had begun a weekly meeting to pray for the peace of Jerusalem (Psalm 122:6) in 1844. Casper continued the meetings, where the family and others gathered specifically in prayer for the Jewish people. The meetings ended on February 28, 1944, when Nazi soldiers came to the house to take the family away.

Corrie's first prison assignment was a narrow cell, which she shared with four other women. When the matron determined she was quite ill, Corrie was transported to the hospital. The doctor diagnosed her with pre-tuberculosis, hoping that she would be allowed to stay in the hospital. It was not to be; Corrie was taken from the hospital and returned to the prison, but not before one of the nurses had slipped her a small packet containing soap, safety pins, and four individual booklets containing the Gospels.

Corrie gradually recovered from the influenza and began to wonder what had happened to the other people from Haarlem who had been transported to the prison. On Hitler's birthday, she had the opportunity to gather information. While the wardens celebrated, the prisoners were able to shout back and forth to each other and gather yearned-for knowledge of loved ones. She learned that her sister, Betsie, was still at Scheveningen, her brother Willem had been released, and her sister, Nollie, had been discharged almost a month before. It would be much later that Corrie learned of her father's death.

Shortly after the celebration, the door to Corrie's cell cracked open, and a package landed on the floor with a thump. She was overjoyed to discover that it was from Nollie. Inside, she found a light blue embroidered sweater. It was like being enfolded in the comfort of Nollie's distant arms. The package also contained cookies, vitamins, a needle and thread, and a bright red towel.

As Corrie wrapped the items back up in the brown parcel paper, she noticed a discrepancy in the return address. Carefully removing the stamp, she found a joyous message: "All the watches in your closet are safe." Corrie rejoiced; all six of the Jews they had been hiding had safely escaped the secret room. This, no doubt, helped her through the following four long months in solitary confinement, in which her only contact was an ant that had found its way into her cell. She was grateful to God for friendship with even one of His smallest creatures. She shared crumbs from her daily ration of bread with the tiny insect.

Corrie knew that eventually, she would face a hearing at the hands of a Gestapo interrogator. Finally, on a cool May morning, she was summoned from her tiny room. She was led through a labyrinth of halls and a courtyard sparkling with the drizzle of rain before entering one of the huts where the hearings were held. As she awaited her fate, she prayed, "Lord Jesus, You were called to a hearing too. Show me what to do."

The inquisitor, Lieutenant Rahms, noticed that Corrie was shivering from the cold and built a fire in the stove. He drew a chair forward, motioned for Corrie to sit, and gently questioned his prisoner. For the next hour, he probed, feinted, and parried in the dance to gain Corrie's trust and glean information from his affection-starved detainee. He began, "I would like to help you, Miss ten Boom, but you must tell me everything."

Corrie was glad that among the drills practiced in her home in Haarlem was one of answering questions if captured by the Gestapo. Her training stood her in good stead. The officer questioned her about the ration cards and how they were obtained. She was relieved that she did not know how they had been stolen. When asked about her other activities, Corrie launched into a description of her work with the girls' clubs and with the mentally disabled. The lieutenant had no idea why she found that so rewarding.

Rahms chided her for her waste of time with the disabled. Corrie responded, "God loves everyone, even the weak and feeble. The Bible says that God looks at things very differently from us." The officer abruptly ended the session and sent Corrie back to her cell. From that time forward, as long as Corrie was in Scheveningen, the lieutenant helped her as much as possible. He arranged for her to be allowed to see her family, using the pretext of the reading of Casper ten Boom's will. While they were all together, Willem slipped Corrie a small, compact Bible secreted in a pouch that she could wear around her neck.

Although the lieutenant could supply aid, he unfortunately did not have the authority to allow her and Betsie to return home. Nevertheless, Corrie spent time reading the precious Gospels that had been smuggled to her. She rejoiced that Jesus' death, though meant for evil, brought forgiveness to all who accepted His gift. She prayed that God would use her troubles to bring good to someone.

CHAPTER TEN

THE EXAMPLE OF CORRIE TEN BOOM

*He who dwells in the secret place of the Most High
Shall abide under the shadow of the Almighty.*
—PSALM 91:1, NKJV

In June 1944, the prisoners languishing in their cells at Scheveningen were told to pack what few belongings they had, then were lined up and marched to a train awaiting them at the station. As she stood in line to board, Corrie saw Betsie down the platform. Suffering from pernicious anemia from childhood, Betsie had been denied medication. Corrie saw at once how very ill she had become, and she wriggled her way through the throng to reach her sister. They embraced with the joy of knowing they were together, at least for the moment.

The train chugged down the line toward a labor camp in the south of Holland. The prisoners were assigned to barracks and forced to work long, hard hours. Corrie was dispatched to the building where Phillips radios were made for German aircraft. She did her work in the Phillips factory with great diligence. Day after day, she made as many mistakes as she dared while assembling the radios.

Life in the camp was exceedingly hard, and execution of the male prisoners was the order of the day. Yet Corrie and Betsie survived. Betsie taught Bible classes to those who gathered around each night. Eventually, a faint hope blossomed as word seeped through the camp that the Allies had invaded Europe. Rumors that Allied forces were nearing Holland swirled through the prison like leaves flying in the autumn wind. The sounds of explosions filled the air, but they were later confirmed to be the work of Germans destroying bridges and railroad lines.

Late one evening, the loudspeaker in the men's camp blared out name after name and then just as quickly fell silent, as if the life had been squeezed from it. A sense of foreboding settled over the women's camp when, suddenly, the twilight was filled with the sound of volley after volley of gunfire. When the guns were finally silenced, more than seven hundred captives lay silent on the killing field.

The next morning, the women were again commanded to gather their belongings and report for roll call in a field outside the camp. As noon approached, the women were ordered to line up and marched to a railroad siding. Betsie clung to Corrie's arm, wheezing and gasping for each breath. Corrie slipped an arm around her and half carried her precious sister the final quarter mile to their destination. As the two sisters glanced around, they could see perhaps a thousand weary, hungry, thirsty, bedraggled women standing in single file along the railroad track.

Corrie looked around for the train that was to take them to their next destination but saw only what she described as "small, high-wheeled European boxcars" stretching out of sight in both directions. Soldiers marched down the line of women, stopping at each car to throw open the sliding door. Horrified, Corrie realized that they were to be herded into the small boxcars like so many cattle. Each car, which normally would have held only thirty or forty, was soon packed with eighty or more women. Those in the car with Corrie and Betsie developed a plan that would allow them, at least, to sit on the floor. With little food or water and no toilet facilities, the car soon reeked of human waste.

For three days and nights, the train slowly made its way across the border from Holland into Germany. At last, the lurching locomotive screeched to a halt, and the doors were opened. The women scrambled out into the sunlight and were at last able to drink their fill of water. They were lined up again and then marched through the countryside to the crest of a hill, where they could see their destination: Ravensbrück! Its reputation had reached Holland long before Corrie and Betsie were incarcerated. It was infamous as an extermination camp for female prisoners.

For the first two days in the compound, surrounded by grey concrete walls intersected by gun towers, the women were forced to stay in the open. Rain poured down on them, turning the ground into a quagmire of mud. When it wasn't raining, the sun beat down mercilessly with nothing to shade the desperate women. Finally, they were processed, forced to disrobe, prodded through showers, and issued thin dresses and worn shoes.

Corrie wondered how she would be able to secure Betsie's much-needed sweater and prevent the confiscation of her beloved Bible. Then, she saw an opportunity to hide them behind a bench in the latrine area. She prayed that her subterfuge would not be discovered as she and Betsie later made their way through two searches. At last, they exited the building with Betsie's sweater tied around Corrie's waist and the Bible dangling between her shoulder blades beneath her dress. Corrie gave the sweater to Betsie as soon as she safely could, and she put it under her dress so the guards could not see it.

The two sisters were then crammed into a barracks designed to hold 400 people. Now, it was home to over 1,400 women forced to sleep on rickety platform beds swarming with fleas. Yet, in this desperate room, Betsie and Corrie retrieved their beloved Bible from its hiding place and proceeded to teach the Gospel of Jesus Christ to these starving women. Betsie would read in Dutch, translate into German, and the words would flow back through the crowd in French, Polish, Russian, or Czech, coming full circle back to Dutch.

The indignity of the regular Friday searches revealed a dynamic truth about Christ's sacrifice that neither Corrie nor Betsie had ever conceived. As they stood naked and shivering before the leering eyes of the German guards, a passage from the

Bible came alive for Corrie. She realized that Jesus, too, had been stripped of His clothing. Corrie later wrote:

> I had not known—I had not thought . . . The paintings, the carved crucifixes showed at least a scrap of cloth. But this, I suddenly knew, was the respect and reverence of the artist. But, oh, at the time itself, on that other Friday morning, there had been no reverence. No more than I saw in the faces around us now. I leaned toward Betsie, ahead of me in line. Her shoulder blades stood out sharp and thin beneath her blue-mottled skin. "Betsie, they took His clothes, too."[47]

A Catholic theologian, Monsignor John M. Oesterreicher, wrote of the forced nakedness of the Nazi prisoners in terms of self-worth:

> The forced nakedness of the prisoners was an attempt to divest them of their dignity as persons. Clothes not only protect and adorn the body, they also bespeak the spirit of man, his sense of beauty, his style, his respect for himself, his reverence for others. In short, clothes mark a man as a civilized being. When the victims were compelled to undress, they were robbed, therefore, of their part in civilization. They were thrown into a mass of like men, all drained of initiative, and the last flicker of resistance was snuffed out.[48]

Each morning, Corrie, Betsie, and the other women were rousted out of bed for roll call at 4:30 by the sound of riding whips striking the side of the building. Conditions inside were so deplorable, filled with the sharp odor of unwashed bodies, strangling dust, crawling lice, and swarms of fleas, that the guards refused to go inside. Everyone had to be outside and ready for work. If even one person was missing, all the women were forced to stand stick straight for hours until all were counted again and again.

Corrie and Betsie were assigned to work in the nearby Siemens factory, pushing a cart laden with heavy metal plates to a railroad siding and then unloading it. Their eleven-hour days were broken only by a meager lunch of thin soup and a boiled potato. Corrie and Betsie felt blessed, for those who did lighter work received no lunch at all.

As the desperate days mounted, Corrie found that she was more often forced to share her hoard of liquid vitamins she had managed to hide for Betsie. The bottle had been given to her before she left Scheveningen. Corrie was stunned when she realized that though she often shared the precious drops with as many as twenty-five women in a day, the contents never ran dry. She was reminded of the woman in the Old Testament, the widow of Zarephath, whose cruise of oil held a perpetual supply as long as there was need of it—all because she willingly shared all that she had with the prophet Elijah.

One day, one of the nurses from the infirmary, a young Dutch woman, smuggled a bottle of vitamins to Corrie. She rejoiced to be able to refill her small bottle. God's provision was truly confirmed that night as she held her bottle upside down to drain the last drop. No matter how long she held it or how many times she tapped the bottom, the bottle refused to give up another single drop. As God provided the new, the old ran dry.

When prisoners became ill with a fever of more than 104 degrees Fahrenheit, they were taken to the camp hospital. No treatment was given to them even at the hospital, so when it grew too full to receive more patients, the weakest and sickest were placed in carts and taken to the ovens that dominated the center of the camp. The ten Boom sisters had truly reached Hell on Earth, yet they continued praising God for His care. No matter where Betsie found herself, she talked about Jesus to those nearby—standing in line at the dispensary, performing the backbreaking work assigned to her, waiting for her daily ration of bread—she spoke of her Lord and His desire to come into their lives.

Corrie recalled how, as the women labored in the prison yard one day, Betsie was maliciously lashed by one of the guards. She refused to allow Corrie to give in to hatred, rather praying for her captors as much as she prayed for the captives surrounding her. As the ruthlessness increased, Betsie's faith seemed to grow exponentially. She seemed to move even closer to God, her suffering but a small thing in light of His sacrifice.

When she returned to the barracks, Betsie told Corrie of her longing to have a place where people wounded in body and spirit could come to be healed after the war. One night, as the sisters lay side by side in the barracks, Betsie told Corrie more of her dream:

It's such a beautiful house, Corrie! The floors are all inlaid wood, with statues set in the walls and a broad staircase sweeping down. And gardens! Gardens all around it where they can plant flowers. It will do them such good, Corrie, to care for flowers. [49]

Betsie's desire was to tell people of the goodness of God—of what a good and wonderful Father He is. She wanted to teach people that hatred and bitterness must be left behind. Like the apostle Paul, she yearned to forget "those things which are behind," and to reach "forward to those things which are ahead," and to "press toward the goal for the prize of the upward call of God in Christ Jesus" (Philippians 3:13-14, NKJV).

Later, Betsie revealed another vision to Corrie, one of a concentration camp. It had been cheerfully painted, flowers ringed its periphery, barbed wire was gone, and guards no longer paraded on its walls. It would house the people who had been vilely treated by Hitler's minions or whose lives had been infiltrated by his evil. They would once again be taught to be loving and kind to those around them.

As the fall days shortened into winter's icy blast, Betsie became increasingly ill. Before long, her body began to fail, and she coughed up blood. She was not a candidate for hospitalization, as her temperature lingered at 102 degrees. Then one fateful night, it finally topped the 104 mark, and she was placed in the hospital. Corrie accompanied her as, with the unexpected help of one of the more brutal matrons, Betsie was taken from the barracks on a stretcher to the hospital. The night was heavy with sleet as Corrie walked beside her sister and tried to shield her from the cold onslaught. When Corrie returned to the dormitory, her dorm mates assaulted her with inquiries about her beloved sister.

Daily, Corrie sneaked over to the hospital to stand outside the window where she could see her sister. One day, she peered through the dirty glass and saw only an empty bed. She slumped as she trudged away from her place of vigil. Suddenly, she heard, "Corrie!" She turned to see the young Dutch nurse, Mien, who had provided so much assistance to those prisoners in the barracks. She grabbed Corrie by the arm and dragged her back to the hospital. "You have to see this," she pleaded. As the two neared the place where Betsie's body lay, Corrie looked at her face, and there was Betsie of Haarlem. Gone were the lines of grief and hunger and disease. Betsie's face was one of repose, of peace, of radiance. At last, she was home with her earthly father and her heavenly Father. Corrie took time over the next days to share Betsie's miraculous transformation with her dorm mates.

One morning at roll call, Corrie heard, "Prisoner ten Boom report after roll call." She thought surely her time must be up. Would she be punished for sharing the Gospel with others, or would she be shot? When she arrived, she learned that she was to be released, but her hopes were dashed when she was ordered to report to the hospital for swelling in her feet. Corrie spent weeks hospitalized before she was declared well enough to leave. Finally, her medical release was stamped.

In a shed near the front gate, she was given new clothes: undergarments, a wool skirt and silky blouse, sturdy shoes, a hat, and a coat. When she was handed a document that stated she had never been ill while in Ravensbrück, she gladly signed the form. She was overjoyed when her watch—a gift from her father—was returned, along with her mother's ring and a few Dutch guilders.

At last, the heavy gates swung open, and about a dozen inmates marched through them. Corrie thought there must have been some mistake. Surely, she was being taken to the Siemens plant to work or a local munitions factory. But instead of turning right toward the workplaces, the group was directed left toward the train station. After a grueling trip with many delays, Corrie reached Berlin on New Year's Day 1945. She and Betsie had both been liberated—Corrie to life anew and Betsie to life everlasting.

After Corrie crossed the border into Holland, she spent almost two weeks in a local hospital, recovering her strength from the cruel ordeal she had suffered. One night, she was smuggled to Willem's home onboard a truck ferrying food and supplies. Sometime later, Corrie learned that she had been released from Ravensbrück by a clerical error, and a week after her departure, all women her age in the camp were brutally slaughtered.

As soon as she was fit enough, Corrie began to share her story with others. When the war ended, she shared Betsie's vision of a place of asylum with a lady, Mrs. Bierens de Haan, whose son had been miraculously returned from a German prison camp. She was so grateful for his return that she gave Corrie her home for Betsie's legacy. It was a place of peace and comfort where the wounded and scarred—physically and emotionally—could receive succor.

The story of Corrie's wartime experiences began to reach other countries. She was invited to speak in America, England, and many other nations. The most difficult place for her to go was Germany, a land scarred by bombs and hatred. Its cities were heaps of rubble, and the citizens' minds and hearts were covered with the ashes of despair. Corrie knew that the Lord would "give them beauty for ashes, the oil of joy for mourning, [and] the garment of praise for the spirit of heaviness" (Isaiah 61:3, NKJV) if only the German citizens would surrender their lives to the living Lord.

In Corrie's own words, she described an encounter with one of the guards from Ravensbrück:

> At a church service in Munich, I saw the former SS man who had stood guard outside the shower room . . . He came up to me and said, "How grateful I am for your message, Fraulein. To think that He has washed my sins away!" He thrust his hand out to shake mine . . . I, who had so often preached the need to forgive, kept my hand at my side . . . I breathed a silent prayer: Jesus, I cannot forgive him. Give me Your forgiveness. As I took his hand, the most incredible thing happened . . . a current seemed to pass from me to him, while into my heart sprang a love for this stranger that almost overwhelmed me.[50]

A Christian organization in Germany providing relief to the German people asked Corrie to help run a camp for those whose lives had been wrecked under Hitler's malevolent rule. When she arrived, she was stunned to see living proof of Betsie's vision spread out before her. It was the abandoned concentration camp of which she had dreamed. Bales of corroded barbed wire surrounded its dull, dreary barracks. Upon its paths of coal ash had trodden the feet of prisoners destined for death. Inside the empty barracks stood row upon row of cots. If they could talk, oh, what tales of bravery, courage, despair, faith, or hopelessness they would be able to relate!

Corrie began to share Betsie's plan with her companions. They would need brightly painted window boxes filled with flowers, paint the color of sunshine for the inside walls, and the color of trees on the outside. And, of course, the horrid barbed wire must go before anyone would be allowed onto the grounds. That place must be a place of refuge, peace, and renewal.

Corrie was further able to spread the Good News of God's faithfulness and love to those around her. For over thirty years, she traveled from country to country, calling herself "a tramp for the Lord." She shared Betsie's story and her own experiences at the hands of their captors while spreading the Gospel. She traveled to communist countries that others avoided as being too risky, and she wrote numerous books. Perhaps the most well-known was *The Hiding Place*, which later became a movie produced by Dr. Billy Graham. As her fame spread, so did her ministry.

Cornelia ten Boom suffered a debilitating stroke in 1978 that robbed her of the ability to communicate. She died on her birthday, April 15, 1983, at the age of ninety-one. Certainly, no Jew who was saved because of the sacrifice of her family, all the Jewish women with whom she and Betsie shared the Gospel and ministered to in the prison and concentration camp, and even the Germans who received the Lord due to their testimony will ever forget her, Betsie, or her family.

Corrie's favorite Psalm was the ninety-first:

> "He that dwelleth in the secret place of the most High shall abide under the shadow of the Almighty. I will say of the Lord, He is my refuge and my fortress: my God; in Him will I trust."

Indeed, she did abide under His shadow and trust Him!

Suppose Christians who are able to bless the house of Israel withhold that blessing, especially by not reaching out to those who are suffering from terrorist attacks, such as the ones that happened during the Holocaust. How will Jews ever know that real Christians are different than those who claim His name but kill Jews? To comfort the house of Israel is our duty and our privilege:

> *But when He saw the multitudes (the Jews), He was moved with compassion for them, because they were weary and scattered, like sheep having no shepherd* (Matthew 9:36, NKJV).

But thou, O LORD, shalt endure forever; and thy remembrance unto all generations. Thou shalt arise, and have mercy upon Zion: for the time to favor her, yea, the set time, is come (Psalm 102:12-13, KJV).

CHAPTER ELEVEN

GOD HAS PRESERVED ISRAEL

Behold, He who keeps Israel Shall neither slumber nor sleep. The Lord is your keeper; The Lord is your shade at your right hand. The sun shall not strike you by day, Nor the moon by night. The Lord shall preserve you from all evil; He shall preserve your soul. The Lord shall preserve your going out and your coming in From this time forth, and even forevermore".

—PSALM 121:4-8, KJV

God has not permitted any power to totally exterminate the Jews, although no people have been plagued, persecuted, pursued, and pressured more throughout their history. Many attempts at annihilation have been made but have ended in utter failure, defeat, and humiliation.

ANTI-ZIONISM *is* ANTI-SEMITISM

Author George Gilder wrote:

> In *Dialogues and Secrets with Kings,* published after the 1967 war, the very first official...PLO leader, Ahmad Shukeiri, said, "I frequently called upon Arabs to liquidate the state of Israel and to throw the Jews into the sea. I said this because I was—and still am—convinced that there is no solution other than the elimination of the state of Israel."[51]

Take a step back in time and look at Egypt and Pharaoh's edict concerning the Israelites:

> *So Pharaoh commanded all his people, saying, "Every son who is born you shall cast into the river, and every daughter you shall save alive"* (Exodus 1:22, NKJV).

Following Pharaoh's brutal treatment of the Children of Israel, God sent Moses to deliver His people from their harsh existence under the Egyptian ruler. To change the heart of the Pharaoh, God sent a series of ten plagues against the captors. The first three curses affected the comfort of the Egyptian people. By turning the water into blood, He denied them what was needed for cleansing and drinking. The Nile, also worshipped as the giver of life, became instead an agent of death. Secondly, their homes were invaded by frogs. (I have never understood why, as Moses asked Pharaoh when he would like to be rid of the frogs, he said, "Tomorrow." Why did he want to spend another night with slimy, green amphibians?) Thirdly, lice invaded the land, attacking the Egyptians.

When Pharaoh continued to refuse to let God's people go, a second trifecta of plagues was unleashed on the land. They targeted Egypt's false gods. The fourth plague was that of flies, perhaps to let it be known that one of their gods, Beelzebub, lord of the flies, could not rescue them from Jehovah's wrath. The fifth plague decimated their herds of cattle. Again, Jehovah proved He was greater than Apis, the sacred bull worshipped by the Egyptians. And the sixth challenged the claims of Egyptian medical shamans by causing a horrific outbreak of incurable boils. Still, Pharaoh was not moved to release the people to Moses, God's chosen leader.

The last set of three plagues was designed to bring death and desolation as hail rained down on the land, flattening crops and killing more cattle. That was followed by a plague of locusts that stripped any green vegetation left after the hailstorms. Then darkness descended upon the land—so comprehensive that the Bible says:

> *During all that time, the people could not see each other, and no one moved. But there was light as usual where the people of Israel lived* (Exodus 10:23, NLT).

In Carlsbad Caverns, New Mexico, at one point during the tour, the guide asks everyone to sit. The lights are turned off in the cavern, and for a few moments, the darkness is complete. You literally cannot see your hand held in front of your face. God caused just such a blackness to cover the land of Egypt for three long days. Not a chariot moved; not a shaman prognosticated; no fishermen fished, and no merchant plied his trade.

With a still obstinate Pharaoh refusing to heed the warnings of Moses, God brought forth the tenth and final plague: the death of all the firstborn in Egypt—at least among those not safe beneath the blood covering of the Passover lamb.

Theologian Arthur W. Pink wrote of the tenth plague:

> One more judgment was appointed, the heaviest of them all, and then not only would Pharaoh let the people go, but he would thrust them out. Then would be clearly shown the folly of fighting against God. Then would be fully demonstrated the uselessness of resisting Jehovah. Then would be made manifest the impotence of the creature and the omnipotence of the Most High.[52]

Psalm 78 summarizes the battle between God and Pharaoh:

> *He cast upon them the fierceness of His anger, wrath, and indignation, and tribulation, by sending evil angels among them. He made a way to His anger; He spared not their soul from death, but gave their life over to the pestilence, and smote all the firstborn in Egypt, the chief of their strength in the tabernacle of Ham* (Psalm 78:49, KJV).

The ruler who had so persecuted the children of Abraham, Isaac, and Jacob, who had ordered every Hebrew male child tossed into the Nile River, lost every eldest son in the land. For some families, it might have meant the death of every male in the household—grandfather, father, eldest son, grandchild. But Jehovah God didn't stop there: while pursuing the Hebrew children into the wilderness, the entire Egyptian army was drowned in the Red Sea as Pharaoh watched helplessly. God had inexorably triumphed over the enemy of His children:

> *Then Moses and the children of Israel sang this song to the LORD and spoke, saying: "I will sing to the LORD, For He has triumphed gloriously! The horse and its rider He has thrown into the sea!* (Exodus 15:1, NKJV).

The Old Testament book of Esther paints a beautiful picture of God's deliverance of the Jews from the menace of antisemitism. Esther, a lovely young Jewish girl, was torn from her home and taken captive to the palace where a tyrannical ruler had banished his queen from the royal throne and initiated a search for her successor. The king was captivated by Esther and chose her to be his new queen. Of course, there was also a dastardly villain, Haman, who desired to perpetrate genocide against her Jewish people.

> *Then Haman said to King Ahasuerus, "There is a certain people scattered and dispersed among the people in all the provinces of your kingdom; their laws are different from all other people's, and they do not keep the king's laws. Therefore, it is not fitting for the king to let them remain"* (Esther 3:8, NIV).

Esther's uncle, Mordecai, challenged Esther to approach the king (a move that could be punishable by death) and ask for the salvation of her people. In encouraging her to do so, Mordecai confronted Esther with these timeless words:

> *For if you remain completely silent at this time, relief and deliverance will arise for the Jews from another place, but you and your father's house will perish. Yet who knows whether you have come to the kingdom for such a time as this?* (Esther 4:14, NIV).

Esther's response to Mordecai was magnificent in its faith:

> *Go, gather all the Jews who are present in Shushan, and fast for me; neither eat nor drink for three days, night or day. My maids and I will fast likewise. And so I will go to the king, which is against the law; and if I perish, I perish!* (Esther 4:16, NIV).

With great trepidation, Esther approached King Ahasuerus. Miraculously, he granted her an audience. The plan for the destruction of the Jews by the foul villain, Haman, was thwarted, and the king issued a decree throughout the land, allowing Esther's people to defend themselves if attacked. Because of this decree, the Jews overcame every enemy and lived in peace (Esther 8-9). Yet another attempt by Satan to annihilate the Jews was foiled.

Another major example was Satan's endeavor to destroy the Jews during World War II. German leader Adolf Hitler declared the Jews were not the Chosen People; the Aryan race was. He determined to resolve what he called the "Jewish problem."

Hitler, born in Braunau am Inn, Austria, on April 20, 1889, was the son of Alois Schickelgruber Hitler and Klara Pölzl, both from a remote area of lower Austria. Hitler's father had been born out of wedlock to a young peasant woman, Maria Anna Schickelgruber. It was not until Alois was in his thirties that his father returned to the village, married Maria Anna, and changed the young man's last name to Hitler. Had he not come forward to claim an inheritance, Johann Hitler's grandson would have grown up as Adolf Schickelgruber. (One can't help but wonder if he would have had the same impact and garnered the same notoriety had he retained that name rather than the more familiar Adolf Hitler.)

As a child, Adolf was angry and sullen, undependable, short-tempered, and indolent. He was antagonistic toward his father, a strict disciplinarian, and intensely devoted to his industrious mother. The young Hitler "took singing lessons, sang in the church choir, and even entertained thoughts of becoming a priest."[53] He was devastated when his mother died during his teen years.

At age sixteen, Adolf made his way to Vienna with dreams of becoming an artist. He applied to the Viennese Academy of Fine Arts but was roundly rejected as lacking artistic talent by that august body. He survived in the large cosmopolitan city by doing odd jobs and selling sketches in backstreet pubs. Between drawing patrons, he would spout political rants of his ostentatious dreams for a superior Germany to anyone too drunk to walk away.

Adolf was enchanted with the manipulative methods of Vienna's mayor, Karl Lueger, and quickly adopted his affinity for antisemitism with its fanatical demand for "purity of blood."

From the eccentric teaching of an excommunicated monk, Jörg Lanz von Liebenfels, to those of German Nationalist Georg von Schönerer, the impressionable young Hitler adopted the belief that the Jewish people were responsible for anarchy, dishonesty, and the ruin of civilization, government, and finance. According to those so-called "learned men," the purpose of the Jew was to completely weaken Germany and dilute the superior Aryan race.

Hitler enlisted in the Sixteenth Bavarian Infantry Regiment during World War I, where he served as a dispatch runner. He was awarded the Iron Cross for bravery but was caught in a gas attack shortly before the end of the war. He spent months recovering from the effects, including temporary blindness. After his recovery, he was delegated the job of joining and spying on various political factions in Munich—among them the German Workers' Party.

Hitler joined the other forty members in 1919, and the name was changed shortly thereafter to the National Socialist German Workers' Party. By 1921, he had claimed chairmanship of the organization and began to dazzle crowds with his formidable gift of oratory. Soon thereafter, the party adopted a new logo—the swastika—which Hitler believed symbolized the triumph of the Aryan man. It also adopted a new greeting, *"Heil!"* and eventually *"Heil, Hitler!"* (This can be translated as "Hail Hitler," or more ambiguously as "Salvation through Hitler.")

The mustachioed little man mesmerized his listeners with his gravelly, impassioned voice—never mind that his speeches contained little of actual value. Near the end of 1921, he had come to be known as *der Führer*. He formed gangs to maintain control at his assemblies and to apply goon-squad tactics to disrupt those of his adversaries. These were the beginnings of the infamous storm troopers, the SS, Hitler's black-shirted and dreaded bodyguards.

Although British Prime Minister David Lloyd George was driven from office in 1922 by the opposition party and would never hold another government position, he stirred a bit of controversy even in his retirement years when, in 1936, he traveled to Berlin to meet with Adolf Hitler. Upon his return to England, he wrote an article for the *Daily Express*, in which he gushed:

> I have now seen the famous German leader and also something of the great change he has effected. Whatever one may think of his methods, and they are certainly not those of a parliamentary country, there can be no doubt that he has achieved a marvelous transformation in the spirit of the people, in their attitude towards each other, and in their social and economic outlook. . . . One man has accomplished this miracle. He is a born leader of men. A magnetic and dynamic personality with a single-minded purpose, a resolute will, and a dauntless heart.[54]

Of course, by the time Adolf Hitler breached the Munich Agreement, Lloyd George was no longer a proponent of appeasement or the German leader's tactics.

CHAPTER TWELVE

REVIVING ISHMAEL

*Oh people of the book, do not go beyond the bounds in your
religion and do not say about Allah anything but the truth.
There is no God but Allah He has no co-partner.
The messiah, Jesus, son of Mary, is but a messenger of
Allah and His word which he cast upon Mary and a spirit from
Him. So believe only in Allah and of his messenger
but do not say three (trinity) and it will be better for you.
Allah is only one God far be it from His glory that He should
have a son. Verily the religion in Allah's sight is Islam.
Translation of an inscription in Arabic from the wall of
The Dome of the Rock Mosque The Temple Site, Jerusalem.*
—QUR'AN, SURA 2:193

*You declare, my friends, that you do not hate the Jews,
you are merely anti-Zionist. And I say, let the truth ring forth
from the highest mountaintops. Let it echo through the valleys
of Gods green earth. When people criticize Zionism,
they mean Jews. Zionism is nothing less than the dream and
ideal of the Jewish people returning to live in their own land.*
—MARTIN LUTHER KING[55]

ANTI-ZIONISM *is* ANTI-SEMITISM

It may seem strange that no one was very concerned about how the Arabs would react to a Jewish homeland in Palestine when the Balfour Declaration was written, but there wasn't much to be concerned about at that point. The Turks, not the Arabs, controlled Palestine, and Britain hoped to liberate it by the end of World War I. The Arabs, on the other hand, were scattered throughout the region with no central leadership or apparent nationalistic leanings. Thus, no one foresaw, in 1917, the war that would erupt almost the same hour that a Jewish state was declared three decades later. This is because while Isaac was struggling to be reborn into statehood, Ishmael was finding his legs again after being knocked from the height he had reached at the dawn of the second millennium AD.

The Islamic world was at its height in the early part of the second millennium, excelling beyond all others in arts and sciences. Islam was expanding on all fronts—into Northern Africa, Europe, and the Near East. Since all other cultures were infidels and barbarians to them at this point in history, Muslims cut themselves off from the rest of the world and basked in their own glory. Because of this isolationism, the kingdoms of Islam failed to notice when Europe emerged from its Dark Ages into the Renaissance, the Reformation, and the technological revolution of the early industrial age in the West.

In fact, until the late eighteenth century, only one Western book was ever translated into a Middle Eastern language, and that was a medical book on syphilis, which they allowed because, after all, they felt the disease had come from the West.[56]

Earlier in the rise of Islam, Western Christianity had been the greatest threat to its spread, but as it seemed to be fading with the crumbling of the Roman and Byzantine Empires, Arabs had little trouble thwarting the West's Crusaders. In their view, Christians would eventually fall to the sword of Allah as all the other religions were at the time. China was too remote to be concerned with yet, Africans were easily made into slaves, and India and the Near East were in the process of being Islamized. Muslims grew content to conquer the world little by little by the wisdom of Allah. After all, they saw their eventual dominance was inevitable.

For the Muslims, Judaism and Christianity are foundational religions that the revelations of the prophet Muhammad in the Qur'an brought to completion in much the same way that Christians believe that Jesus brought to fulfillment the Old Testament and its covenants with Abraham, Moses, and David. After all, all of these men were prophets mentioned in the Qur'an. What was true of these religions Allah had incorporated into the Qur'an, and what was false was left out. Thus, the threat of Christianity was not a threat of conversion (for why would someone return to the old, incomplete revelations of the Bible when they had the complete revelation of the Qur'an?) but of power, technology, and conquest. Buddhism, Confucianism, and the other religions of the East had not produced these things as well as Christianity had, so they posed a much smaller threat. Muslims were not afraid of ideas at this point—for their culture was so much more advanced—but of Europe's military might. Over time, most Muslims even developed a tolerance for Christians and Jews as monotheists and "People of the Book" because they were mentioned in the Qur'an.

However, the West's culture and ideas soon rose and eclipsed those of the Islamic empires as Arabs and Persians fell to fighting. Author and Islamic history expert Bernard Lewis notes that had it not been for the Ottoman Empire's differences with Persia, Europe may well have become part of their empire in the mid-1500s.[57] However, the Ottomans fought with the East instead of the West, and the struggle continued for centuries, keeping their attention focused away from Europe. The Ottoman Turks were Sunni Muslims, and those of Persia, Egypt, and the Arabic Peninsula were Shi'ites. In response to the Shi'ites casually converting those of the Ottoman extreme east to their "denomination" of Islam, Ottoman Sultan Selim I (and subsequent Ottoman rulers) invaded. At its height in the late 1600s, the Ottoman Empire stretched east to the Caspian Sea, engulfing the westernmost parts of Persia (today Iran), South to the base of the Red Sea and along the Asir Mountains (thus they controlled Lebanon, Syria, Palestine, Egypt, Iraq, Kuwait, and edges of the Arabian Peninsula), West in North Africa nearly to Morocco, and north to Hungary and the provinces on the northern shores of the Black Sea. The bulk of the center and southern edges of the Arabian Peninsula, however, a vast desert at the time, remained free, and the Arabs of that region became tribal, nomadic, and divided over the centuries before World War I.

However, as Zionism was rising in the West and Britain was encouraging Jews to look to Palestine as a possible new homeland with the Balfour Declaration, men such as T.E. Lawrence

(Of Lawrence of Arabia fame) and Harry St. John Bridger Philby were organizing the Bedouin Arabs to help Britain oust the Turks from the Middle East. While the bulk of this was structured by Lawrence with Sharif Hussein as the "documented" puppet leader of the Arab nation (in other words, he was leader on paper only for official British purposes), Philby was sent to clean up a bit of muck hampering that cause. A small group of dissident Muslims from an extremist sect were running terrorist raids on Hussein's forces. Philby was sent to dissuade their leader, a Muslim ruler of the extremist Wahhabist sect named Abdul Aziz Ibn Saud, from doing this and to join the British cause. Ibn Saud, as the West came to know him, eventually went on to establish the nation of Saudi Arabia, and all of its leaders today are his direct descendants.

In the mid-1700s, Muhammad ibn Abd al-Wahhab formed this fundamentalist sect and propagated it to the Saudis by making an alliance with Muhammad Ibn Saud in 1744.

It appears that Muhammad Ibn Saud even married ibn Abd al-Wahhab's daughter, so the Saudi royal family of today actually has ibn Abd al-Wahhab as an ancestor. Ibn Abd al-Wahhab preached that Islam was deteriorating because it was being infected with heresy from outside religions—a form of polytheism (shirk). Things such as the veneration of the early Islamic disciples, worship of sacred trees, and the like were all forms of idolatry—and, again, polytheism. In his Book of Tawhid, ibn Abd al-Wahhab wrote, "Shirk is evil, no matter the object, be it king or prophet, saint or tree or tomb."[58]

Since there was not a large enough Christian or Jewish populous in the Middle East to turn his attention to, they attacked other Arabs who had "apostated" from true, traditional Islam. To justify this, Ibn Abd al-Wahhab reinterpreted the ideal of jihad. For most Muslims of his day, *particularly* the Shi'ites, jihad (which literally means "struggle") was described as the spiritual struggle towards holiness and included missionary outreach, but it no longer necessarily called for battles. However, Ibn Abd al-Wahhab taught his followers that for the prophet Muhammad, jihad had been a "holy war upon the infidels," and it had never changed. Those who were of false faiths—including Muslims who had perverted their religion with outside influences—should either be converted or killed, and conversion was definitely the secondary goal. So polytheists, called *mushrikun*, were considered less than human, cattle to be slaughtered in sacrifice to Allah, the one true god. Women, children, the elderly, and the defenseless were no exception. The Spanish Inquisition had nothing on Wahhabism. Under Ibn Abd al-Wahhab's doctrines, committing mass murder became a way of getting closer to God.

With the strength of the Saudi armies, Ibn Abd al-Wahhab soon established a nationalist Arab state in the Najd (the region in the central Arabian Peninsula around Riyadh). From here, they waged a war to purify Islam, among other things, sacking the Shi'ite holy city of Kerbala in 1802 (which was still part of the Ottoman Empire and is part of Iraq today), destroying its religious shrines and temples, and ruthlessly slaughtering the Shi'ites as infidel polytheists. He even went so far as to destroy the tombs of the first disciples of Muhammad as they were being venerated in a similar fashion to those of Christian saints. In their raids, they cold-bloodedly murdered thousands: men, women, children; the young, the elderly, and the pregnant were all executed mercilessly.[59]

In 1803, the Wahhabis captured Mecca and even threatened to take Damascus from 1803-1805. Eventually, they were pressed back and retreated to Riyadh, which they set up as their capital in 1824 and recaptured much of the previously occupied land. However, the dynasty fell into civil war after 1865 (the same year the US Civil War ended), and their kingdom was divided among the Ottomans and various clans. The Saudi royal family fled into exile in Kuwait. However, they would rise again. As a young man, Abdul Aziz Ibn Saud retook Riyadh in 1902, and by 1906, his forces controlled the Najd region and were establishing themselves as a force to be reckoned with, even though they were still small. Ibn Saud's forces showed the same brutality in their warfare that their Wahhabi predecessors had a century earlier.[60]

For Ibn Saud and his predecessors, the extreme fundamentalism of Wahhabism was an incredible tool for religious and political control. Isolationistic and nostalgic by nature, Wahhabism built a longing in its followers to return Islam to its former greatness. It created a romance around the Bedouin lifestyle and the glory of the ancient Arabic royal courts.

One thing to note about this Muslim fundamentalism is that culture, government, and religion are inseparable for them. The idea of the separation of church and state was neither introduced by our forefathers nor modern liberals but by Jesus Himself when He said, "Render to Caesar the things that are Caesar's, and to God the things that are God's."[61]

Christianity was to be of a spiritual kingdom that superseded and influenced the natural through a change in the people's hearts, while Islam is a religion of natural laws of government and culture that would determine the spiritual. Thus, Christian fundamentalists can deal with the heart issues of the Bible through a more literal interpretation of it and apply them to any culture. Still, they do not try to return to the dress and cultural practices of Jesus and the disciples. Wahhabists, however, not only return to a more literal interpretation of the Qur'an but also to the culture and practices of when those Scriptures were written. Thus, progress and modernization are seen with great suspicion as temptations and corruption. Ibn Abd al-Wahhab preached an ascetic and legalistic doctrine that rejected all luxury, dancing, gambling, music, and the use of tobacco, among other things. Such a belief system could not exist within another but must pervade and dominate—thus, its intolerance and desire to take the whole world back to the ninth and tenth centuries. Being backward by its very essence, all that is modern was seen as perversion (except, of course, modern weapons that can lead to the ascendancy of Wahhabism), and those who propose such are followers of "the evil one."

Government and conduct in most Muslim countries today are based upon Sharia Law, which is derived from four principal sources: 1) the Qur'an; 2) the Sunnah, a collection of actions and sayings of the prophet Muhammad; 3) ijma, meaning "consensus," which refers to the consensus over the centuries of the schools of law, but can also refer to the consensus of the Muslim community; and 4) qiyas, reasoning by analogy, in which jurists and scholars formulate new laws based on the Qur'an or the Sunnah. Wahhabists, however, reject ijma—there is no room for consensus or other opinions. Law is thus handed down from the Qur'an by clerics/judges/leaders, called ulema, scholars called a mufti, or in decrees, called fatwa. Such declarations are binding and not debatable. The populace needed no education besides these *fatwas*, and, as a result, over half of the population in most fundamentalist Muslim countries today cannot even read the Qur'an for themselves. Thus, Ibn Saud could rule without opposition with a religion that enforced his absolute authority.

Outsiders, especially modern Europeans, were viewed quite dogmatically as infidels, and contact with them was seen as risking contamination. Thus, when European Jews reached the shores of Palestine to build homes and set up shop, they were an incredible threat to the Wahhabist way of life. And with no great love for ruling by consensus, democracy was no welcome neighbor either. The British and the Balfour Declaration were nothing Ibn Saud wanted to see setting up shop next door.

Despite this, however, Philby and Saud hit it off—probably because they could be mutually beneficial to one another. It appears that Philby helped make Ibn Saud king of Saudi Arabia, and Saud helped make Philby rich. Perhaps part of it was also that Philby had an equally strong contempt for the Jews. They formed a lasting partnership that would empower Ishmael with both the hope and the means to return Islam to greatness. What Ibn Saud and Philby began in World War I led a straight and clear path to September 11th and the war we are fighting against terrorism.

During World War I, Lawrence and Philby fell in love with the Arab cultures and ways, went "native," and felt that Britain promised independence to Arabia if it helped defeat the Turks and Germans. Thus, they promised their Arab counterparts everything they wanted in exchange for their loyalty. As a result, each of them took it as a slight betrayal when Britain adopted the Balfour Declaration and a full betrayal when Britain refused to move significantly on Arab independence. In the eyes of Great Britain, the Arabs were a rag-tag lot that couldn't hold a government together if it were handed to them on a silver platter and, therefore, weren't worth the trouble of empowering, so they refused to let go of the strings they had on its leaders.

While Lawrence took this as an affront, he remained loyal to the crown; for his part, Philby decided to turn traitor. He had fallen in love with the Arab ways and its harems and preferred that in many ways to ever returning to England, though he did from time to time to keep up appearances. Philby was, above all, an excellent spy (as was his son, Kim Philby, who became the most infamous Soviet double-agents in British history). Unfortunately, he turned those skills on his government and used them to help Ibn Saud and line his own pockets.

After the First World War, Ibn Saud began to call for the overthrow of the British puppet leaders in the region. Philby, who had actually been fired for his outlandish attitudes and outspokenness on behalf of the Arabs, managed, with Lawrence's help, to stay in the Middle East as a chief British representative in Amman, Transjordan. Thus, he was in a perfect place to feed Ibn Saud the intelligence he needed to overthrow the puppets Philby was supposed to be helping. Ibn Saud took Jabal Shammar in 1921, Mecca in 1924, Medina in 1925, and Asîr in 1926 with remarkable swiftness, ultimately proclaiming himself king of Al Hijâz. In 1932, after unifying the conquered territories, he declared Saudi Arabia a nation.

However, Saudi Arabia remained somewhat of a backwater until its oil deposits were discovered in 1938. Saudi Arabia played both sides of World War II until it was obvious the Allies would win, and declared war on Germany and Japan in March 1945. Thus, by the time Israel declared herself, Ibn Saud had collected a decade of oil money. By then, US companies had paid $53 million in royalties, quadrupling to $212 million by 1952.[62]

This might be left at the feet of Philby and the British had it not been for the partnership they had with two American brothers, John Foster and Allen Dulles. The two lawyers' connections with Germany between the world wars helped to fund the Nazi Party, whose connections with the oil companies delivered power to Saudi Arabia. That move wrested Middle Eastern oil rights from the British, giving them to US companies. Foster and Dulles began political careers that blossomed under President Eisenhower: one became Secretary of State and the other Director of the Central Intelligence Agency.

The Washington Dulles International Airport was named in honor of Secretary of State John Foster Dulles because of his strong stand against Communism—and despite his and his brother's connections with and support of the Nazis throughout World War II. According to Supreme Court Justice Arthur Goldberg, who had served in US intelligence during the Second World War, "The Dulles brothers were traitors" because they had given aid and comfort to US enemies before and after World War II.[63]

In May 1933, an agreement was reached in Berlin between Hjalmar Schacht, Hitler's economics minister, and John Foster Dulles, the international attorney for dozens of Nazi enterprises. This new pact called for all Nazi trade and commerce with the US to be coordinated with The Harriman International Co., headed by Averell Harriman's first cousin, Oliver. Max Warburg and Kurt von Schroeder were also involved in the negotiations.

As war approached, the links between the Rockefellers and the Nazi government became firmer.... Schroder, Rockefeller and Company Investment Bankers was formed as part of an overall company that Time magazine exposed as "the economic booster of the Rome-Berlin Axis." The partners in Schroder, Rockefeller and Company included Avery Rockefeller and Kurt von Schroder of the BIS and the Gestapo in Cologne. Their lawyers were John Foster Dulles and Allen Dulles of Sullivan and Cromwell. Allen Dulles (later of the Office of Strategic Services) was on the board of Schroder.

According to *The Splendid Blonde Beast: Money, Law, and Genocide* by Christopher Simpson, a bonds issue arranged by the Dulles brothers helped jump-start German industry and, in fairly short order, provided the underpinning for German rearmament.

Tolerance of European fascism was common in political circles of the 1920s and 1930s. Major American business leaders maintained rich financial ties to Hitler's Third Reich. Among these prominent Americans were Republicans Allen and John Foster Dulles. The Dulles brothers reflected the country club antisemitism prevalent in upper-crust society at that time.

John Foster Dulles saw Hitler's aggression as a legitimate German reaction to the World War I punitive peace terms. Historian Robert E. Herzstein wrote that Dulles believed "the Axis powers were trying to redress an awkward balance in international relations.... Hitler's attacks on the Jews and his growing propensity for territorial expansion seem to have left Dulles unmoved," Herzstein reported.

The Dulles brothers built investment ties between their US clients and major German firms, such as I.G. Farben, a principal supporter of the Third Reich, Loftus and Aarons reported [in *The Secret War Against the Jews*, St. Martin's Press, 1994]. One of Allen Dulles's clients was Prescott Bush, father of the future president. Bush was drawn into business with Nazi front companies by his father-in-law, George Herbert Walker, whose Hamburg-Amerika shipping line was identified by a 1934 congressional investigation as a cover for I.G. Farben.

After the congressional disclosures, "instead of divesting the Nazi money, Bush hired a lawyer to hide the assets," Loftus and

Aarons wrote. "The lawyer he hired had considerable expertise in such underhanded schemes. It was Allen Dulles."

Later, Allen Dulles used his senior position within the wartime Office of Strategic Services, the CIA's forerunner, to help Nazi businessmen smuggle their wealth to safe havens in Argentina. After the war, Dulles and other US intelligence officials also assisted Nazis in escaping across "ratlines" to South America, supposedly so the Nazis could be helpful in anti-Soviet strategies.

Most of the evidence of Nazi collaboration by the Dulles brothers and others was kept secret at the time. But some senior figures inside the Roosevelt-Truman administrations fumed over these Nazi dealings. In an interview before his death, former Supreme Court Justice Arthur Goldberg, who served in US intelligence during World War II, stated bluntly: "The Dulles brothers were traitors," according to Robert Parry, Springtime for Appeasers, Consortium News, December 2, 1999.

On October 20, 1942, under the Trading With the Enemy Act, the US Alien Property Custodian seized the Union Banking Corporation (UBC) shares, of which Prescott Bush was a director and shareholder. The largest shareholder was E. Roland Harriman. (Bush was also the managing partner of Brown Brothers Harriman, a leading Wall Street investment firm.)

The UBC was established to send American capital to Germany to finance the reorganization of its industry under the Nazis. Their leading German partner was the notorious Nazi industrialist Fritz Thyssen, who wrote a book admitting much of this called *I Paid Hitler*.

Among the companies financed was the Silesian-American Corporation, which was also managed by Prescott Bush and his father-in-law George Herbert Walker, who supplied 'W' with his name. The company was vital in supplying coal to the Nazi war industry. It, too, was seized as a Nazi front on November 17, 1942. The largest company Bush's UBC helped finance was the German Steel Trust, responsible for between one-third and one-half of Nazi iron and explosives.

Prescott Bush was also a director of the Harriman Fifteen Corporation (this one owned largely by Roland's brother, Averell Harriman), which owned about a third of the Consolidated Silesian Steel Corporation, the rest owned by Friedrich Flick (a member of Himmler's "Circle of Friends" who donated to the SS).

Republican presidential candidate Bush's great-grandfather, Bert Walker, helped organize the Harriman investment in the Hamburg-America Line of ships, of which grandfather Prescott became a director. It was seized on August 28, 1942, because it was used to give free passage to Nazi propagandists and had earlier shipped guns to the Nazi's private armies to assist their takeover of Germany.

Prescott's father, Samuel P. Bush, owned Buckeye Steel Castings Co., which made parts for the Harriman brothers' father's (E.H. Harriman) railroads. Harriman's financing for the railroads came largely from William Rockefeller, shipping the oil of his brother John D. Rockefeller, the founder of Standard Oil. (This commenced the two Georges' involvement in the oil business.) [Source: Richard N. Draheim]

As a member of the Wall Street legal firm of Sullivan and Cromwell, John Foster Dulles represented several large German corporations, including IG Farben. According to Loftus and Aaron, one of his nefarious projects was to prevent the seizure of the Kaiser's property by the US Alien Property Custodian through personal contacts and bribes.

He also represented wealthy American clients whom he persuaded to invest in the German industry. These were some of the same clients involved in the round-robin of reparation payments known as the "Dawes Plan," whereby loans were made to Germany to pay reparations to Britain and France. The medium of exchange was gold. These gentlemen eventually made huge profits on the loans. The plan was devised by the Dulles Brothers, who incidentally also sat on the boards of German banks and IG Farben, the largest corporation in Germany. IG Farben later manufactured Zyklon B, the poison gas that was used in the extermination of the Jews.

In the 1930s, the Dulles Brothers continued their duplicitous projects by encouraging their Western clients to contribute to the Nazi Party as well as the Nazi war machine in return for financial favors.

During the '20s, one of Hitler's ploys was to attack the industrial corporate structure of Germany as part of the Jewish international conspiracy to destroy the country. Dulles' client IG Farben, one of the largest chemical companies in the world, was at the top of the list. At one point, Hitler threatened to dismantle the company. In 1933, when Hitler needed additional votes to assume power, a meeting was held with Hitler, Goring, and several German industrialists. The purpose was to persuade Hitler to cease his propaganda attacks against the corporate structure, particularly IG Farben. A deal was finally made. The industrialists donated 3 million marks to the Nazi party in return for cessation of harassment. Of course, included in the agreement was the eventual dismissal of all Jews.

After World War I, American companies were encouraged by the Dulles brothers through the Wall Street firm of Sullivan and Cromwell to invest heavily in German industry. German companies likewise invested in American companies. It was "a revolving door." IG Farben, for example, owned large blocks of stock in American oil companies. In exchange for gold payments, American industry exchanged important industrial information with the German industry, including technological patents. Foster Dulles, in 1934 drafted an agreement between Standard Oil of New Jersey (Rockefeller) and IG Farben to provide the Nazi war machine with synthetic oil and rubber patents. Farben manufactured the products using slave labor at Auschwitz, the notorious death camp. So, while John Foster Dulles sat on the board of directors of IG Farben, the company contributed to the genocidal policies of the German government by working slave laborers literally to death for profit.

They used legal technicalities and personal connections to impede the prosecution of German corporations that had used slave labor to produce war materials. In addition, they were able to prevent the prosecution of Nazis, who were known mass killers.

They personally interceded on their behalf and were instrumental in arranging their escape from Germany and southeast Europe to the US, our Allies, and South America. Under the Freedom of Information Act, the supporting documents for these statements of fact are filed in the historical archives of this country and are now available.[64]

This is one of John Foster Dulles' infamous quotes:

> "I am aware how almost impossible it is in this country to carry out a foreign policy [in the Middle East] not approved by the Jews. Former Secretary of State George Marshall and former Defense Secretary James Forrestal learned the. . . . terrific control the Jews have over the news media and the barrage the Jews have built up on congressmen . . . . I am very much concerned over the fact that the Jewish influence here is completely dominating the scene and making it almost impossible to get Congress to do anything they don't approve of. The Israeli Embassy is practically dictating to the Congress through influential Jewish people in the country."[65]

John Foster died in 1959. Allen was eventually forced to resign as director of the CIA by President Kennedy because of the Bay of Pigs debacle. Still, he was ultimately appointed by President Johnson as a member of the presidential commission that investigated Kennedy's assassination.

Despite all of this, however, the Middle East of the 1950s became a checkerboard of the Cold War. As independence from imperial powers was found and Arabs began to adopt self-rule rather than British protectorate status, two trends started in the Middle East, one toward Arab nationalism and modernization following the vision of Egyptian President Gamal Abd al-Nasser, and the other towards the nostalgic Wahhabian vision of the monarchies of the region. Saudi Arabia, of course, was foremost among this latter group. The monarchies of Saudi Arabia, Iraq, Iran, and Kuwait also had a legitimate edge over the nationalists because they controlled the oil. The Cold War further polarized the region. Because of the influence of American oil companies, the US supported the monarchies, and though Presidents Eisenhower and Kennedy had made solid efforts to court Nasser, Egypt and Syria moved to the Soviet side of the table, having received most of their military technology from them.

Thus, the checker pieces of the Cold War began jumping as East and West played their game: Britain signed the Baghdad Pact in 1955 with Iraq, Iran, Turkey, and Pakistan in an attempt to keep these nations pro-Western. In 1956, Britain moved with France and Israel to invade the Sinai Peninsula and precipitate the Suez Crisis. In response to these maneuvers, Egypt and Syria formed the United Arab Republic in 1958, which would eventually be the alliance that initiated the Six-Day War in 1967 and the Yom Kippur War in 1973. In response to that, Jordan and Iraq formed the Arab Union of Jordan and Iraq that same year, joining together their Hashemite kingdoms, and Nuri as-Said, former premier of Iraq, was named premier of the new joint nation. Nasser responded to this by calling upon the people, police, and military of Iraq to overthrow their pro-Western government. This resulted in the July 14, 1958 coup d'état that put the military in control of the country and dissolved the Arab Union. Iraq withdrew from its own Baghdad Pact in 1959.

This made for an odd trend: the US favored the regressive regimes over the progressive ones. While both were dictatorships and repressive, America was supporting the side of Ishmael that would produce terrorism and continue pushing the Middle East back to the Middle Ages, not the side that would move his descendants towards modernization and a better standard of living. As America had depleted its oil reserves in Oklahoma and Texas to win the Second World War, Middle Eastern oil, particularly that from Saudi Arabia, Iran, Iraq, and Kuwait, had become of great interest, if not a necessity, to keep the US economy prospering. As America paid richly to pump the crude to keep its economy thriving, it was also funding a growing underground movement against Israel and stability in the region.

Through it all, Saudi Arabia maintained the neutrality Ibn Saud had exhibited during World War II and waited to see what would become of it all under Ibn Saud's second son, King Saud (Ibn Saud died in 1953). Though Saudi Arabia had no love for the fledgling Jewish state, at this time, it was more concerned with its aggressive neighbors, particularly the Hashemite kingdoms of Jordan and Iraq on their northern border. Under King Saud, Saudi Arabia plunged into financial disarray despite the continual flow of oil money into the region. King Saud was eventually deposed and replaced by his younger brother, Faisal bin Abdul Aziz, in 1964. The Wahhabi ulemas had a good deal to do with this change in leadership, and Faisal wouldn't forget it. Where Saud's government had grown soft and more open, Faisal would return the country to its ultra-conservative Wahhabist roots. According to the advice of King Faisal's maternal grandfather, who raised him after Faisal's mother's death when he was six, "Saudi Arabia should lead the Arab world, and the ideology of Wahhabism should be exported."[66]

Though Faisal's grandfather died not long after giving him this advice, it appears that it was never forgotten. It also seems that Faisal was more like his father, Ibn Saud than his older brother had been. But Faisal exhibited the clever, behind-the-scenes Ibn Saud savvy rather than the cutthroat invader who had retaken Mecca and Medina. He would use his influence and the power Wahhabism gave him, not their military might, to promote Saudi interests. Thus, it was that, just as Ibn Saud had only supplied two Saudi brigades to help fight the Jews in their war for independence in 1948-1949, so Faisal would only supply one for the Six-Day War in 1967, and that division would not even see action. Saudi Arabia would, however, benefit from Israel's victory in more ways than one. With Egypt embarrassed and weakened, Nasser pulled his troops from Yemen, where he had hoped to begin a coup that would deliver the Arabian Peninsula into Pan-Arab Nationalist control. With Nasser's withdrawal, Saudi Arabia's southern borders were again secure.

However, King Faisal showed no gratitude for this. He soon found another way to undermine the Israeli cause, and those of the Arab states that might rival Saudi in the Middle East, by financially supporting an upstart organization called Fatah (The Movement for the National Liberation of Palestine), headed by an Egyptian named Yasser Arafat. Fatah and brother organizations would use Saudi money to destabilize Jordan and eventually force Jordan to use its full military might to oust them from their country during the "Black September" of 1968. However, the Fatah would still go on to take full control of the Nasser-created Palestine Liberation Organization (PLO) in 1969, combining several terrorist groups under one umbrella.

All the while, Saudi Arabia kept solid relations with the US. Oil flowed to America, American money flowed into Faisal's coffers, and from there, US dollars flowed to promote and export Wahhabism—the doctrine of Ishmael's hatred for Israel and the West.

CHAPTER THIRTEEN

Exporting Hate

*As for Ishmael, I have heard thee: Behold,
I have blessed him, and will make him fruitful,
and will multiply him exceedingly; twelve princes shall
he beget, and I will make him a great nation.
But my covenant will I establish with Isaac.*

—GENESIS 17:20-21

The Six-Day War of 1967 and the Yom Kippur War of 1973 not only defended Israel but also turned the tide in the Arabic world from the progressive, pro-socialist Pan-Arab-nationalists to the regressive, pro-western monarchies. As the Arab nationalists following the Nasser flag failed again and again to defeat the small sliver of a country of Israel and ended up losing more and more control over the area in the process, Saudi Arabia sat back quietly and paid thugs to keep its interest on the rise. This money also acted as protection money to keep targets such as the TAPLINE (the Trans Arabian Pipeline that passed from Sidon in Lebanon, through the Golan Heights, and on into Saudi Arabia) off of the terrorists' lists of targets (though it did eventually close down when Lebanon collapsed in 1983). As the PLO took prominence over terrorism in the region, Saudi Arabian princes and kings became Arafat's most faithful supporters.

While King Faisal had temporarily suspended oil exports to the US and Great Britain during the Six-Day War, the results were minimal, and Faisal didn't yet see oil could be used as a weapon. However, the world changed greatly from 1967 to 1973. By that time, both Saddam Hussein, who was vice-president of the regime that had toppled the Iraqi monarchy in 1972, and Colonel Muammar Qaddafi, whose regime took power in June of 1973, had nationalized all oil interests within their borders. The Organization of Oil Producing Countries (O.P.E.C.) was at its height. While Saudi Arabia was content to sit on the sidelines as the Yom Kippur War erupted on October 6, 1973, and sat on its hands through most of the struggle, King Faisal decided to finally step in when it looked like all was lost as Israeli troops under the command of Ariel Sharon crossed the Suez Canal on October 16 and were within 63 miles of the Egyptian capital in Cairo by October 20. So, on October 20, Faisal cut off oil supplies to the US and urged the rest of O.P.E.C. to do the same. They did. On the 21st, he cut off the oil to the US sixth fleet in the Mediterranean. Suddenly, Israel's allies were urging her to sign a cease-fire.

Though the war ended with neither side conceding defeat, the only real winners were the Saudis, who had won without firing a shot. They had shown the other Arab nations they had power; the pan-Arab Nasserites and Syrians did not. This might have had enough of a ripple effect on its own, but the embargo would have an unexpected additional benefit: oil prices soared. Saudi oil revenues in 1972 had been $2.7 billion; however, in 1973, they went to $4.3 billion, and in 1974 skyrocketed to $22.6 billion.[67] Suddenly, Faisal had nearly unlimited resources with which to propagate Saudi and Wahhabist interests.

Saudi Arabia soon had the leading economy among Muslim countries, so it became a destination for Muslims who could not find decent-paying jobs in their own countries. Wahhabist ulemas would put this to work for them. These immigrants would be indoctrinated with Wahhabism while they were in Saudi, and eventually, when they had made enough money, they would return to their own countries with a "renewed" mind. Wahhabism would become the world cry for Islamic ascendancy to a place of dominance in the world system. Saudi Arabia became the ideal of every other Muslim nation, and Saudis preached Wahhabism as the belief system that Allah blessed so richly. The Muslim world looked to Saudi Arabia for both financial deliverance from poverty and enlightenment. Wahhabism was introduced as the seed of revival to true Islam.

Additionally, Saudi Arabia controlled the holy cities of Mecca and Medina, where every Moslem had to travel at least once in their life as part of the Hajj (which means "pilgrimage"), one of the five pillars of Islam. This gave them another way of showing the rest of the world what "true" Islam was. Pilgrims were introduced to extreme-fundamentalist Wahhabi doctrine as a return to the true Islam of Muhammad. As interest in it grew, Wahhabism spread throughout the Muslim world. It became a standard curriculum in schools, mosques, and universities—Saudi grants and donations to Islamic charities ensured this.

The West glossed this over, calling the move "Islamism." The US State Department, intelligence community, and other concerned branches of the government paid little attention. In a relativist culture of "separation of church (religion) and state," Islamism was viewed simply as a cultural movement to uplift the spirits of some of the poorest nations in the world. For them to think that a religious teaching could actually be dangerous bordered too closely on intolerance (the greatest sin of political correctness) and went against the grain of the relativistic ecumenicalism of the "global village." We would not, in fact, begin to take notice of it until the attacks of September 11th, and even then, it would take more than two years before any government agency publicly announced that Wahhabism might be a threat.[68] Until that day, no one in the US government was willing to suggest that someone could hate us enough to hijack a plane and commit suicide in the hope of killing thousands. They assumed anyone on such a mission would lose their resolve before carrying it through. They were wrong. They had totally underestimated the narcotic power of Wahhabism and the hatred it created.

The Yom Kippur War also brought other changes in the Islamic world and the Middle East. After Egypt and Syria's defeat in a conventional war, it became evident, especially when the US began to back Israel as a military ally and bolster her military with advanced US weaponry, that there was little chance of winning a direct conventional war against Israel. Despite having only one-eighth of one percent of the land of the Arab states, this little country was much more than a David against their Goliath. Somehow, Israel had become the Middle Eastern superpower, especially since it was the only country in the region with the atomic bomb. This brought about the concern that Israel might attack Iraq with nuclear weapons if provoked during the 1991 Gulf War, thus again causing America to rush weaponry to defend Israel—this time the Patriot missile—in exchange for Israel's promise to stay on the sideline. As a result, Israel absorbed thirty-nine missiles without firing back once while keeping Baghdad in her nuclear crosshairs the entire time.

All this began because of a 1974 meeting in Rabat, Morocco, the Arab League appointed the terrorist organization, the PLO, as the sole, legitimate representative of the Palestinian people and an Egyptian-born, Mohammed Abdel Rahman Abdel-Raouf Arafat al Qudwa al-Husseini, as its leader. We know him as Yasser Arafat.

Another result was also the brightest ray of hope we have seen in the Arab-Israeli conflict in the last Century, the peace treaty and "normal relations" between Egypt and Israel that returned the Sinai Peninsula to Egypt on the guarantee that it remains demilitarized. Yet even in this were signs of dissension. After Egyptian President Muhammad Anwar al-Sadat made his unprecedented trip to Israel in 1977 and became the first Arab Leader to address the Israeli parliament, known as the Knesset,

ANTI-ZIONISM *is* ANTI-SEMITISM

I asked Prime Minister Menachem Begin what he had thought of the Egyptian leader in an informal meeting we had some time later. He responded, "I didn't like his tie, and I didn't like his letter." I didn't know what he meant at the time but felt it was inappropriate to pursue it at that moment. Later I discovered that as Sadat addressed the Knesset, he wore a tie with a dazzling pastiche of large Nazi swastikas up and down it. I also discovered that, as rumors spread in 1953 that Adolph Hitler may have escaped capture and was alive and well in Brazil, an Egyptian weekly, Al-Musawar, asked its leaders what they would write to the Führer if they could. Sadat (who had helped in Nasser's coup to oust King Faruk) replied, "I congratulate you with all my heart because, though you appear to have been defeated, you were the real victor. You were able to sow dissensions between Churchill, the old man, and his allies on one hand and their ally, the devil, on the other.... That you should become immortal in Germany is reason enough for pride. And we should not be surprised to see you again in Germany or a new Hitler in your place."[69] Prior to this event, in the midst of World War II, Sadat had even spent time in jail for his openly pro-Nazi stance and frank endorsement of Hitler in British-ruled Egypt. Sadat would thus sign a peace treaty with Israel, wearing his antisemitism at the same time.

Yet despite this, Sadat was assassinated in 1981 for his efforts at bringing peace to the Middle East. "Normal relations"—the establishment of embassies and exchange of ambassadors as opposed to "normalization," which would include that but also open trade and transportation between the countries—broke down as Egypt withdrew its ambassadors to Israel in 2001. Sadat's move did, however, set a precedent that would be followed by the Jordanians when they signed a peace treaty with Israel in 1994.

Until Trump established the Abraham Accords in 2020, Egypt and Jordan were the only two Arab countries to agree to such treaties; the rest of the Arab nations retained the right to remain openly hostile towards Israel. However, antisemitism is starting to take back its ground in Egypt as more and more of it appears in their media.

If direct military confrontation was not the answer to defeating Israel, however, what was? Ayatollah Khomeini provided part of the answer to that question in toppling the Shah, and the PLO provided the rest in their toppling of Lebanon. The Arabs would fight a war of attrition against Israel, defeating her little by little and destroying her will to fight back. This occurred through spreading the virus of rabid antisemitism and asymmetrical terrorism. Khomeini showed how to unify secular, social, and religious groups in their hatred for the Shah and the US and used it as a political and military tool to overthrow the government—all started while he was not even in the country. With the storming and capture of the US Embassy on November 4, 1979, he showed that the West was far from all-powerful. Suddenly, Islam became the David beginning to defeat the new Goliath—the "Great Satan" of America and "the illegitimate offspring of the Little Satan," the nation of Israel.

The surprise of the revolution to Washington and Langley didn't help things much. When the Mossad reported to the

Americans in 1978 that the Shah Muhammad Reza Pahlavi's position in power was shaky and would not hold, they rejected it, giving continual forecasts that he would cling to power. When he fell roughly a year later, it was not only shocking to them but extremely embarrassing. Unfortunately, this would not be the last event of this magnitude that the CIA would fail to correctly warn their President about.

Despite the US's surprise, the Saudis welcomed the overthrow in more ways than one. Saudi Arabia benefited from the Iranian revolution as it cut off Iranian oil to the West. Saudi oil revenues again grew disproportionately as a result, just as they had after the O.P.E.C. embargo of 1973: their royalties were $32.2 billion in 1978, $48.4 billion in 1979, and $102.1 billion in 1981.[70] As a result, between 1982 and 2002, 1,500 mosques, 210 Islamic centers, and 2,000 Muslim schools were built in non-Muslim countries to promote Wahhabism. The Saudis also donated academic chairs for Islamic studies to Harvard Law School and the University of California in Berkley and grants supporting Islamic research at American University (in Washington, D.C.), Howard University, Duke, and Johns Hopkins.[71] In a two-year period in the 1980s, according to Muslim World League internal documents, the Saudis spent $10 million to build mosques in the United States.[72] Since 1973, Saudis have spent $87 billion to spread Wahhabism throughout the US and the Western Hemisphere.[73] Thus, Khomeini provided Saudis with an example and furthered their means.

The Saudis also started their arms purchases from the United States about this time. It was in February of 1978 that Jimmy Carter informed Congress he wanted to sell fifty F-15 fighters to Saudi Arabia. Despite objections from Israel, pro-Israel lobbyists, and demonstrators marching in the streets with signs saying things such as "Hell No to the PLO" and "Aid to Israel! Best Investment for America," the sale was eventually approved.[74] America was now selling advanced arms to both prophetic brothers.

The PLO and Hezbollah ("Party of Allah") contributed to the rise of Islamism by creating something that eventually became known as "asymmetrical terrorist attacks." The term asymmetrical was used because their attacks were disproportionately one-sided: these were not battles with visible soldiers on each side wearing distinguishing uniforms shooting at each other over a no-man's land; these were sudden, surprise kamikaze attacks that were aimed to kill as many as possible with no opportunity to retaliate because there was no one alive to shoot back at. Under their careful manipulation of zealous minds, they had created a new "H" bomb—the "Human" bomb. It could be used to zero in on any target with greater precision than any of America's smart bombs and cost millions less—unless, of course, you included that lost life the bomb was strapped to, a cost that those who send them never considered.

Using these H-bombs, the PLO and Hezbollah showed how to use asymmetrical terrorist tactics to scare an enemy into retreat. I was in Beirut in October 1983 when two truck bombs were used against the US and French troops stationed there. The explosions killed 241 US military personnel and fifty-eight French paratroopers. I remember the chaos and panic that rippled through the streets that day. The result was that the foreign troops withdrew. Lebanon was turned into a terrorist incubation center where Christians were killed, and children in daycare centers and kindergartens were taught the glory of being martyred for Allah as suicide bombers against Israel. America had lost our first significant battle in the war on terrorism, and we didn't even know we were at war.

Yet, while Wahhabism focused its hatred on the West, it felt no better about the Communist East. Thus, when the Soviets invaded Afghanistan at the end of 1979 to help protect the Soviet puppet government there from the Mujahadeen, or Mujahidin (from the Persian for "warriors") rebel uprising, the twenty-three-year-old heir of the largest construction business in Saudi Arabia, along with many others, left the Middle East to fight for the freedom of these Islamic brothers in Afghanistan against their government and the Soviets. He received Saudi, Pakistani, and US support to fight a guerilla war of nomads against sophisticated Soviet military might. The Saudis gave $4 billion in aid to the various Afghan rebel groups between 1980 and 1990, not including the amount they gave through Islamic charities and the private funds of the princes.[75] This construction engineer also received special training from the CIA and created a network throughout the Muslim world to successfully recruit fighters and equipment to join the rebels' cause and push back the Soviet infidels. After nearly a decade of fighting, the Soviets finally withdrew in February of 1989, showing they were no longer able to move into a region and suppress an uprising as they had throughout the Soviet

Bloc countries in previous decades. As a result, Soviet Republics began to secede from the USS.R. one by one by declaring their independence. Moscow had no resolve to fight a civil war to bring them back into their Soviet Union, and as a result, the Berlin wall came down on November 9, 1989, and the Union of Soviet Socialist Republics dissolved completely in December of 1991.

However, the fighting in Afghanistan did not end with the Soviet withdrawal as rebel forces continued their drive to take over the government that had precipitated the Soviet intervention. The government held out against these forces for some time until, before its demise, the Soviet Union signed an agreement with the United States to stop giving aid to either side. Over the next few years, various groups claimed control until a Wahhabish movement headquartered in Herat called the Taliban finally won out and set up a government. This movement was organized with the help of the Saudi construction engineer, who was suddenly a George Washington to the Arab world, as he had not only toppled the Soviet Union but also made way for the first Wahhabist government outside of Saudi Arabia. The name of this new Muslim folk hero was Osama bin Laden. With the help of the Taliban and Saudi funding, Afghanistan was set up as a terrorist-incubating state with its own special terrorist training camps.

Intoxicated by his success in vanquishing the Soviets, bin Laden would turn his attention to the only remaining superpower that threatened the Wahhabist worldview: the United States. The incredible network that bin Laden had formed to defeat the Soviets became al Qaeda ("The Base") in 1988. Thus began more than a decade of violence against the US that would not really be noticed until fifteen Saudis and four other Muslim al Qaeda terrorists highjacked four US airliners and crashed them into the World Trade Center towers and the Pentagon on September 11, 2001.

All the while, Saudi Arabia sat back and watched, quietly funding terrorism and coercing more and more advanced military hardware and protection from the United States to keep its oil flowing in our direction. Saudis even let the US launch attacks on its Muslim neighbor Iraq in 1991 and 2003 from their soil in defense against tyranny and terrorism, all the while hiding that their true intention was to weaken the Hashemites and sitting back while others on both fronts died for the strengthening of Saudi Arabia. The threat to them was real. However, in 1991—Saddam Hussein could easily have pushed through Kuwait to Riyadh if he had so desired because of Saudi Arabia's poor defensive ability. While they had some of the most sophisticated US weapons available, their troops weren't combat-ready and could hardly operate the weapons effectively. America, for its part, pulled it off beautifully. There was no more than a bump in the US economy as gas prices temporarily soared in response to the possibility that the wars might bring shortages; then, it returned to normal. As was expressed by Martin Indyk, a former US Ambassador to Israel, "We've struck a Faustian bargain, turning a blind eye to Saudi Arabia's domestic policies . . . and a blind eye to Saudi Arabian efforts to export Wahhabism."[76]

In roughly that same period (1990-2001), the Saudis were the number one world customer for advanced US conventional weaponry, with sales totaling over $45 billion. Saudis have also invested about $200 billion back into the US economy. However, despite having the most sophisticated weaponry in the region, without mercenaries or US troops to operate and maintain them, they are little more than fancy and extremely dangerous toys to show off. Like much else in Saudi Arabia, great sums of money have been spent to look good, but no infrastructure has been built to maintain them. Saudi Arabia's wealth is based solely on its oil reserves, but all those billions have created no lasting industry in the country, and no Saudis have been trained to run anything. The entire country is kept going by engineers and experts from the West and cheap labor from the rest of the Muslim world. Saudi nations have not benefited much from the reign of the House of Saud. Instead of creating more wealth and raising the standard of living in the country, Saudi riches have instead been wasted on the opulent lives of their government officials (almost all of whom are relatives of the 7,000-member strong royal family), and on exporting the hatred of Wahhabism.

Right after the Iraqi invasion of Kuwait in August of 1990, Osama bin Laden offered the aid of his well-trained Mujahideen forces to protect his Saudi homeland from Saddam Hussein, continuing his march through Kuwait to Riyadh. This would keep Saudi Arabia free of the possible infidel infection of letting Western troops into the country to defend it. The Saudi Government did not take Bin Laden seriously, and soon, the US troop movements began into Saudi Arabia that would form the invasion force of Desert Storm. Thus, the presence of American troops in his homeland became another mark against the United States for bin Laden, against what he must have seen as obvious Western corruption of Saudi leadership. This is further evidenced by the fact that bin Laden became more and more critical in his comments about the Saudi regime to the point that the Saudi government revoked his citizenship in 1994. There is also good evidence that this sentiment motivated al Qaeda members to carry out the four bombings in May and November of 2003 in Riyadh that murdered forty-two, mostly Muslims (only eight of the victims were Americans), and wounded hundreds in the pursuit of chasing all Westerners from Saudi soil.

In April of 1991, Ishmael's rage became more consolidated and focused. From the 25 through the 28 of that month, radical Islamic groups that sympathized with Iraq during Desert Storm convened in Khartoum at the invitation of Hassan al-Turabi. Islamic militants called the National Islamic Front (N.I.F.) toppled the Sudanese government in June of 1989, and Sudan moved into the Islamist world (after the Soviet withdrawal from Afghanistan, bin Laden made trips to Sudan to help organize the N.I.F.). Many of the groups attending received Saudi financial support. Fifty-five nations were represented, including several from the Middle East: HAMAS (an acronym for the "Islamic Resistance Movement"), Islamic Jihad, Yasser Arafat, and bin Laden. Bin Laden even set up residence in Khartoum from 1991 until he was expelled in 1996 (at which time he returned to Afghanistan to set up new headquarters for al Qaeda). In those few years, he initiated various businesses as money-collecting fronts for al Qaeda.

What these groups all had in common was their hatred for the United States and its Middle East protégé, Israel. From it came the Popular Arab and Islamic Congress (P.A.I.C.), which met every couple of years until Sudan closed its offices in Khartoum in February of 2000. In a parting shot, al-Turabi blamed the US chiefly, among other nations, for the shutdown because the United States "is well known for its hostile attitudes towards Islam."[77] In that period, P.A.I.C. became a terrorist' convention where they could make new relationships and alliances, share bomb-making secrets, coordinate efforts and logistics, and encourage one another in their hatred. Al Qaeda blossomed due to the connections bin Laden made there and at the next conference held in January 1993. On his own, Bin Laden would coordinate efforts with Hezbollah in 1992, and Hezbollah would attend P.A.I.C.'s 1995 conference. PAIC became a "Who's Who?" of international terrorists.

It was about this time as well, during President William Clinton's early watch, that the United States received its second wake-up call from bin Laden's organization: the February 26, 1993 truck bombing of the World Trade Center (the first was the 1992 attack on the Goldmore and Aden Hotels in Yemen that temporarily housed US Marines on the way to Somalia). While this first W.T.C. attack went relatively unnoticed, it was the seeds of the eventual September 11 attacks, and not only in the location. The actual aim of the bombing was to topple the towers and kill as many as 250,000.[78] If they had succeeded in even one percent of this instead of only killing seven, we would be remembering February 26, 1993, not September 11, 2001. Instead, however, because our president at the time was more occupied with implementing his economic program than keeping America safe, no one else paid much attention to the bombing either. In his regular President's Radio Address the day after the bombing, President Clinton mentioned the "tragedy" (he never once used the word "bomb" or "terrorist" in the address) and never mentioned the incident in public again. Neither did he ever visit the site of the blast. As the author of *Losing bin Laden*, Richard Miniter, put it about Clinton's inability to deal with bin Laden throughout his presidency:

> In 1993, bin Laden was a small-time funder of militant Muslim terrorists in Sudan, Yemen, and Afghanistan. By the end of 2000, Clinton's last year in office, bin Laden's network was operating in more than fifty-five countries and already responsible for the deaths of thousands (including fifty-five Americans)....
>
> Clinton was tested by historic, global conflict, the first phase of America's war on terror. He was president when bin Laden declared war on America. He had many chances to defeat bin Laden; he simply did not take them. If, in the wake of the 1998 embassy bombings, Clinton had rallied the public and the Congress to fight bin Laden and smash terrorism, he might have been the Winston Churchill of his generation. But, instead, he chose the role of Neville Chamberlain (whose appeasements of

Hitler in Munich in 1938 are credited with paving the way to the Nazi invasion of Poland that began World War II the next year).[79]

The 1993 W.T.C. bombing had been planned and organized by Sheikh Omar Abdel Rahman, who said,

> The obligation of Allah is upon us to wage jihad for the sake of Allah.... We have to thoroughly demoralize the enemies of Allah by blowing up their towers that constitute the pillars of their civilization ... the high buildings of which they are so proud.

In an uncompromising fit of moral relativistic blindness, they marked across the top of the boxes "Irrelevant religious stuff," dismissing the very reason for the attacks and failing to connect them to the worldwide Wahhabist movement that had fueled it. They saw Rahman's group as a fanatic splinter group, much like Jim Jones and the Branch Davidians of Waco, Texas, they faced only a few days after that bombing.

Rahman, who was involved in the assassination of Egyptian President Anwar Sadat, came to America in 1990, free to set up his terrorist shop in New Jersey. A PBS special aired in 1994 documented a quilt-work of Islamic groups and terrorist sponsors that had sprung up across America since the Iranian revolution. These groups include arms of Islamic Jihad, HAMAS, and Hezbollah, with cells in New York, Florida, Chicago, Kansas City, and Dallas. The groups hide behind a smoke screen of small businesses and religious and charitable groups. These team members work in the US to raise funds, recruit volunteers, and lay plans for terrorist missions for the ultimate battle against "The Great Satan." Their primary objective was to succeed in the mission without being blamed, to realize widespread media coverage, and to maximize psychological and economic damage through terror.

In October of the same year as the first World Trade Center attack, US troops had been sent on a humanitarian mission to Mogadishu, Somalia. I was there shortly afterward when two Blackhawk helicopters were shot down, and a roughly twenty-hour firefight ensued in which nineteen American soldiers and over a thousand Somalis were killed. Shortly after this, President Bill Clinton decided to pull out of Somalia. Evidence was later found that the Somalis who had shot down the helicopters had received training from bin Laden's forces that had become adept at bringing down advanced Soviet helicopters in their fighting in Afghanistan with rocket-propelled grenades. Bin Laden eventually admitted his involvement in Somalia in an interview on CNN. The terrorists considered it a glorious victory.

Thus, in 1993, Ishmael's hatred for his half-brother was in full bloom and empowered by oil royalties paid by the US, trained and experienced in toppling superpowers, organized and coordinated by organizations such as P.A.I.C., terrorist-harboring states, businesses, and charities in the US, all aimed at attacking America and Israel. Another piece of the puzzle leading to September 11th was the December 1994 attempt by the Algerian Groupe Islamique Armé's hijacking of an Air France plane they planned to crash into the Eiffel Tower. Most in the group were Arabs who had fought in Afghanistan. The plan failed, however, because none of the hijackers could fly the plane, so it landed in Marseilles instead, where it was stormed by French police. No direct connection was made to al Qaeda, but the attempt alone must have seeded the idea for September 11th and cautioned them to make sure there were terrorists on board who could fly the airliner, even if they didn't know how to land it. If nothing else, America was now directly in the crosshairs of prophetic radical apocalyptic Islamic rage.

Yet we were also at a crossroads between the two brothers. In September of that same year, I sat in the audience as President Bill Clinton celebrated on the White House lawn for what he called "a brave gamble for peace," where he forced—standing with his thumb in the Prime Minister's back—Israeli Prime Minister Yitzhak Rabin to shake hands with PLO Chairman Yasser Arafat—who had probably just shaken Osama bin Laden's hand in the same way only months before—over a blank sheet of paper that represented the Declaration of Principles—or Oslo Accords—that led to Israeli concessions to the Palestinian Authority that would only be answered with more H-bombs in Jerusalem and Tel Aviv. The paper lay on the same table over which President Jimmy Carter had presided as Menachem Begin and Anwar Sadat had signed the Peace Treaty between Israel and Egypt in 1979. President Clinton later described it as one of "the highest moments" of his presidency as the two "shook hands for the first time in front of a billion people on television. It was an unbelievable day."[80]

It was indeed an "unbelievable day" and a defining moment for the forty-second President of the United States, but hardly in the terms he described them. America had not only negotiated an official agreement between a democracy and a terrorist organization but also sent a signal to radicals worldwide that terrorism pays.

CHAPTER FOURTEEN

Treason

America will never be destroyed from the outside.
If we falter and lose our freedoms,
it will be because we destroyed ourselves.
—ABRAHAM LINCOLN

All nations before him are as nothing; and they
are counted to him less than nothing, and vanity.
—ISAIAH 40:1, KJV

Almost exactly a year before the September 11th attacks, on September 8, 2000, President Bill Clinton welcomed an incredible assembly of world leaders made up of dignitaries, ambassadors, and heads of state who were attending the United Nations Millennium Summit to a reception held in one of the most remarkable places in New York City: The Temple of Dendur, a Nubian shrine honoring the Egyptian goddess Isis. The temple was rebuilt stone by stone in the Sackler Wing of the Metropolitan

Museum of Art, which is a glass room large enough to fit a house and overlooks Central Park. It was disassembled in the 1960s to preserve the ancient site, as the Aswan Dam project would have covered it in water. It was given to the United States in 1965 as a gift of friendship from Egyptian President Gamal Abd al-Nasser and awarded to the Met the same year that Nasser provoked the Six-Day War.

The symbolism of the event and the location seems to speak volumes about the Clinton presidency, not only the symbolism of meeting with the UN members in a room housing a gift from a man who hated Israel, but also the symbolism of the temple itself. The temple was erected roughly fifteen years before Christ's birth as a Roman tribute to Egyptian heritage and even depicts the Roman Emperor Caesar Augustus (the emperor responsible for Mary and Joseph going to Bethlehem for Jesus' birth)[81] sacrificing to the Egyptian gods alongside other pharaohs, symbolizing the supremacy of such gods to even the greatest world leaders of that day. Isis, to whom the temple is dedicated, has been one of the most enduring goddesses of all time, being the great mother-goddess, maternal spirit, enchantress, goddess of magic, and protector of the dead: an archetype identified with Mother Earth, the earth goddess, Gaia, and similar worldly traditions. In their words, she symbolizes Spiritus Mundi, the "spirit of the world." If ever there was a gathering that epitomized the moral relativity of Bill Clinton's eight years in office, this was it—perhaps even going one step further than the day he lied before a federal grand jury concerning his sexual harassment of Paula Jones.

Many liberals gloss over the issues surrounding Bill Clinton's impeachment as a right-wing Republican witch hunt to oust a progressive, educated, highly intelligent, and charismatic world leader—the man who has come the closest in history to bring peace to the Middle East and the president who presided over the greatest time of prosperity in American, if not world, history. "So the man had a few sexual scandals, so did President Kennedy, and look at what a great man he was!" Yet, as often happens, they have their facts confused. William Clinton wasn't impeached for having an affair with Monica Lewinsky or even using his position as governor to sexually harass Paula Jones. He was impeached for placing his hand on the Bible, promising to "tell the truth, the whole truth, and nothing but the truth," and lying to cover up his own indiscretions. If the man would lie to do that, what else would he be willing to lie about? If he were willing to twist the reasoning of moral judgment to justify perjury ("That depends on what your definition of 'is' is..."), what else would he do to achieve the goals he set for himself? And would this president's lack of moral judgment make him a danger to the citizens of the United States?

As the facts come out about him and his actions during his presidency, it appears that he was indeed willing to lie about and justify a great deal more to carve a place in history for himself. Yet history will not remember President William Jefferson Clinton nearly as fondly as he would have liked, and, unfortunately, his sexual behavior will probably almost be lost in the gravity of what he did to America. If America falls into obscurity in the events of the final chapter of the Bible, it will have been Bill Clinton, his policies, moral relativity, and favoring of globalization and the UN over strengthening and protecting America that weakened our stability to enable that landslide. "Treason" may not be a strong enough word for what he did to America during his presidency.

Clinton's strengths were his uncanny charisma and his ability to make people hear what they wanted to hear in what he was saying without ever saying it. He also had an incredible aptitude always to know the pulse of American opinion and act to stay in the graces of the whims of popular sentiment. A large part of this was because of his unprecedented use of focus groups and skillful exploitation of their findings. Focus group research is done by taking random collections of people into a room for a two or three-hour session, giving them a small hand-held computer device on which to indicate their responses, and showing them videotaped speeches and addresses. They rate what they saw and heard to indicate what they liked the most and least. Then, the gestures, phrases, and expressions that got the highest approval ratings could be incorporated into the next speech or debate to elicit the greatest positive response from the audience. Clinton's solutions for the problems he faced in his initial election concerning his dodging of the draft, his affair with Gennifer Flowers, and other concerns that voters had about his moral character were all solved through intense focus group research. He mastered the art of "spinning" issues to put them in their best possible light and thus make his corruption and immorality palatable to the American public.

This was also something he used widely during his presidency—in his first year, he worked with more different focus groups than George H. W. Bush did during his entire four-year term as president. Through it, Clinton became a master of manipulating image and public opinion. He maintained a high approval level throughout most of his presidency while selling the United States and its allies down the river.

One of President Clinton's greatest hopes was to go down in history as the man who finally solved the Arab-Israeli conflict in the Middle East. To do this, he used his tremendous aptitude for image transformation to change the terrorist and murderer Yasser Arafat into a "freedom fighter" and a diplomat. Arafat became the most welcomed foreign leader to the White House during the Clinton years. It also seems likely that Arafat got some coaching from Clinton and his advisors on what to say, how to speak, and what to do to help in this metamorphosis.

I remember sitting next to Jim Wright, a former congressman and Speaker of the House, as Arafat spoke to an audience on the lawn of the Rose Garden at the September 1993 meeting when Arafat and Rabin shook hands. In his speech, as one reporter put it, Arafat said:

> "I assure you that we share your values of freedom, justice, and human rights for which my people have been striving," . . . his reading glasses and soft tone belying his ogre status. "Our two peoples want to give peace a chance," he said to applause

from a crowd of 3,000, a Who's Who of the American establishment...

"We are relying on you, Mr. President, and all the countries who know that without peace in the Middle East, peace in the world is incomplete."[82]

Afterward, former Congressman Wright turned to me and said, "Wasn't Arafat's speech brilliant? He is a charming fellow, and I used to not like him."

Such comments leave me astounded at how well glitz can sell over substance. Yasser Arafat has left a trail of blood behind him since he first got involved with Fatah in the 1960s, with some of his most recent actions being his renewed call for a million martyrs—suicide bombers—to march on Jerusalem and kill innocent men, women, and children. However, all of this magically disappeared as Arafat and his entourage marched into the White House on thirteen different occasions during the Clinton era as welcome guests to negotiate the release of "Palestine's occupied territories."

Clinton aimed to hold both brothers' hands as he walked them through the "peace" process—and he did so by legitimizing one and applying pressure upon the other. One of the other things he did to legitimize Arafat, perhaps with further aid from his focus groups, was to change the language of the discussion. The PLO would no longer be referred to as "terrorists" but as "freedom fighters" or "militants." Somehow, the building of Israeli settlements on the West Bank became morally equivalent to suicide bombers murdering innocent people in major Israeli cities as each was pitched as the reason that negotiations were continually failing.

A clear example of the Clinton administration's moral makeover happened in 1997, when Sara Ehrman, a co-founder of Americans for Peace Now who became a senior advisor to Clinton, organized a conference call in New York between Secretary of State Madeleine Albright and some American Jewish leaders. Among the participants was Ken Bialkin, who noticed this tendency on the part of the Clinton administration. He asked Albright, "How can you compare building the settlements [in the West Bank] to Arafat's terror? You are creating moral equivalence."

The conference call ended, and everyone hung up. However, one participant remained on the line and recorded the rest of what was said. Sarah Ehrman angrily asked her friend Steven Cohen, who had been Shimon Peres's contact man with the PLO during the 1980s, "How is it that there are people here asking such embarrassing questions? Don't they realize that Arafat has no choice but to use terror?"[83]

He had no choice? The PLO and similar organizations have no choice but to send some of their most dedicated youth to murder innocent people by committing suicide? Then what are the peace talks about? Do Arafat and the other Arab nations really want peace with Israel? If so, why have they rejected it time and again? Why did they reject it in Madrid in 1981 when they were offered ninety-five percent of the lands won in the Six-Day War? Why did they renew their intifada after they were given the Gaza Strip, Jericho, and Bethlehem if what they really want is peace? Do they really have no option but to renew violence time and again after Israel makes concessions to them?

On the other hand, the Palestinian Authority—whose strings are pulled by Arafat and the PLO—has yet to honor its word in any of these negotiations and blames the continued violence on the Islamist "splinter groups" of Islamic Jihad and Hamas—many of whose attack were, however, coordinated with Arafat and the PLO before being carried out. Wouldn't a better choice be to follow through on what they have promised, as Israel has done, rather than breaking agreement after agreement by reinitiating the violence time and again? As Democratic Congressman Elliot Engel from New York put it:

> It's not poverty; it's fanaticism that causes terrorism. They are the product of a system that hates the Jews. Islamic Fundamentalism is against anything Western. Israel has the right to go after the terrorists everywhere. The fight against terrorism is a fight for world survival. We must speak with moral clarity—there is no equation between suicide bombers and Israeli actions.[84]

We must realize that moral relativism has given birth to this mess, not "the love of truth" that provides moral clarity. It is the United States that has raised Ishmael's hopes. He thinks we will help him get it all, so he won't settle for anything less than one hundred percent of what Israel won in 1967, and after that, he will continue to work to get what Israel won in 1948.

As author Alan Dershowitz said in the first pages of his book, *Why Terrorism Works*:

Terrorism is often rationalized as a valid response to its "root causes"—mainly repression and desperation. But the vast majority of repressed and desperate people do not resort to the willful targeting of vulnerable civilians. The real root cause of terrorism is that it is successful—terrorists have consistently benefited from their terrorist acts. Terrorism will persist as long as it continues to work for those who use it, as long as the international community rewards it, as it has been doing for the past thirty-five years.[85]

Why does terrorism work? Because we try to appease it! We pay attention to it and let its perpetrators make valid representatives of their causes even if the people they claim to represent do not. We let their acts of violence get them more concessions or prompt intensification of negotiations. Whenever the violence increases, we go out of our way to get them more concessions. So why should they stop?

It was in doing just this—validating the PLO's acts of violence by pandering all the more earnestly to them—that Bill Clinton and his obsession with going down in history as the author of peace in the Middle East caused an unremitting erosion in Israel's negotiating positions with the Arab world in the 1990s. When Israel was forced to fight against terror—striking back at military targets to disable terrorists, not randomly to create an equal number of innocent Palestinian victims—he did not give it his full backing.

As Israel was the center of it all, it was also the main focus of Clinton's pressure to force agreements. According to Oslo, Israel would negotiate separate peace accords with Jordan, Syria, and the Palestinians, yet only one of these was ever signed, and that was with Jordan on October 26, 1974. For Syria, Israel's deportation of 415 Hamas members in December 1992 precipitated a crisis in continuing the talks, so they demanded that the PLO be part of their negotiations and that the PLO also be given the power of veto. The fate of the Golan Heights was also a major issue as these mountains provide a natural protective barrier from which to launch attacks as Syria had done in the Six-Day War. Rabin himself had stated during his election campaign in 1992 that "to come down from the Golan Heights would be a betrayal of Israel's security." So, at least for the meantime, Rabin saw no mutual basis upon which Jerusalem could negotiate with Damascus.

In the wake of signing the Oslo agreements, however, Clinton formulated a comprehensive peace plan for the Middle East, and Syria was the main objective. So, in 1994-1995, he pressured contacts between Israel and Syria to go into high gear. As a result, a peace agreement appeared to be taking shape. The proposed peace settlement, which included a full Israeli withdrawal from the Golan Heights, awakened tremendous opposition within the Israeli populace. In the context of the contacts with the Syrians, Yitzhak Rabin gave President Clinton what became known as the "deposit," a paper that stated that if all of Israel's security needs were addressed and its demands regarding normalization and a withdrawal timetable were met, it would be willing to carry out a full withdrawal on the Golan Heights. The paper was not a diplomatic commitment but rather was intended only to inform the president of what Israel would be willing to have as its final position to ultimately attain a peace agreement. According to a different version, Rabin was willing later on to explicitly mention the June 4, 1967 borders.

To this day, it is not yet clear how this "deposit" was born. It is quite possible that in the relationship between the Israeli prime minister and an American president constantly pressuring for "progress" with the Syrians, the Israeli prime minister was forced to reveal a position of this kind. In how Clinton later acted, it appears that Clinton's role in the "deposit" may well have been greater than Rabin's. However, the result was that the Clinton administration was willing to exploit Rabin to attain Israel's withdrawal from the Golan Heights and a subsequent peace agreement. Clinton betrayed Rabin and showed the Syrians the deposit that had been intended for his eyes only. But it was Rabin instead who was seen as a traitor and was assassinated by an Israeli extremist on November 5, 1995. What Clinton had called his "brave gamble for peace" did not pay off for Rabin due to Clinton's double-handedness. I remember standing at Rabin's state funeral and watching a tiny bead of sweat roll down Bill Clinton's face as he looked on. He looked sullen and tired but not remorseful. The damage done to the negotiations was irreversible and talks with the Syrians deteriorated from there until they finally ended in late 1998.

When Benjamin Netanyahu ran for Prime Minister in 1996, Clinton did not find him as malleable as Rabin. In fact, Netanyahu posed such a barrier to Clinton fulfilling his dreams for history that he did something unprecedented: he sent his own democratic campaign advisors to try to help Netanyahu's incumbent opponent, Shimon Peres, win the election (Peres had been foreign minister and an integral part of the peace negotiations under Rabin. After Rabin's assassination, he became leader of their Labor party and prime minister).

Why did Clinton see Netanyahu as such a threat to his plans? Binyamin Netanyahu was a man who saw that the problems in the Arab-Israeli conflict could not be solved without moral clarity, and he also saw through Clinton's double-talk. He would not sell Israel's security down the river for repeatedly violated agreements from Arafat and the Palestinian Authority. The violence was renewed in a series of murderous bus bombings in February and March of 1996.

Netanyahu was already leading Peres in the polls because the Israeli public, though they didn't know it at the time, found that Clinton's "peace" process had an evil twin: Palestinian suicide attacks. When Netanyahu and his Likud Party spoke of security, they liked what they heard as opposed to the Labor Party's "peace" process that only led to more violence. For his part, Clinton viewed the Likud Party and its leader, Netanyahu, as a Middle Eastern chapter of the Republican Party. Unfortunately, due to the Clinton administration's double-dealing and pressure, Netanyahu would not be able to deliver the security that he had promised Israeli voters.

A few weeks before the elections, Rahm Emanuel, Clinton's senior advisor on internal affairs, arrived in Israel. Emanuel, by the way, comes from an Israeli family of former Irgun members—the Israeli resistance movement of the 1940s. He came to hear assessments as to what could be expected in the elections and to coordinate the possibility of helping Peres's campaign with his staff. The American embassy in Tel Aviv invited several Israeli political experts, such as Yitzhak Herzog, Yaron Ha'ezrahi, Rafi Smith, and others, for a meeting with Rahm Emanuel. Only one of those invited to the meeting dared disagree with the consensus in the room, maintaining that the question was not if Binyamin Netanyahu would win the election but rather by how much. Everyone laughed, including Emanuel.

That same individual happened to bump into Emanuel on a plane to Washington, where they had many hours to argue. "Get used to the idea that soon there will be a new sheriff in town," he told Clinton's top advisor, telling him about the policies that Netanyahu planned to introduce after the election, based on what Netanyahu wrote in his book, *A Place Among the Nations*. When the two parted company in Washington, Emanuel said, "Tell your friend that if he dares to act according to what you have described—we will kick him in the --- so hard, and he will be so miserable, that he won't know what hit him."[86]

Netanyahu, however, held the day and won the election. The confrontation between Clinton and Netanyahu on the personal-political level became evident immediately during Netanyahu's first state visit to Washington as prime minister in the summer of

1996. For the first time, Clinton encountered a head of state standing next to him during a press conference whose sound bites were better than his and who gave a more impressive appearance. Telling the truth makes a difference. He found it virtually intolerable. Afterward, when Netanyahu spoke before Congress and received a standing ovation, especially from the Republican wing, Clinton began to treat the prime minister not as the person expressing the Israeli people's will but as if he were head of the opposition party. Ultimately, Clinton made every effort to undermine Netanyahu while he was in office.

American-Israeli relations in the mid-nineties should be viewed in the context of Clinton's overall policy, which may be defined as conciliatory towards terror and all potential aggressors. If Arafat wanted faster action or more concessions from Israel in their talks, all that had to happen was for the violence to increase. He could blame Netanyahu for moving too slowly (while he, in fact, moved backward), and Madeline Albright and the Clinton team would start scrabbling and chastising the Israelis. Clinton didn't care about Israel's security and Palestinian violence. He cared about keeping the "peace" process going because it bumped up his approval ratings and acted as a diversion from his moral scandals. Clinton demonstrated laxness in the war against terror (as evidenced by his continually ignoring the growing threat of al Qaeda), and he was largely responsible for creating an environment friendly to terror and the creation of destructive trends in the world. During his term, the United States' systems and will to deter terrorism deteriorated, as did Israel's.

Clinton made only a gesture to respond to the Iraqi assassination attempt on former President George H.W. Bush in Kuwait in 1993 (blowing up an empty Iraqi government building in the middle of the night with cruise missiles), and he made virtually no attention to the first World Trade Center bombing that took place that same year. This was followed by a series of terror attacks that peaked with the attack in Dhahran, Saudi Arabia, in which nineteen Americans were killed. The year 1998 saw mass terror attacks in Kenya and Tanzania, in which 224 were killed, and almost 5,000 were injured as the US Embassies in Nairobi and Dar es Salaam (which, oddly enough, translates as "Haven of peace") were attacked with truck bombs almost simultaneously. Clinton's response—the firing of cruise missiles on insignificant targets in Sudan and an empty terrorist attack in Afghanistan (poor judgment on Clinton's part led to bin Laden being tipped off about the attacks and escaping by minutes)—sent the message that the Clinton administration only wanted to do enough to make it look like he was taking action to keep American public support.

Once Americans returned to their lives, thinking he was taking care of things, he went back to his agenda and forgot about the terrorist threat. Subsequently, seventeen Americans were killed and thirty-seven more injured aboard the USS Cole when a suicide bomber hit it on October 12, 2000, as it sat refueling in Aden, Yemen. It was the deadliest attack on a US warship since World War II. Clinton's continual weakness in the face of terrorists proclaimed an "open season" on Americans throughout the world.

In 1999, Clinton tried to restore American deterrence of violence and the appearance of our military strength during the war in Kosovo. The massive air strike on the Serbians instead sent a positive message to Yasser Arafat and a negative one to Israel, without Bill Clinton even intending to. It was a pro-Muslim war (the Kosovars were largely Muslim, while the Serbs were Orthodox Christians), and Arafat could see himself in the Kosovo Liberation Army (KLA) militants fighting to free Kosovo at a time when, for many in world opinion, Israel found itself pushed into the role of a Serbian-type aggressor.

Israel also showed Clinton raw data that proved that Arafat had given the green light to the renewal of terror attacks by the Hamas. Israel had monitored the talks that Arafat held with the Hamas leaders in Gaza on March 12-19, 1997. Based on that information, the then head of Military Intelligence, Moshe Yaalon, determined that Arafat had indeed approved and sanctioned these terror attacks on Israel. Clinton could have been expected to respond to this very harshly. However, he did nothing because he was unwilling to abandon Arafat, who was part of the Oslo legacy and "peace process" to which he was committed.

In 1999, President Clinton made even more blatant use of his special position in the eyes of the Israeli public to undermine Netanyahu's standing and cause him to lose the election. Psychologically, Israel's unique relationship with the United States is one of the most important underpinnings of Israel's national security. If this relationship were to be viewed by the Israeli public as being shaken due to a particular individual, even if this had no objective basis in reality, it could result in serious public stress. Right at the start of the 1999 election campaign in Israel, Clinton sent a very clear message as to what he wanted: he sent the team that had run both of his successful election campaigns to lead Ehud Barak's campaign.

This team was James Carville, Stanley Greenberg, and Bob Shrum, a team worth more than a million dollars, and regarding the activities for which the three were responsible, much more than that. Stanley Greenberg had already been involved in figuring out ways to win against Netanyahu in 1998. He kept close contact with Barak. As the most prominent figure among the three, Greenberg did public opinion surveys and analyzed focus group data. While the general opinion in the US and Israeli press during 1998 was that Netanyahu would be in power for at least four more years, Greenberg found and told Barak that there was a way to beat Netanyahu. The main idea was to cross the security image threshold and stick to the economy and social affairs—the same strategy Clinton had won with in the United States behind his sleight-of-hand slogan "It's the economy, stupid!" by keeping America focused on their pocketbooks. At the same time, he did whatever he wanted while they weren't looking. That was the main input of "the Americans," said Tal Silberstein, one of Barak's top advisors for the campaign. "They structured the research, they came with the insights, and we adapted it to Israel."[87]

Some of the top donors to the Democratic Party and Clinton's campaigns were mobilized for Barak's campaign as though this was another election the Democrats must win.

Overall, the Labor Party spent between $50 and $80 million on its anti-Netanyahu campaign, roughly ten times what Netanyahu's own Likud Party spent. In early 2000, the state comptroller of Israel produced a report that in doing so, the Labor Party had grossly violated strict Israeli campaign finance laws. The government fined the campaign an unprecedented $3.2 million and is still following through on a criminal investigation of Barak's "One Israel" campaign financing.[88]

Clinton personally contributed to Ehud Barak by continuing his warm meetings with Arafat in the White House while freezing out Prime Minister Binyamin Netanyahu and receiving Barak and Yitzhak Mordechai, both of the candidates running against Netanyahu in the election. "Clinton helped Barak more than he had to," says one of Barak's men.[89] The fact that Arafat had become the White House's most welcome official guest (he could have also been awarded the Blair House's frequent-guest prize) was interpreted in the Israeli media to the detriment of Netanyahu rather than of the American president. The result of all those efforts was the collapse of the Israeli political center, with six percent of Netanyahu's voters moving over to the other side, causing a change of government in Israel.

Clinton, now with his new Israeli Labor Party partner, continued his intensive race to curry favor with the most extreme leaders in the Arab world and attain his long sought-after "peace." The timetable of the new Israeli prime minister regarding the peace process on both fronts, the Palestinian and the Syrian, was now pinned to that of the American President, who had only one more year in office. This became evident in the Camp David initiative of July 2000. Politically, it was very risky for Barak to rush to Camp David, but the partnership with Clinton dictated a tight schedule.

The results regarding both the Syrians and the Palestinians were disastrous. Syrian President Hafiz al-Asad, although he had an Israeli agreement in his pocket to return to the June 4, 1967 lines, refused to sign it, and negotiations over parts of the Sea of Galilee and the Northern mountainous part of the Jordan River began. Exactly the same thing happened with the Palestinians, who got everything they demanded, only to present new ultimatums backed by an onslaught of terror, the like of which had yet to be seen in the region. Of Clinton's appeasement policies, it has already been said that the road to hell is paved with good intentions. It's not enough to imagine. More than three months after the Palestinians began a Second Intifada against Israel (September 2000) with an increased wave of bloody suicide bombings, Arafat was still a welcome guest in Clinton's White House.

On January 2, 2001—when the lame-duck president was supposed to be getting ready to vacate the White House to make way for the about-to-be inaugurated President George W. Bush, and about half a year after Israel's prime minister had presented the most far-reaching concessions ever offered the Palestinians— President Clinton came up with yet another peace initiative, this one involving even more far-reaching Israeli concessions than those Israel's Prime Minister Ehud Barak had agreed to at Camp David and Arafat had refused. The Second Intifada was having its desired effect.

President George W. Bush observed afterward that Clinton's final plan was the work of two "desperate people"—Clinton and Barak. One wanted to leave behind a legacy of peace in the Middle East when he completed his presidency in addition to his personal need to clear his name after the Lewinsky affair. In contrast, the other needed a peace agreement in order to survive the next elections. Arab sources show that Clinton's far-reaching offer involved an extraordinary new development: it gave Arafat almost everything he wanted, including ninety-eight percent of the territory of Judea, Samaria, and Gaza, all of East Jerusalem except for the Jewish and Armenian quarters, Palestinian sovereignty over the Temple Mount, conceding only the right of Jews to pray there, and a compensation fund of $30 billion.

Arafat landed at Andrews Air Force Base. From there, he went to the Ritz-Carlton Hotel, where he met with the ambassadors of Saudi Arabia and Egypt. They promised to back him up if he agreed to the Clinton plan and warned him that he would receive no backing if he went back to war. When Arafat left the hotel for the White House and his meeting with Clinton, it was clear that he could only give two possible answers: yes or no. Arafat was late returning. Clearly, the meeting was not going as planned. Clinton told Arafat: "It's five minutes to midnight, Mr. Chairman, and you are about to lose the only opportunity that your people will ever get to solve their problem on satisfactory ground by not being able to make a decision.... The Israelis accepted."[90]

The Saudi ambassador, Prince Bandar, knew that Arafat was responsible for causing the Clinton offer to fail and told him that missing the opportunity was not just a tragic mistake but also a crime. Nevertheless, the next evening, a spokesperson representing Clinton said that Arafat had agreed to accept Clinton's proposals as the basis for new talks—in other words, he would not sign the agreement and expected yet more concessions to be made. This pattern of willingness to negotiate endlessly with enemies, even when they were already shooting, was one of the trademarks of Clinton's presidency and, in particular, characterized his relations with Israel. On the eve of the 2001 elections, Eyal Arad, Ariel Sharon's strategic advisor, described Clinton and Barak as two children in a playground playing with a barrel of gunpowder.

Bill Clinton was a president who could not stand being disliked, even by his enemies or those he had betrayed. Saudi Ambassador Bandar said of Clinton, "He gets excited by the possibility of talking to his enemy and converting him. If Clinton leaves office . . . and doesn't have a relationship with Cuba, North Korea, Iran, or Libya, he will feel internally that he has not accomplished his mission."[91]

In September 2003, almost three years after leaving office, Clinton visited Israel to express his continued solidarity with Israel—even if it was only with a particular part of the Jewish state. He came to celebrate Shimon Peres' eightieth birthday.

I was in Jerusalem at the King David Hotel at the time to speak at a world summit on winning the war on terrorism through moral clarity. I spent the evening with dear friends Benjamin and Sarah Netanyahu. Benjamin, a former prime minister and presently Minister of Finance, was also a keynote speaker.

He said, "Mike, are you going to the party in Tel Aviv?"

I said, "No chance. How about you?"

He replied, "Are you kidding? No chance."

I asked Benjamin, "Remember when he was pressuring you to give up more land to the PLO, and the meeting was cut short because the Monica Lewinsky scandal had broken?"

I added, "It just hit me! The date that the report was submitted to Congress was September 11, 1998. Very interesting! By the way, I heard a rumor that Monica is in the air and on her way to Jerusalem. Is that true?"

Benjamin responded, "Yes, it is. President Clinton had better not stay too long."

However, that same evening we spoke, another telling moment occurred across town, further revealing Bill Clinton's relativism and worldview. At a certain point in the celebrations for Peres' party, which was in the midst of a renewed onslaught of mass terrorist attacks and murders in Israel, dressed to kill, Bill Clinton got up on the stage. He burst into song, crooning John Lennon's 1971 hit, "Imagine," which could be considered the moral relativists' anthem.

> Imagine there's no heaven,
> It's easy if you try,
> No hell below us,
> Above us, only sky,
> Imagine all the people
> Living for today...

Imagine there's no countries,
It isn't hard to do,
Nothing to kill or die for,
No religion too,
Imagine all the people
Living life in peace . . .

Imagine no possessions,
I wonder if you can,
No need for greed or hunger,
A brotherhood of man,
Imagine all the people
Sharing all the world . . .

You may say I'm a dreamer,
But I'm not the only one,
I hope some day you'll join us,
And the world will live as one.[92]

CHAPTER FIFTEEN

THE MEDIA WAR AGAINST ISRAEL

He who says to the wicked, "You are righteous,"
Him the people will curse; Nations will abhor him.
—PROVERBS 24:24, NKJV

Thus, as the nation that helped the Jews find a state of refuge in the land that had been theirs two millennia before and as the nation that had raised Ishmael's princes from obscurity with the power of the petrodollar, America stepped out of the eye of the prophetic storm on September 11, 2001, and into the fury of the hurricane. It was also the day that the beautiful economic house of cards the Clinton administration took credit for began to topple. The nation went from a time of unprecedented hope and economic confidence to despair in a matter of an hour.

The elections of 2000 were filled with debate about what America should do about its incredible budget surplus: Pay down the national debt? Save Social Security? Give tax cuts back to the taxpayers? 1998 and 1997 were the first back-to-back years the government had budget surpluses since 1957. January 2001 estimates projected that by 2010, the US government could have as much as $5.6 trillion in surplus income to work with. However, by March of 2002, that forecast dropped to $1.6 trillion. In 2000, the United States budget had a surplus of $237 billion, which fell by almost half to $127 billion in 2001, even though the attack hit us three-quarters of the way through the year, and to $158 billion in the red in 2002, and hit another record deficit of $374.2 billion in 2003 in the wake of the Iraqi war. In early 2003, national forecasts for 2010 were cut from the $1.6 trillion surplus to a deficit of $4 trillion, a drop of $9.6 trillion from the 2001 estimate.

When the stock market reopened on Monday, September 17, after the attacks, it saw record losses in the first few hours of trading. Not only did the US economy take a dive, but also those of countries worldwide that depend largely on the US consumer market. In the weeks following, it rebounded, only to be hit again and again as the consumer confidence of the 1990s had apparently been misplaced. Tech stocks corrected themselves from being grossly overvalued. Corporate accounting scandals hit companies like Enron, WorldCom, and Tyco. America had been robbed by the inflated economic optimism preached in the 90s and by corrupt corporate leaders. At the same time, the airline industry took a hit due to the attacks, and United Airlines was knocked into filing for Chapter Eleven Bankruptcy.

However, one industry did boom—the security industry. Americans have spent more trying to stay safe in recent years than ever before. The new Department of Homeland Security (DHS) created by the Bush administration was allotted $37.70 billion for its 2003 budget—an increase from $19.5 billion in 2002. This was, of course, a department that didn't even exist as Bill Clinton finished his second term, and it was a yet greater expense to be covered by US taxpayers.

Yet, eclipsing all of that were the lives that were changed forever that day—the children who lost mothers or fathers, those who lost a spouse, a friend, or a son or daughter. I can remember driving home a few days after the attacks and listening to the account of a father, such as myself, only with younger children, calling his sister in the minutes before the second tower fell and giving her a final message to pass along to his wife and children. My eyes welled with tears for the first time since the tragedy had struck. For the first time, I felt the real loss and madness of those attacks. Innocent lives were scarred in an instant because of jealousy and a murderous doctrine of hatred. I am not sure there has been a moment that better defined the senselessness and horror of terrorism. Unfortunately, that has not been the only time I have experienced such moments.

Thus, the moral clarity that could have prevented the September 11 attacks could have also saved us tremendous amounts of money in the long run. However, it might have cautioned the economic growth that had been based on deception during the 1990s. Unfortunately, despite the increased awareness of our real needs brought about by September 11th, our deep ties to Ishmael still cloud our vision. It appears that warning signs continue to be ignored.

One example is that a group of Americans on a federal commission tried to sound a warning twice: In September 1999 and January 2001, just 11 days after the Bush inauguration. The first report was a preliminary by former Senators Gary Hart and Warren Rudman, co-chairs of the United States Commission on National Security, given to then-President Bill Clinton. It stated: "Americans will likely die on American soil, possibly in large numbers," as the result of terrorist attacks. This warning was virtually ignored by top officials and the news media. The commission continued its work, however, and on January 31, 2001, seven months before the attacks on the World Trade Center and the Pentagon, Hart and Rudman presented the commission's final report of 150 pages to newly elected President Bush. It was called "Road Map for National Security: Imperative for Change." In it, the commissioners reissued their warning and a detailed plan of action to make America safer from terrorism. Again, the report was ignored—until after the September 11th attacks.

Yet this relativity continued. On April 24, 2002, some seven and a half months later, an eight-plane Saudi delegation set down at Ellington Air Force Base in Houston, Texas, to meet with President George W. Bush at his "Western White House" in Crawford. It propagated what should have been an international incident, but instead became a State Department cover-up. Why? Because among the passengers in Crown Prince Abdullah's entourage was one person on the FBI's most wanted list and two others on the terrorist watch list. The FBI was ready to storm the plane in the interest of national security and arrest the three; however, the State Department had other priorities—after all, it had been the State Department that had issued them visas in the first place. Thanks to the State Department's intervention, the planes left without incident, though thanks to the FBI and the Secret Service, they got nowhere near Crawford, Texas. The planes left with the three terrorists that had easily been within US grasp.[93] Moral relativity had won the day again—economics and oil carried more weight than national security.

Even worse than this, perhaps, was the Visa Express program that gave Saudis US visas through travel agents rather than through a trip to the embassy, as is the system everywhere else in the world. At least three of the fifteen Saudi terrorists of September 11th entered the US via Visa Express, yet the program continued to run uninterrupted through September 11, 2001. It took another 10 months and extreme media pressure to finally shut it down.

In the wake of September 11th, the Saudis hired several public relations firms to clean up their image in the eyes of the US public. Justice Department filings reveal they spent some $17 million on this. The firms they hired include one of Washington's most prominent, Patton Boggs, which reportedly received some $200,000 monthly. Patton Boggs is especially known for its contacts among Democrats. Thomas Hale Boggs, Jr., a well-connected Democratic lobbyist, founded it. His father, Representative Hale Boggs, was the majority leader, and his sister was journalist Cokie Roberts.

The New York Times reports that the Saudi government has also hired Akin, Gump, Strauss, Hauer & Feld, a firm founded by Robert W. Strauss, the former head of the Democratic National Committee, paying out $161,799 in the first half of 2002. Frederick Dutton, a former special assistant to President John F. Kennedy and a long-time adviser to the Saudis, received $536,000 to help manage the Saudis' handling of the aftermath of September 11th and has an ongoing contract with them.

The Saudi government has run hundreds of television and radio commercials in virtually every major American media market and placed advertisements in publications like People magazine and Stars & Stripes, presumably for the US troops in Iraq. The latter is apparently an effort to make up for Saudi reluctance to respond to President George W. Bush's call for support on Iraq—and the Saudi memory lapse regarding how the US saved the kingdom from extinction at the hands of Saddam in the Gulf War of 1991.

The Saudis also hired three well-connected Washington lobbying and law firms to advance their cause. One firm, paid over $420,000 in 2003, is headed by former Representative Thomas Loeffler, a top contributor to President Bush when he was governor of Texas and a major fund-raiser in Bush's presidential campaigns.

Ex-Washington officials are also paid handsomely from the Kingdom's coffers. This list includes Spiro T. Agnew, Jimmy Carter, Clark Clifford, John B. Connally, and William E. Simon. The Washington Post lists other former officials, including George H.W. Bush, who have found the Saudi connection "lucrative." It also quotes a Saudi source saying that the Saudis have contributed to every presidential library in recent decades.

Amnesty International, however, reports 123 executions in 2000 in Saudi Arabia, some on charges of sodomy and "sorcery." The body of one of those put to death, an Egyptian national, was reportedly crucified following his execution. There were thirty-four reported cases of amputation last year, seven of which were cross amputations (of the right hand and left foot). Another Egyptian national had his left eye surgically removed as a punishment handed down by a court in Medina. Flogging continues to be a punishment widely imposed. Two teachers, arrested following demonstrations in Najran, were reportedly sentenced to 1,500 lashes each, with the sentence carried out in front of their families, students, and other teachers. Torture of prisoners, including the use of electro-shock, is common.

We have got to emerge from our slumber. All is not well. We cannot be taken in by appearances any longer. Obviously, it wasn't enough to find out that fifteen of the nineteen September 11 terrorists were Saudis nor that Saudi Arabia was the largest supporter of al Qaeda. These considerations have been overlooked to keep the oil that lubricates our national economy flowing. We have accepted the cultural unconsciousness of the last decade, which has repeatedly said, "Everything will be all right. The economy will recover. Go back to sleep."

The ebbs and back currents of prophecy are starting to disappear as the various currents come together and flow more and more quickly towards the rapids ahead. As we proceed towards the next key events of prophecy, it is easy to look at the present world stage and see the players slipping into position:

1) Israel

As we have seen, against all odds and vast opposition, the Jews were pulled from obscurity, and Israel reborn. In that, Israel had much to thank America for. It now also stands on the world stage as a nuclear power, and one that has on more than one occasion brandished that power in the wake of invasion and possible defeat (the Yom Kippur War of 1973 is the most blatant example of this). Israel seems ready today to take on the world if need be—and she may soon have to.

2) The European Union (EU)

The nations occupying the same lands as the Roman Empire have traditionally been seen as the "ten toes" of Nebuchadnezzar's dream, as revealed in Daniel 2:31-45. However, this mixture of iron and clay, representing the alliance of two things that cannot truly mix like—oil and water—may more likely be the alliance of two forms of government that are so different they do not easily mix—such as Middle Eastern monarchies and European democracies—whose leadership is based in the lands of ancient Rome.

Whatever this alliance is, it seems likely the EU will be at the center of it. As a member of the Quartet (The US, EU, UN, and Russia) that tried to force the Road Map down Israel's throat, it can easily be seen as part of the end-times government that will ratify a false seven-year peace agreement with Israel.

3) The United Nations

This second member of the Quartet has become a major proponent of the Arab League and anti-Semitic thought in the past decades. While it has done everything to fester the Palestinian refugees' plight since the War for Independence of 1948, it has also spoken with one voice time and again against Israel. Of all the nations cited for Human Rights violations, Israel stood unique under their scrutiny, not North Korea, China, Sharia Law nations, or any other. This masquerade extends even further when terrorist-supporting states such as Syria become the head of the Security Council or countries such as Libya become the head of the Human Rights Commission. No wonder the United Nations Human Rights Commission proclaims that the Palestinians can use "all available means, including armed struggle" to regain their "occupied territories"—a clever endorsement of suicide bombings.

At an Anti-Racism Conference in Durban, South Africa, in 2001, the entire conference banded together to condemn one nation as blatantly racist—Israel. The only democracy in the Middle East committed to civil rights, the rule of law, and Arab participation in democratic government was accused of genocide, ethnic cleansing, and apartheid.[94] Israel and the United States walked out on September 4th, exactly a week before the attacks on the World Trade Center and the Pentagon—the only two nations willing to acknowledge the lunacy and prejudice of the entire proceedings. During the conference, the streets were filled with banners reading, "The blood of the martyrs irrigates the tree of revolution in Palestine" and "George W. Bush: Palestinian blood is on your hands." It is too easy to see that this organization has changed greatly from its original intent and will be a puppet of Ishmael's vengeful whims in the latter days of the earth.

4) Russia
Since the fall of communism in Russia, we have been contented to no longer view this superpower as a threat. The Cold War (which some have called World War III) may have ended, but if the world edges towards another, World War IV may be fought over control of the world's oil supplies. If so, this former superpower will be a key player (especially considering it may be harboring oil reserves that could rival those of Saudi Arabia, Iraq, Iran, and Kuwait, once considered to be as much as two-thirds of the world's remaining oil reserves). As a third member of the Quartet, the once leader of the Communist world, a nuclear power, and the probable coalition leader of the Gog and Magog that will sweep down from the North to attack Israel, its side in the final conflict also seems evident.

5) China and the East
These nations can also be seen easily fitting into an anti-Israel coalition because of their links to the Former Soviet Union and utter dependence on outside sources of oil. We also know from

Revelation 16 that the "kings of the east" will join with those of the river Euphrates (Babylonia) in the final battle.

6) The Terrorists

Their most vocal plea has been for the destruction of Israel and the return of the third holiest site in Islam, Jerusalem (and in particular the Temple Mount), to Arab control. Most experts agree that the war they began with the US on September 11 will never truly end. As they have lumped us together with Israel in the fight, it is easy to see them and their antisemitism (which is again infesting Europe and Russia as it did at the dawn of the twentieth century) as the glue that binds the anti-Israel coalition together in the last battle.

7) The United States

America stands in the gathering clouds of this storm. As a member of the Quartet, we were the only one who really had the voice to urge Israel's acceptance of the Road Map; however, our strategic alliance with Israel also makes us her greatest defender. Our choice of allegiance will determine our position in the last days: will the growing liberal tendencies of our nation pull us to join the EU, UN, and Russia in a globalization move that will, in the end, force a false peace on Israel and begin the Tribulation? Or will we, with our moral clarity, large Jewish populace, and Christian consciousness, align ourselves so closely with Israel in the final conflict that we are literally indistinguishable from her in the final chapter of Bible prophecy?

As you should be able to tell from this brief summary of the players, such a decision will be one we make ourselves, not one imposed by outside nations. While outside forces will influence us, either through negotiations or terrorist attacks, the final decision is up to us. What will we do? Will we trade our freedom away for cheap oil, globalization, and moral relativism, or will we stay the course our forefathers began and hold to the Bible as our guide? Will our nation be on God's side in the final conflict? Will we give in to the lunatics, liberals, and liars in weakness? Or will we stand strong and seek a revival of moral clarity in our land?

CHAPTER SIXTEEN

THE BATTLE LINES ARE DRAWN

Arabs may have the oil, but we have the matches.
—ARIEL SHARON, to a colleague while touring Dimona—Israel's nuclear facility[95]

Jerusalem represents the earthly point where God came into contact with man and where eternity crossed history.
—POPE PAUL VI, Jerusalem, 1964

But I have chosen Jerusalem, that my name might be there; and have chosen David to be over my people Israel.
—2 CHRONICLES 6:6, NIV

The battle lines for the future battle of Armageddon have already been drawn by UN resolutions, terrorist demands and intents, and US acquiescence along the Israeli boundaries of June 4, 1967, declaring the Golan Heights, the Gaza Strip, the West Bank, and East Jerusalem and the Temple Mount "Occupied Territories." To this point, on three different occasions from

1991 to 2001, the PLO has been offered basically all of that, minus control of East Jerusalem—each time they have refused and escalated their violence. The conclusion is only too obvious: the PLO will not sign any "final" agreement with Israel until that agreement includes their control of East Jerusalem. The battle line is indeed drawn through the heart of Jerusalem: the old city and the Temple Mount.

Both Israel and the Palestinians declare Jerusalem their capital, and while the US hesitated to relocate its embassy there until 2020, the subtle message was that we could not choose sides. With the move of the embassy to Jerusalem, President Trump took sides and drove a stake in the heart of the "two-state solution." The PLO and Palestinian Authority claim to have a capital of a state that has never existed, while every shovel of dirt moved in Jerusalem uncovers more evidence it has been the capital of Israel for nearly 3,000 years.

I met with Mayor Giuliani in New York to discuss Jerusalem, and asked him what were the most important things Jerusalem and New York had in common. He answered:

> The most important thing we share is that we both live in freedom. We are both blessed with freedom and democracy. Much of the world doesn't have freedom and democracy. Because we share the same principles on which government and society are based, then all of the other friendships become even stronger.

> The relationship of blood also exists between New York and Jerusalem. There are so many who have family in both places.
>
> We have the relationship of religious significance for Jews, Christians, and Muslims—the historical significance and the reality that we are two of the world's great cities. Jerusalem is older than New York. A good deal of the world passes through both places. We share great bonds.

New York and America indeed hold a great bond with Jerusalem—the city that will be the center of the whole earth's attention in the final days.

Even after decades of visiting Israel and studying the conflicts and prophecies surrounding her, I still don't fully comprehend why this is the case. While the Temple Mount is the holiest place in Judaism and perhaps second only to Golgotha (just across from it) to Christians, it is considered the third holiest place in the world to Muslims. However, neither Palestine (Filistin) nor Jerusalem (al-Quds) is mentioned in the Qur'an (the holiest being Mecca and the second holiest Medina). For the Jews, it is the place of which God said, "In this house [the Temple], and in Jerusalem, which I have chosen before all the tribes of Israel, will I put my name forever."[96]

Why has Jerusalem been a bone in the throat of the world? Why is such a tiny city the front-page headline of world news? It is because of an ancient prophecy whose fulfillment Jehovah himself will guarantee!

Every nation that has come against Jerusalem has been cursed, the latest being Babylon. In 586 B.C., the Babylonian army besieged Jerusalem, and the Temple was ransacked. On Friday, April 11, 2003, the Iraqi National Museum in Baghdad was plundered by a lawless society. More than 170,000 ancient and priceless artifacts were stolen. These relics covered the entire 7,000 years of Babylonian history.

Saddam Hussein, who claimed to be Nebuchadnezzar incarnate, ended up cursed just as the first Nebuchadnezzar was cursed. Saddam should have read his Bible. Who would ever have believed that the man who caused nations to tremble would end up with matted hair, a nasty, unkempt beard, and a diet of rotten food in a dirty hole in the ground? Bums living under bridges look better than Hussein did when captured.

For decades, I have challenged leaders in America not to touch Jerusalem. I remember standing up to Robert McFarland, the National Security Advisor to Ronald Reagan. McFarland had said, "The status of Jerusalem must be determined by negotiations."

I said, "Excuse me; I have the book on Jerusalem. Jehovah is not negotiating with you or anyone else."

In Madrid, I was the first to challenge then-Secretary of State James Baker over Jerusalem. I asked, "Why can't America recognize Jerusalem as Israel's capital?" Baker was hot at my remarks and said he refused to be entangled in a fruitless debate: the status of Jerusalem should be determined by negotiations.

Why have I been so concerned? There is no city in the world on which Jehovah pronounces a blessing on those who bless it and a curse on those who curse it. The nations that divided Jerusalem will be cursed beyond their ability to comprehend. If that happens, no amount of prayer or repentance will reverse the curse on that nation. Once prophecy is touched, Jehovah's anger will boil over.

The revelation is amazing. Presidents have placed their hands on the prophecy of King Solomon[97] as they were sworn into office. They trusted that Jehovah would bless America and their term in office. It is unlikely, however, that any have read another prophecy by the same king found in 2 Chronicles 6:6: "But I have chosen (*bachar*) Yerushalayim, that my name (*shem*) might be there." This amazing prophecy denotes that Jerusalem is the only city in the world where Jehovah has chosen to place His name.

Is it important that Jerusalem not be touched? Yes, one thousand times, yes! Heaven and earth met in Jerusalem (the coming of Jesus Christ) and will meet again (His return). The prophecies say Jerusalem will be united—not divided—when the Messiah returns. He is not coming back to a Muslim city.

At the end of the age, Jerusalem will be the center of all prophecy.

> *I saw the Holy City, the new Jerusalem, coming down out of heaven from God, prepared as a bride beautifully dressed for her husband* (Revelation 21:2, NIV).

As the prophet Amos proclaims,

> *The LORD also shall roar out of Zion, and utter his voice from Jerusalem* (Joel 3:16, NIV).

The prophet Zechariah declares:

> *I will return to Zion and dwell in Jerusalem* (Zechariah 8:3, NIV).

It is no coincidence that the first words of the New Testament are:

> *A record of the genealogy of Jesus Christ, the son of David, the son of Abraham* (Matthew 1:1, NIV).

David was the first king of Jerusalem, a forerunner of the true King of Jerusalem, Jesus Christ.

The final battle of the Ages will be over Jerusalem. If America chooses to line up against the Scriptures, America will find herself fighting against Jehovah and will definitely lose!

Satan's challenge to Jehovah can be found in Isaiah 14:12-15:

> How you have fallen from heaven, O morning star, son of the dawn! You have been cast down to the earth, you who once laid low the nations! You said in your heart, "I will ascend to heaven; I will raise my throne above the stars of God; I will sit enthroned on the mount of assembly, on the utmost heights of the sacred mountain. I will ascend above the tops of the clouds; I will make myself like the Most High." But you are brought down to the grave, to the depths of the pit.

Notice he says he will sit on the Temple Mount in Jerusalem, on the north side. Yet Jehovah says, "You will be cursed and brought down to the lowest pit of hell."

Most wars have been fought over ownership disputes, land, and property. Personal battles have raged over someone illegally using the name of another person to write a check or buy goods. It is called "fraud." The person who commits fraud can be punished. America even has laws granting citizens the right to bear arms to protect their property. Jerusalem's title deed does not belong to anyone but exclusively to Jehovah. He placed His Name there!

A brilliant and respected scholar I have known for decades told me: "If you look at a satellite image of the City of Jerusalem, you will see the tetragrammaton JHVH. It is clearly visible in the photo. What does JHVH mean? Those four Hebrew characters compose the word *Jehovah*—the name of God! Yes, God's Name is mystically inscribed in the very city of Jerusalem."

The prophets also declare that,

> Then shall the LORD go forth, and fight against those nations, as when he fought in the day of battle. And his feet shall stand in that day upon the mount of Olives, which is before Jerusalem on the east, and the mount of Olives shall cleave in the midst thereof toward the east and toward the west, and there shall be a very great valley; and half of the mountain shall remove toward the north, and half of it toward the south (Zechariah 14:3-4, NIV)

Anti-Zionism is Anti-Semitism

It's amazing that several administrations of the United States, supposedly a Christian nation, have wanted to divide Jerusalem and give East Jerusalem to a terrorist regime, the PLO, to become an Islamic state.

The same scholar who told me about his discovery in the satellite image of the City of Jerusalem also told me:

> "The geological formation created by the Kidron Valley between the Mount of Olives and the Treble Mounts, the Tyropoeon Valley and the Hinnom Valley (Gehenna), which lies at the bottom of the Temple Mount, and sweeps northward, forms the Hebrew letter *Shem* that looks like a warped 'W.'"

He said it years before the internet, but numerous websites now highlight the stark and easily discernible letter shape. God's name is buried in the very geological foundations of Jerusalem—and cannot be removed. He carved into stone this fascinating and prophetic sign concerning ancient Jerusalem and man's futile battle over it. Jerusalem is biblically, historically, and geologically "the city which I have chosen for Myself, to put My name there" (1 Kings 11:36).

There is, indeed, in ancient prophecy, a curse that Jehovah will place on the nation that divides Jerusalem:

> Behold, I will make Jerusalem a cup of trembling unto all the people round about, when they shall be in the siege both against Judah and against Jerusalem. And in that day will I make Jerusalem a

burdensome stone for all people: all that burden themselves with it shall be cut in pieces, though all the people of the earth be gathered together against it. In that day will I make the governors of Judah like an hearth of fire among the wood, and like a torch of fire in a sheaf; and they shall devour all the people round about, on the right hand and on the left: and Jerusalem shall be inhabited again in her own place, even in Jerusalem. In that day shall the Lord defend the inhabitants of Jerusalem; and he that is feeble among them at that day shall be as David; and the house of David shall be as God, as the angel of the Lord before them (Zechariah 12:2, 3, 6, 8, NIV).

And this shall be the plague wherewith the Lord will smite all the people that have fought against Jerusalem; Their flesh shall consume away while they stand upon their feet, and their eyes shall consume away in their holes, and their tongue shall consume away in their mouth. And Judah also shall fight at Jerusalem; and the wealth of all the heathen round about shall be gathered together, gold, and silver, and apparel, in great abundance (Zechariah 14:12,14, NIV).

According to Genesis 22, this is the location where Isaac was to be offered to God as a sacrifice before the angel stayed

Abraham's hand. Echoing the jealousy of Ishmael—the eldest but not favored son- Muslim tradition holds that Ishmael, not Isaac, was offered here. It is also said to be the place from which Muhammad ascended one night into heaven for a special visit. Muslims do not refer to the area as the Temple Mount, but as the Noble Sanctuary.

The Mosque of Omar, more commonly known as the "Dome of the Rock," is built over the rock upon which Abraham reportedly laid Ishmael to sacrifice him (some believe this is also the location of the altar of the first two Hebrew Temples—though this may be more because of the Crusader's confusion of it with the temple of Solomon than actual archeological evidence). It was built sometime around AD 700. Caliph Omar I, the successor to the prophet Muhammad, took Jerusalem in AD 637. This is the Golden Dome, which you see in all modern photographs of Jerusalem that show the Temple Mount. Though it is the most famous of the two mosques of the Noble Sanctuary because of its brilliant dome, it is not considered the holiest.

That attribute rests with the second mosque on the Mount, called the al-Aqsa Mosque (which means "the farthest place of worship of the One God," referring to its distance from Mecca when it was built); it is just to the south of the Dome of the Rock. It is the largest mosque in Jerusalem. This mosque was built soon after the Dome of the Rock and is dedicated to Muhammad's "night visit" to heaven. It supposedly rests upon the place from which he took that journey.

This location also became the focal point for the beginning

of the Second Intifada, which is also called the al-Aqsa Intifada because it began when Ariel Sharon visited this holy site. Though the violence had already started in smaller outbreaks some days before this, on September 28, 2000, it reached new heights after Sharon stood at the door of the al-Aqsa Mosque. Though Sharon entered none of the mosque buildings on the Temple Mount, his mere presence on the Noble Sanctuary (all of which Arabs consider a mosque) caused an eruption of shouting and rock throwing that resulted in twenty-eight Israeli policemen being injured, three of whom had to be hospitalized. There were no reported Palestinian injuries on the day of Sharon's visit. The next day, however, significant orchestrated violence erupted after the Muslims' Friday prayers, resulting in deaths and casualties on both sides. It began the worst period of Palestinian violence in Israeli history. From September 29, 2000, to September 11, 2002, Israel saw 427 civilians and 185 members of Israeli security forces killed and 3,202 civilians and 1,307 security members injured. (Numbers usurped in the attacks of October 2023.)

Though the violence had probably already been set to start because Arafat had just walked out on Camp David talks with Israel in July, the fact Sharon's visit to the Noble Sanctuary was used to catalyze the violence in earnest is a testament to how close to the heart of the conflict control of the Temple Mount really is. It has also been the site of other outbreaks of tension between Palestinians and Jews, such as the one on September 24, 1996, that led to four days of fighting with tanks and helicopters brought in for support, ending with more than seventy dead and hundreds wounded. The pretext of that fighting was opening a new exit to the Hasmonean Tunnel. This archeological site runs along the Western Wall and runs under part of the Old City of Jerusalem because, at the time, visitors had to enter and exit through the same opening.

It has traditionally been believed that the Dome of the Rock will have to be removed before the third and last Temple can be built. It's a prophecy well known to the Arabs and a reason for their further distrust of Jewish custody of the Mount. However, some believe that the original site of the Temple may have been on the northern part of the Temple Mount, which is open, not in the south where the Dome of the Rock sits today. If this is the case, it is possible that the Temple could be rebuilt without harming the two mosques, which would be more peaceable considering the importance of each to the Jews and the Muslims. One way or the other, it seems likely that the rebuilding of the Temple will be one of the bargaining chips used by the anti-Christ to draw Israel into the seven-year peace pact with him.

Thus, Jerusalem is edging its way back to being the center of world attention, even as it is already the center of Jewish and Muslim attention. As it does, the fate of Jerusalem will become the greatest reason for hope in the world as the seven-year pact is signed and the Tribulation begins. It will also be the site of the final breakdown of hope when the anti-Christ enters the rebuilt temple and desecrates it, marking the beginning of the Great Tribulation. If the spirit of anti-Christ truly is behind the actions of the PLO and other terrorist groups, and I firmly believe it is, that adds a spiritual dimension to why Jerusalem is so key to the Palestinian Authority's acceptance of a treaty with Israel and why it is such a sticking point for anyone proposing peace for the region. It is about much more than how many have died in suicide bombings or Israeli police actions. This conflict is about who controls the center of the world and the rock upon which God first cut a covenant with humanity.

Not only has the line firmly been drawn, but both sides also know what they are willing to sacrifice to get what they want: the Palestinians to chase Israel from their land and the Jews to protect their place there. Though America and the USSR. wished to avoid an arms race in the Middle East, they could not at the same time maintain their loyalties. So the Soviets armed Nasser's Pan-Arabists, and the United States eventually promised to keep Israel one step ahead of her neighbors after the Yom Kippur War.

This proved more difficult as America also agreed to supply weapons to Saudi Arabia, Egypt (after Sadat signed a treaty with Israel in 1978), The United Arab Emirates, Kuwait, Bahrain, Jordan, Oman, Lebanon, Qatar, and Yemen (in that order according to sales from 1990 to 2001).[98] If any one of these got an advanced weapons system (missiles, planes, ships, tanks, etc.), the US was obliged to offer the same or better to Israel. From 1990 to 2001, the US sold $79.4 billion in arms to these Arab nations. This easily rivals the $81.3 billion the US has granted Israel since 1976, much of which was economic aid and loans, not arms sales. In roughly the same period, since 1991, the US has specifically given Israel $18.1 billion in weapons and military aid.[99] Thanks to us, those on both sides of the line running through Jerusalem are well prepared to wage conventional warfare to control it.

So far, the edge has been to the Israelis, not only because we have promised to keep them one step ahead in this race to obtain US arms but because of Israel's nuclear strike potential. Almost from Israel's rebirth, which was only three years after the bombing of Hiroshima and Nagasaki, Prime Minister David Ben-Gurion saw that nuclear power could be useful in making the Negev desert bloom by supplying it with electricity and powering desalinization plants to provide it with drinking water. However, as author Seymour Hersh put it, "Nuclear power was not Ben-Gurion's first priority; the desert would glow before it bloomed."[100] Ben-Gurion had his eyes set on Israel becoming a nuclear power.

Throughout his contacts with the United States, Ben-Gurion would continue to push for the US's promise that Israel could find sanctuary under the umbrella of America's nuclear weapons. He could never get this promise. Thus, Israel began a cat-and-mouse game with her most sought-after ally as, on the one hand, she tried to get the US to promise its protection; on the other, she developed protection of her own.

By 1953, Israel's Weizmann Institute had developed an improved ion exchange mechanism for producing heavy water and a more efficient method for mining uranium, which it bartered with the French for a formal agreement to cooperate in nuclear research. By 1958, Israel had begun construction of its own nuclear facility near the Negev Desert town of Dimona, which they based upon their visits to the French nuclear research facility at Marcoule. Perhaps by then, Ben-Gurion had realized that the US was not as interested in Israeli security as he had hoped after Eisenhower's reaction to the Suez Crisis. Israel would continue her research for a decade before the first nuclear bombs would begin rolling out of Dimona in 1968. The facility went into full-scale production at that point, turning out four or five bombs a year.

During this time, through every means possible, the US tried to figure out just what was going on at Dimona, and Israel tried to hide it. However, evidence seems to suggest that the US had a pretty good idea of what Dimona was for, but it looked the other way, knowing that Israel didn't have much choice. Some members of Congress even supported Israel's actions. A few days before meeting with President Kennedy to further discuss the Hawk missile purchases, Shimon Peres met with Senator Stuart Symington, a Kennedy supporter and ranking member of the Senate Armed Services Committee. As Peres told his biographer, Symington said, "Don't be a bunch of fools. Don't stop making atomic bombs. And don't listen to the administration. Do whatever you think best."[101]

However, this struggle didn't come without its political casualties. In the spring of 1962, President Kennedy was pushing hard on Prime Minister Ben-Gurion for some solid answers about Dimona, or at least solid promises that its research was not for military purposes. Ben-Gurion held his ground. According to Yuval Neeman, a physicist and defense ministry intelligence officer who was involved in Israel's nuclear weapons program, "It was not a friendly exchange. Kennedy was writing like a bully. It was brutal."[102]

As a result, Kennedy shut Ben Gurion out amid a growing threat. In April, Iraq joined Egypt and Syria in the short-lived Arab Federation, making the threat of another Arab invasion, such as that of the War of Independence, much more likely. Author Seymour Hersh described the situation:

> He instinctively turned to Washington and proposed in a letter to the President that the United States and Soviet Union join forces to publicly declare the territorial integrity and security of every Middle Eastern state. "If you can spare an hour or two for a discussion with me on the situation and possible solutions," Ben-Gurion asked, "I am prepared to fly to Washington at your convenience and without any publicity." Kennedy rejected Ben-Gurion's offer of a state visit and expressed "real reservations," according to Ben-Gurion's biography, about any joint statement on the issue with the Soviets. Five days later, a disappointed Ben-Gurion sent a second note to Kennedy: "Mr. President, my people have the right to exist ... and this existence is in danger." He requested that the United States sign a security treaty with Israel. Again, the answer was no, and it was clear to the Mapai Party that Ben-Gurion's leadership and his intractability about Dimona were serious liabilities in Washington. Golda Meir acknowledged

to Ben-Gurion's biographer, "We knew about these approaches. . . We said nothing, even though we wondered."

A few weeks later, on June 16, 1963, Ben-Gurion abruptly resigned as prime minister and defense minister, ending his fifteen-year reign as Israel's most influential public official.[103]

By 1973, Israel had about twenty-five nuclear warheads with three or four missile launchers in place and operational at Hirbat Zachariah. Israel also had mobile Jericho I missile launchers at her disposal. Israel had the capability of launching nuclear weapons and hitting targets as far away as Tbilisi and Baku in southern Russia. Damascus and Cairo were within easy range.

When the Yom Kippur War broke out, the United States was slow to respond as the attacks began. Several sources suggest that Nixon and Kissinger planned to let Israel get a severe bloody nose before the US responded to teach her a lesson. However, at this point, Israel developed what became known as "the Samson Option." Once the United States discovered this, it pulled out all the stops to help Israel win a conventional war that would prevent the possibility of nuclear proliferation starting in the Middle East.

The Samson Option emerged from Israel's determination that there would never be another Holocaust at the hands of a foreign power. As the Jews had done at Masada, it was better to die at their own hands rather than be captured by an oppressing force, whether that should be the Romans, the Germans, or the Arabs. However, it was not Masada but Samson from whom they took their example. In his last hour, a blinded and weakened Samson was marched into the temple of Dagon as a display to the Philistines of their pre-eminence over the Jews. As the mocking catcalls fell upon him, Samson prayed, "O Lord GOD, remember me, I pray thee, and strengthen me, I pray thee, only this once, O God, that I may be at once avenged of the Philistines for my two eyes."[104] Then, placing his hands firmly on two pillars supporting the roof of the temple, he prayed again, "Let me die with the Philistines,"[105] and with all of his might, pushed the columns over, bringing the roof down upon himself and all of the Philistines who had ridiculed him. The Bible tells us that in this final act, he killed more Philistines than he previously had in his entire life.

The "Samson Option" thus illustrated Israel's willingness to bring the world into a nuclear war and destroy much of it rather than allow another holocaust at the hands of an anti-Semitic nation. Israel knew the consequences of attacking Egypt and Syria—the Soviet Union would launch an all-out nuclear attack on Israel. Armageddon would come early. Thus, Israel armed and aimed her nuclear missiles at Egyptian and Syrian military headquarters near Cairo and Damascus just a few days into the war. Israel didn't know what else to do and was losing confidence fast. They were already willing to seriously consider using their weapons of last resort a few days into the war. However, to prevent that, the United States came dramatically to Israel's aid to keep the war conventional.

By 1979, Israel was routinely gathering US satellite intelligence to target cities in the Soviet Union. Israel had learned a key fact that the United States and Soviet Union also learned in the Cold War: in a nuclear war, it doesn't matter how many times you can blow up your enemies, only that you can blow them up. Israel had entered the world of nuclear superpowers.

Thus, in essence, what victory Israel won in the Yom Kippur War was won by staring down the barrel of a nuclear missile launcher. Since Israel had nuclear weapons and her neighbors did not, this further bolstered her position as a nation that could not be defeated in open warfare. If the Arabs developed nuclear weapons, however, this distinct advantage would be lost. So it was that on June 7, 1981, Israel used US F-15s and F-16s that had been purchased "for defensive purposes only" to take out the Osirak nuclear reactor that was twelve miles southwest of Baghdad before it became operational. Israel did not want a Samson vs. Goliath scenario.

Israel knew the seriousness of the strike and was ready for possible retaliation. Before the bombing, they shut down Dimona in case of a counterstrike and left it down for roughly a year. While the world fumed, the US only gave Israel a mild reprimand for this pre-preemptive strike. According to Richard V. Allen, Reagan's national security advisor, when President Ronald Reagan was informed of the attack, the conversation went like this:

> "Mr. President, the Israelis just took out a nuclear reactor in Iraq with F-16s." . . .

"What do you know about it?"

"Nothing, sir. I'm waiting for a report."

"Why do you suppose they did it?"

The President let his rhetorical question hang for a moment, Allen recalled, and added:

"Well. Boys will be boys."[106]

The White House announced that the next installment of a 1975 sale of seventy-five F-16s would be suspended because of the attack. However, two months later, the suspension was lifted with little attention drawn to the fact, and the shipment of four new F-16s was delivered to Israel without incident.

It also appears Israel had found a way to get around restrictions it had been given on the use of America's extremely advanced and secret KH-11 spy satellite system. President Jimmy Carter had agreed the Israelis could receive satellite pictures of areas within one hundred miles of their borders so they could watch for troop movements in neighboring countries that might alert them of a new invasion by Arab forces—thus, again, for "defensive purposes only." However, somehow, they received enough images of Osirak—which is roughly 550 miles from Jerusalem—that they could also launch this surgical strike against Iraq without being detected until they were already upon their target.

Later, in the 1980s, Israel planted nuclear landmines along the Golan Heights. Israel now also has impregnable submarines—each one carrying four nuclear cruise missiles. In June 2000, an

Israeli submarine launched a cruise missile that hit a target 600 kilometers away, making Israel the third nation, after the US and Russia, with that capacity. However, in the spring of 2002, Iran launched a missile that covered a similar distance. When asked about Iran's nuclear capabilities on May 24th of that same year during the Bush-Putin summit in Moscow, Russian Deputy Chief of the General Staff, General Yuri Baluyevshy said, "Iran does have nuclear weapons. Of course, they are non-strategic nuclear weapons. I mean, these are not ICBMs with a range of more than 5,500 kilometers and more."[107] They may not have the range to reach Moscow or Washington, but they could certainly reach Tel Aviv and Jerusalem. Goliath is quickly closing in on Samson's military edge. Again, it doesn't matter how many times you can blow someone up, just that you can.

In November of 1999, I was in Russia and met with a former head of the KGB. I told him, "It is wonderful how the world is now a much safer place to live." He grinned at me and responded, "Listen, the world is not a safer place to live. Our republics are cash-poor and crime-rich. We have thousands of nuclear bombs. Last month in the Ukraine, two bombs were found to be missing. Only the casings were left. When I asked where they were, I was told, 'Russian entrepreneurs.' While your country was celebrating the end of the Cold War, we were panicking over the beginning of the hot war."

I asked him about Israel. He smiled again and said, "Listen, we have been targeting their cities, and they have had their big bomb trained on us for years. So, what else is new?" I knew he was telling me the truth, for I had heard this from a key advisor to two of Israel's prime ministers years before.

The Washington Post reported that:

> In the ethnic conflicts that surrounded the collapse of the Soviet Union, fighters in several countries seized upon an unlikely new weapon: a small, thin rocket known as the Alazan. Originally built for weather experiments, the Alazan was transformed into a terror weapon, packed with explosives, and lobbed into cities. Military records show that at least thirty-eight Alazan warheads were modified to carry radioactive material, effectively creating the world's first surface-to-surface "dirty bomb." Now, according to experts and officials, the warheads have disappeared.

The Samson Option again came into play in the 1991 Gulf War. A senior advisor to Israel's prime ministers, Reuben Hecht, lived in Haifa, the target of a SCUD missile attack during the Persian Gulf War. He said to me, "We have picked up intelligence that Saddam has given the order to put chemical and biological weapons on SCUDs. I need to get into a sealed room quickly. I can assure you, however, that if they hit our cities, Baghdad will be a radioactive dustbowl. Israel has mobile missile launchers armed with nuclear weapons. They are facing Baghdad even as I speak and are ready to launch on command. We are on full-scale nuclear alert." He added, "You know, Mike, this is not to be repeated."

Today, names like Dimona, the Samson Option, Project 700, the Zechariah Project, the Temple Weapons, and Z-Division are all part of one of the most massive nuclear arsenals in the world in Israel. Now, new names are being heard: Pumped X-ray Lasers, Hydrodynamics, and Radiation Transport—the new Armageddon generation of weapons. Israel has over 300 tactical and strategic weapons, including more than 100 nuclear artillery shells, nuclear land mines, and neutron bombs that will destroy biological life without creating an explosion. They also have lasers for their planes, tanks, and electro-magnetic weapons that shut down radar. In November 2003, Israel took her first order of US F-16I fighter jets, the first of 102 she was to receive by 2008, making it the largest arms deal in Israeli history. The new plane could reach nations as far away as Iran and Libya. It had AMRAAM air-to-air missiles and Northrop Grumman APG-68 radar, allowing them to shoot down other jets from over thirty miles away.

At least nine nations currently have the capability of attacking an enemy with a thermonuclear bomb: Russia, the United States, China, Israel, France, Great Britain, India, Pakistan, and, possibly Iran. This gives them all the possibility to unleash a plague of nuclear or neutron bombs that would be very much like what is described in Zechariah 14:12, NKJV:

> And this shall be the plague with which the LORD will strike all the people who fought against Jerusalem:

> Their flesh shall dissolve while they stand
>   on their feet,
> Their eyes shall dissolve in their sockets,
> And their tongues shall dissolve in their
>   mouths.

Others seem to be closing in on it. In the last battle, Russia, the European countries (Great Britain and France), and the Eastern countries (Iran, Pakistan, India, China, and North Korea) will be on the other side opposite Israel. But where will the United States be?

As the terrorist network stands poised against us, it seems only a matter of time and money before one of the missing Soviet suitcase nukes finds its way into their hands. If we don't handle the next steps in the war on terrorism correctly, those Soviet nukes or some of Saddam's weapons of mass destruction that liberals claim "don't exist" will very likely assist in this goal.

Thus far, the war on terrorism has taken us from the attacks of September 11th to victory in Iraq. But we are ultimately to win this war and prevent these weapons of mass destruction from striking our cities. Where do we need to go from here?

We must fall on our faces in prayer and repentance. America has no idea what we could face if the Nation sleeps. George Santayana said, "Those who cannot remember the past are doomed to repeat it."[108]

CHAPTER SEVENTEEN

The New Antisemitism

As our recent history teaches, what begins as a threat to the Jews is soon a menace to the entire world. It is but a short step between a knifing in Jerusalem and a bombing of the World Trade Center in New York.
YITZAK RABIN
The Rabin Memoirs 1979 (reprinted in 1994)

The voice of thy brother's blood crieth unto me from the ground.
—GENESIS 4:10, KJV

As the ink was drying on the newly penned Constitution of the United States, many who had taken part in crafting it saw that the silver lining of its promise for America's future had a dark cloud. An issue had been sorely fought through the proceedings that seemed to burst the young country at the seams before it was even knit together. However, rather than break the new union back into colonies that the British could easily return to conquer one by one, the delegates struck compromises such as the "Three-Fifths Clause." The black cloud that our forefathers saw was the issue of slavery and the hatred and racism that allowed it. It was an issue they felt could have eternal ramifications. Thomas Jefferson described it in this way:

> The whole commerce between master and slave is a perpetual exercise of the most boisterous passions, the most unremitting despotism on the one part, and degrading submission on the other. Our children see this and learn to imitate it; for man is an imitative animal. This quality is the germ of all education in him. From his cradle to his grave he is learning to do what he sees others do.... The parent storms, the child looks on, catches the lineaments of his wrath, puts on the same airs in the circle of smaller slaves, gives a loose rein to the worst of passions and thus nursed, educated and daily exercised in tyranny....
>
> Can the liberties of a nation be thought secure, when we have removed their only firm basis, a conviction in the minds of the people that these liberties are of the gift of God? That they are not to be violated but with his wrath? Indeed I tremble for my country when I reflect that God is just: that his justice can not sleep forever: that considering

> numbers, nature and natural means only, a revolution of the wheel of fortune, an exchange of situation is among possible events: that it may become probable by supernatural interference!
> The Almighty has no attributes, which can take side with us in such a contest. [109]

Jefferson felt that America's racism, despite whatever Christian principles our nation was founded upon, could well bring our nation's destruction, and worse than that a destruction at the hands of a just and moral God. In fact, in the midst of the Civil War, Abraham Lincoln included this thought in his second inauguration address of 1865:

> If we shall suppose that American Slavery is one of those offences which, in the providence of God, must needs come, but which, having continued through His appointed time, He now wills to remove, and that He gives to both North and South, this terrible war, as the woe due to those by whom the offence came, shall we discern therein any departure from those divine attributes which the believers in a Living God always ascribe to Him? Fondly do we hope—fervently do we pray—that this mighty scourge of war may speedily pass away. Yet, if God wills that it continue, until all the wealth piled by the bondmen's two hundred and fifty years of unrequited toil shall be sunk, and until

every drop of blood drawn with the lash, shall be paid by another drawn with the sword, as was said three thousand years ago, so still it must be said, "The judgments of the Lord are true and righteous altogether."

With malice toward none, with charity for all, with firmness in the right as God gives us to see the right, let us strive on to finish the work we are in, to bind up the nation's wounds, to care for him who shall have borne the battle and for his widow and his orphan, to do all which may achieve and cherish a just and lasting peace among ourselves and with all nations.[110]

However, racism lingered into the civil rights movement of the 1960s and still has its foothold in America today, though it has greatly receded into the shadows.

If God's hedge of protection was removed from the Christian nation of the 1860s to the point it allowed the Civil War, what can we expect to happen to us if we tolerate the racism of antisemitism that is arising today in our world just as it did in Germany in the 1920s and 30s?

The Jew hatred of Germany between the World Wars has found a new home in the Arab nations of today. As we have seen from Herzl's experiences in France, Germany was not the only nation in Europe that disliked the Jews, and while that antisemitism was buried under the guilt of the Holocaust, it was not extinguished. Nearly nine decades after the Holocaust, it is beginning to reemerge. Yet today, hatred of the Jews has turned to hatred of the nation of Israel. It is seen as their rightful representation. Hating Jews now hides behind the politics of opposing Israel.

This anti-Zionism is now spread "democratically" by fanatics across the ideological spectrum, from the extreme Left to the extreme Right. Recent comments by Malaysian Prime Minister Mahathir Mohamad at the Organization of the Islamic Conference summit in October 2003 are typical of this:

> I will not enumerate the instances of our humiliation and oppression, nor will I once again condemn our detractors and oppressors. It would be an exercise in futility because they are not going to change their attitudes just because we condemn them. If we are to recover our dignity and that of Islam, our religion, it is we who must decide, it is we who must act. . . .
>
> We [Muslims] are actually very strong. 1.3 billion people cannot be simply wiped out. The Europeans killed 6 million Jews out of 12 million. But today, the Jews rule this world by proxy. They get others to fight and die for them.[111]

Mohamad is a respected national leader who turned his country into the world's 17th-ranked trading nation during his 22 years in power and was the conference host. Yet his comments didn't stop there. He continued with statements that the Jews "invented socialism, communism, human rights, and democracy" to avoid persecution and gain control of the most powerful countries of the world.

While National Security Advisor Condoleezza Rice said of Mohamad's comments, "I don't think they are emblematic of the Muslim world," it seems unlikely that the delegates of fifty-seven nations to whom he spoke would agree with her comments, as they all stood when he finished and clapped loudly, shouting their approval.

Media around the world are noting the rise and new openness of antisemitism that are exemplified by remarks of men such as Prime Minister Mohamad. How different are such remarks from those of Hitler's propaganda secretary Paul Joseph Goebbels on, of all dates, September 11th—but in 1937, not 2001:

> Who are those responsible for this catastrophe? Without fear, we want to point the finger at the Jew as the inspirer, the author, and the beneficiary of this terrible catastrophe: look, this is the enemy of the world, the destroyer of cultures, the parasite among the nations, the son of chaos, the incarnation of evil, the ferment of decomposition, the visible demon of the decay of humanity.[112]

Early in 1937, Goebbels documented a meeting on church affairs, where Hitler freely expressed his world-historical vision. In his diary, Goebbels wrote:

> The Fuhrer explains Christianity and Christ. He [Christ] wanted to act against Jewish world domination. Jewry had him crucified.[113]

This common doctrine of accusing the Jews of responsibility for virtually all the world's ills is resurfacing today in very similar language in the halls of European government, academia, and the media, and with worldwide distribution over the Internet. Of course, if all these ills are because of the Jews, the next logical step is to begin shutting them out of positions of power, taking away what they own, and boycotting their businesses—the first steps Hitler took in 1933. How far is the world, especially those Arab countries that won't even let Jews within their borders, from Hitler's gospel of "redemptive antisemitism," as he expressed it in 1922?

> My first and foremost task will be the annihilation of the Jews . . . until all Germany has been cleansed.[114]

Just as this traditional antisemitism sought to deny Jews their rights as individuals in society, anti-Zionism today attacks the collective Jewish people as a nation. Just as Jews were exploited as scapegoats for their host countries' problems, Israel is being singled out today as the root of all the world's evil—thus what happened at the UN's International Conference on Racism in Durban, South Africa, in August of 2001. As far as the delegates there seemed to be concerned, racism would be a thing of the past if the nation of Israel could be eliminated. Another example of this was Israel's November 2003 General Assembly draft resolution calling for the protection of Israeli children from Palestinian terrorist attacks—the first resolution introduced by Israel to the UN since 1976—which was rejected by the assembly's Social, Humanitarian, and Cultural Committee, even though a similar resolution to protect Palestinian children passed just weeks before.

So-called political opposition to Israel's policies and simple Jew hatred has also become implicitly indistinguishable. Both the opponents of globalization and US intervention in Iraq blame Israel—by attributing these policies to Jewish "control" over Washington as part of the historically antisemitic canard that the Jews aim to take over the world.

What are the Jews usually accused of? How have they curried "control of the world by proxy?" What are their greatest sins? Don't be surprised if you can answer this yourself—you have probably been more exposed to such anti-Semitic propaganda than you have realized. The big three always seem to be: 1) the Jews control the media, 2) the Jews control the money, and 3) the Jews killed Jesus.

Is this true, though? Among the wealthiest people in the world, only six percent are Jewish. Who does control the money? According to a BBC report, seven of the ten wealthiest heads of state in the world are Arabs; none are Jewish. Nor are Jews C.E.O.s of any of the world's ten largest companies.

Do they control the media? Of the ten largest media companies in the world, only one has been run in recent years by a

Jew—the Walt Disney Company—hardly a pro-Israel propaganda machine. In Europe, Russia, China, and many Muslim nations, much of the media is owned by or government-run, and none of the government officials directing them are Jews.

Did the Jews kill Jesus? Read your Bible. The Sanhedrin had to go to the Romans to have Jesus killed. Romans nailed Jesus to the cross, and a Roman spear pierced His side. What of the angry mob that called for his death? I have stood in the courtyard where that happened and you could fit no more than a hundred people in it. The Sanhedrin accounted for at least half that number. That is a pretty small sample for which to blame an entire race.[115] Plus, that was an awful long time again. No one holds the young Germans of today responsible for the Holocaust, and that was less than a century ago. How can we still hold the Jews of today responsible for the act of two thousand years ago? You might as well hold the Italians accountable for the destruction of Jerusalem because Titus was a Roman.

Besides the technicalities, it was the sin of all humankind that hung Jesus on the cross, Gentiles and Jews. Romans 3:23 holds us all responsible: "All have sinned. . . ." Beyond that, Peter told the Jewish crowd at Pentecost, only days after Jesus' crucifixion and resurrection, "Men of Israel, hear these words, Jesus of Nazareth, a Man attested by God to you by miracles, wonders, and signs which God did through Him in your midst, as you yourselves also know—Him, **being delivered by the determined purpose and foreknowledge of God**, you have taken by lawless hands, have crucified, and put to death" (Acts 2:22,23 NKJV, **emphasis** added). It was God's foreknown and foreplanned purpose that Christ should die. Further, Jesus Himself said, "No one can take my life from me. I sacrifice it voluntarily. For I have authority to lay it down when I want to and also to take it up again. for this is what my Father has commanded" (John 10:18 NIV).

While antisemitism is on the rise again in Europe, nowhere is it more vehemently expressed today than in the Arab World and, of all places, in Egypt, Israel's first Arab peace partner. An Egyptian state television mini-series based on the notorious forgery of *The Protocols of the Elders of Zion* is only one example. Egyptian schoolbooks also fill the minds of impressionable youngsters with hate propaganda against Jews. At the same time, state-controlled newspapers publish Nazi caricatures of Jews, and a vast array of anti-Semitic "literature" in original Arabic and translation is readily available in bookstores. The fraudulent Protocols were a runaway bestseller in all Arab states, as is Hitler's *Mein Kampf* in Gaza now. They are illustrated, as are the daily newspapers, with depictions of grotesque hook-nosed, bearded, thick-lipped Jews and Israelis that are indistinguishable from those published during the Holocaust by Nazi propaganda chief Josef Goebbels in *Der Stürmer*.

Just before the visit of Shimon Peres to Cairo on April 29, 2001, the Nasserist newspaper Al-Arabi printed a swastika and a photomontage of Peres in a Nazi uniform on the front page. On April 18, Ahmad Regev, a journalist, wrote in the official Egyptian newspaper Al-Akhbar: "Our thanks go the late Hitler who wrought, in advance, the vengeance of the Palestinians upon the most despicable villains on the face of the earth. However, we rebuke Hitler for the fact that the vengeance was insufficient."

Syrian Defense Minister Mustafa Tlass's 1983 book, *The Matza of Zion*—an Arab variation on the medieval Christian blood libel that also caused the Damascus incident of 1840—accuses Jews of baking Passover matza with the blood of Muslim children. It has just been reprinted. "Sucking the blood of Arabs" has been aired repeatedly in the Arab media, for example, by Palestine Liberation Army Col. Nadir al-Tamimi on Al-Jazeera television on October 24, 2000, and by Egyptian columnist Adil Hammuda, "A Jewish Matza made from Arab Blood," in the government daily Al-Ahram. The Egyptian weekly October has informed its readers about "the loathsome qualities of the Jewish race throughout its long history." Meanwhile, the official Syrian daily Tishrin frequently accuses Israel of fabricating the Holocaust. It should also be recalled that Adolf Eichmann's sadistic deputy, Alois Brunner, found safe haven in Syria.

Holocaust denial is a frequent theme in the Arab media, with The Palestine Times writing of "God's lying people" who are "the Holocaust worshippers,"[116] and the Palestinian Authority's TV channel: "No Chelmno, no Dachau, no Auschwitz, only disinfecting sites ... the lie of extermination." The PA mufti of Jerusalem, Sheikh Ikrima Sabri, explains the Holocaust, stating: "It is not my fault that Hitler hated the Jews. Anyway, they hate them just about everywhere."[117] Other Muslim clerics call upon the worshipers in the mosques to "have no mercy on the Jews, no matter where they are, in any country ... wherever you meet them, kill them."[118]

For their part, Palestinian terrorists practice a form of antisemitism that combines the Nazi dehumanization of Jews with glorying in their murder—supposedly for the sake of peace, resistance, and a Palestinian state. While most European countries have come a long way toward facing their past and ensuring that antisemitism will never again become official policy, the Arab world has done nothing to douse the flames of Jew hatred within their borders.

The official Palestinian Authority TV station broadcasts movies in which children kill Israeli soldiers. Reports broadcast from P.A. summer camps show children training with weapons and singing songs filled with hatred for Jews and songs of praise for the shahids ("suicide bombers"). The studio map of "Greater Palestine" covers the area of the entire State of Israel—but the name "Israel" is not mentioned, and all Israeli cities are presented as the cities of Palestine.

In another obscene denial of the Holocaust, Palestinian Authority spokesmen describe Israel as a "racist country that uses the same method of ethnic cleansing that Nazi Germany used against the Jews." The Jews are presented as the enemies of Islam and called "wild animals," "locusts," "swindlers," "traitors," "aggressive," "war-mongers," "robbers," "sly," "avaricious," "disloyal," and "thieves"—whose end will come as the will of Allah. A typical caricature in one of the official P.A. newspapers shows a dwarf with a Star of David, his face copied from the face of the Jew in the Nazi Der Stürmer, with the caption: "The disease of the century." Another cartoon shows an Israeli soldier barbecuing

Arabs, taking them off the grill, and eating them one by one with relish.

Esti Vebman, an expert on antisemitism from the Institute for the Study of Anti-Semitism and Racism at Tel Aviv University, has been following antisemitism in the Palestinian Authority and the Arab world for years. "Back in the Middle Ages," says Vebman, "the Christians used this motif of poisoning wells. The Arabs are now adopting the Christian antisemitism of the Middle Ages and Nazi antisemitism; they are adding Islamic motifs and integrating it into their anti-Israel propaganda."

Hitler is one of the heroes of Palestinian youth, according to researchers at the University of Hamburg, who conducted an international study on the perceptions of democracy among young people around the world. Booksellers in the territories report that the Arabic translation of Hitler's book *Mein Kampf* is a best seller in Palestinian areas, Egypt, and other Arab nations. The official Palestinian Authority media are in the habit of comparing Israel's actions in the territories with those of the Nazis. Binyamin Netanyahu is frequently portrayed as a Nazi and described as "a Zionist terrorist who is worse than Hitler."

"It was a good day for the Jews when the Nazi Hitler began his campaign of persecution against them," writes Sif Ali Algeruan of Al-Hayat al-Jedida.

> They began to disseminate, in a terrifying manner, pictures of mass shootings in directed at them, and to invent the shocking story about the gas ovens in

ANTI-ZIONISM *is* ANTI-SEMITISM

which, according to them, Hitler used to burn them. The newspapers are filled with pictures of Jews who were mowed down by Hitler's machine guns, and of Jews being led to the gas ovens. In these pictures they concentrated on women, babies, and old people, and they took advantage of it, in order to elicit sympathy towards them, when they demand financial reparations, contributions and grants from all over the world. The truth is that the persecution of the Jews is a myth, that the Jews dubbed "the tragedy of the Holocaust" and took advantage of, in order to elicit sympathy towards them.

Since the beginning of the second intifada in September 2000, Israel has been subjected to a worldwide campaign of delegitimization in the media and international forums by political leaders and intellectuals. Extremists of the Left and Right have joined together in their hatred of the Jewish State, resulting in a dramatic increase in anti-Semitic incidents, including physical attacks on Jews. These attacks on Israel's legitimacy have been accompanied by attacks on Jewish targets throughout the world, particularly in Europe. Antisemitic incidents have included bombings of synagogues and Jewish schools, vandalism and desecration of Jewish cemeteries, death threats, and unprovoked violence against Jews, including murder. These hate crimes against Jewish individuals and institutions are often disguised as "anti-Zionist" actions.

One of the consequences of Palestinian antisemitism has been an increase in attacks on Jewish targets in the Arab world, such as the April 2002 terrorist attack on the ancient synagogue in Djerba, Tunisia, when 12 European tourists, four local Arabs, and a Jew were murdered. In Istanbul in November 2003, twenty-three persons were murdered, six of them Jews, and hundreds wounded in suicide bombing attacks on two synagogues.

The following are excerpts from a report on antisemitism in Europe in 2002 by the European Union's European Monitoring Center on Racism and Xenophobia:

> Physical attacks on Jews and the desecration and destruction of synagogues were acts often committed by young Muslim perpetrators... Many of these attacks occurred either during or after pro-Palestinian demonstrations, which were also used by radical Islamists for hurling verbal abuse. In addition, radical Islamist circles were responsible for placing anti-Semitic propaganda on the Internet and in Arab-language media.... In the extreme left-wing scene anti-Semitic remarks were to be found mainly in the context of pro-Palestinian and anti-globalization rallies and in newspaper articles using anti-Semitic stereotypes in their criticism of Israel.... In the heated public debate on Israeli politics and the boundary between criticism of Israel and antisemitism, individuals who

are not politically active and do not belong to one of the ideological camps mentioned above become motivated to voice their latent anti-Semitic attitudes (mostly in the form of telephone calls and insulting letters). Opinion polls prove that in some European countries a large percentage of the population harbors anti-Semitic attitudes and views, but that these usually remain latent.... Observers point to an "increasingly blatant anti-Semitic Arab and Muslim media," including audiotapes and sermons, in which the call is not only made to join the struggle against Israel but also against Jews across the world. Although leading Muslim organizations express their opposition to this propaganda, observers assume that calling for the use of violence may influence readers and listeners.... We recommend that the EUMC request state authorities to acknowledge at the highest level the extraordinary dangers posed by anti-Semitic violence in the European context.

France, with its large Muslim minority, stands out as the country in which the greatest number and most serious anti-Semitic incidents occurred in comparison with other countries in the world. These included: The physical attack and harassment of Jews all over the country, the torching of synagogues, the desecration of cemeteries, and threats and dissemination of radical anti-Semitic and anti-Israel propaganda. The perpetrators came mainly from among young North African Muslim immigrants.

It should be noted that many attacks were the result of organized action rather than spontaneous mob activity or vandalism, which targeted Jews in reaction to events in Israel and were part of efforts to de-legitimize Israel and Zionism. These attacks were not limited to a focus on Israel. They were blatant manifestations of antisemitism involving incitement to attack Jews everywhere—incitement in mosques and other concentrations of Muslims to attack Jews "because they are responsible for everything 'evil' in the world."

In other European countries, especially those with large Muslim populations, there have been serious physical attacks on Jews, in addition to verbal harassment, graffiti, and cemetery desecrations. Jews have been physically attacked in Belgium, in addition to Jewish community facilities. Universities throughout Europe have become active centers of anti-Semitic and anti-Israel propaganda and threats. In Britain, Jews have been attacked, and synagogues and other community facilities have been desecrated.

Numerous antisemitic incidents have occurred in the Scandinavian countries, especially Denmark and Sweden, whose governments have been extremely critical of Israel. In Germany in 2002, there were a large number of anti-Semitic incidents, including physical attacks on Jews and the desecration of cemeteries by neo-Nazi and Islamic elements.

In Eastern Europe and Russia, antisemitic activities have mostly taken the form of propaganda and demonstrations. In

ANTI-ZIONISM is ANTI-SEMITISM

Russia, Jews were injured, and synagogues and other Jewish facilities were damaged. One Russian innovation was the placing along highways of booby-trapped signs with antisemitic slurs, which exploded when someone would try to take them down. These signs caused one fatality and several injuries in Russia and led to several copycat incidents in Ukraine.

An analysis that appeared in the *London Spectator* regarding the attitude of the British clergy acknowledged: "Animosity towards Israel has its roots in a deep hatred of the Jews."[119] This was echoed by the prominent Italian journalist Oriana Fallaci, who strongly denounced the double standard practiced in Europe today: "One standard for the Jews and another for Christians and Muslims, one vis-à-vis Jewish blood that has been spilled and another vis-à-vis other blood. And there is the lack of proportion between attacks on Israel, which are not political criticism but saturated with anti-Semitic terms, and what Israel actually does."[120]

There is an ironic Jewish joke that defines antisemitism as a disease suffered by Gentiles that is often fatal to Jews. As such, there is not much that is new about the so-called "new antisemitism" of the twenty-first century. One difference, as noted by Israeli parliamentarian Michael Melchior, is the strange coalitions of the new antisemitism. "In the US, for example, there is striking cooperation, especially through antisemitic websites, between neo-Nazis and Islamic fundamentalists," he wrote. "After 9/11, both groups claimed Jews were behind the attacks. That's not a new phenomenon. It was discovered that the Iraqi Embassy in

Sweden had financed neo-Nazi activities, even though neo-Nazis hate the Muslims."

Israeli historian Robert Wistrich has noted that it is radical Muslims and not necessarily white Europeans who are leading the present wave of antisemitism. The Islamic world imported antisemitism from Europe, "converted it to Islam" as part of the Israeli-Palestinian conflict, and exported it back to Europe and the West in general, utilizing the Muslim Diaspora and anti-West and anti-globalization elements.

Regarding the new blood libels of the new century, Wistrich concluded:

> Arab governments are doing nothing against these fabrications, and in essence legitimize them in order to protect themselves from the wrath of their own embittered citizens, deprived of democracy, freedom of speech and basic human rights. Against this background it is clear how millions of Muslims are prepared to believe every falsehood, including the blowing up of the World Trade Center by the Mossad. . . .
>
> This "Semitic" antisemitism is especially threatening when it is on a mission from Allah, and the 1979 revolution in Iran against the "Great Devil" (America and the "Crusader" West) and the "Jewish-Zionist Devil" bears witness to this. This is total war, because it is mainly a religious war.

Antisemitism of this kind has diverted the Jihad from its original objective and turned it into a death cult.

This growing trend is gradually becoming not an echo but an amplification of what happened in pre-World War II Germany. While the cries against the Jews grew louder in Germany, the rest of the world simply shrugged it off with comments such as, "Oh, I don't think that is emblematic of all the Germans." However, it didn't matter if it was or not—their silence made them accomplices in the murders by such "non-representative" Germans. Are we any less guilty if we stand quiet and let the cry to kill Jews grow among Arabs and in Europe, France, Australia, and Brazil? How far do we need to let such blatant hatred go before we should do something about it? My feeling is that it has already gone too far.

There is perhaps no better sign that the spirit of anti-Christ is again on the rise than this reemergence of rabid antisemitism. Satan will, of course, hate Jews first, and then Christians, because they were the first to cut a covenant with God. And we can be no less guilty as a nation for being silent about racism towards Jews than we have been because we acquiesced to racism towards African Americans as our constitution was being written. We realize with Thomas Jefferson that God's "justice cannot sleep forever," and with Isser Harel, "Hitler first killed Jews, then he killed Christians. Our culture and our democracies are the root of the rage. If we're right, they are wrong."

This is why I started the Jerusalem Prayer Team. September 11th, 2001, was a tragic day in American history. The attack was a physical manifestation of a battle that had been lost weeks, months, and possibly years before because of a lack of prayer. Osama bin Laden had been verbally attacking America for years, but the church was asleep. The demonic powers influencing him needed to be violently confronted by holy angels on assignment through the power of prayer, as in the time of Daniel.

Praying for the peace of Jerusalem is not praying for stones or dirt. They don't weep or bleed. It is praying for God's protection over the lives of the citizens of Jerusalem. It is praying for revival. It is praying for God's grace to be poured out on the Bible land and all over the Middle East—prayer that holy angels will defeat demonic powers in a battle that cannot be seen with the natural eye. Mother Teresa was one of the first people to tell me she prayed daily for the peace of Jerusalem according to Psalms 122:6. She said, "Love is not something you say; it's something you do." I believe that with all my heart.

The House of Israel is in a state of terror, as are all the children of the Bible land. They need the Lord to answer them in their day of terror. They need the God of Jacob to defend them. They need help from the sanctuary and strength out of Zion. It is time for us to wake up, but will that awakening be great or rude? According to Genesis 12:3, God told Abraham that He would "bless those who bless you, and... curse him who curses you."[121] Which have we been as a nation: A blessing or a curse to Israel?

Is it possible that America might have been spared the Great Depression if she had not ignored the plight of the Jews? Is it possible that tens of thousands of Americans would not have died in World War II if America had not closed her doors to the House of Israel (Divine intervention)? If so, God-fearing Americans must stand up now before it is too late. "And I will bless them that bless thee, and curse him that curseth thee: and in thee shall all families of the earth be blessed" (Genesis 12:3, KJV).

A FINAL WORD:

5 REASONS TO STAND WITH ISRAEL

There are numerous reasons why, as Christians, you and I should stand with Israel in these last days. The following are just five of the imperatives for championing God's Chosen People:

1. God promises to bless those who bless Israel and curse him who curses Israel. (Genesis 12:3.)

This verse was God's promise to Abraham forevermore. Jehovah would bless those men who bestowed compassion and benevolence upon His people. This was not just an Old Testament command; the New Testament gives several examples of God's generosity to Gentiles who aided the Jewish people—Cornelius in Acts 10, the Centurion in Luke 7, and Julius in Acts 27, the centurion who was charged with delivering Paul to Rome. When the ship on which they sailed ran aground near Malta, he saved Paul from certain death at the hands of the other soldiers onboard. Each of these men, and many others, aided the Jewish people, as have a myriad of others down through the ages and even today.

2. God has raised up intercessors to pray for the Jewish people.

In Numbers, we are instructed how to pray for the Children of Israel:

> *The Lord bless you and keep you; the Lord make his face shine on you and be gracious to you; the Lord turn his face toward you and give you peace* (Numbers 6:24-26, NIV).

When we pray for Jerusalem we are saying, "Maranatha, come Messiah!" The Messiah is indeed coming to Jerusalem! That is something on which both Jews and Christians agree.

3. God has called us to be watchmen on the walls—caretakers of the House of Israel.

Isaiah 62:6-7 (NIV) records: I have posted watchmen on your walls, Jerusalem; they will never be silent day or night. You who call on the Lord, give yourselves no rest, and give him no rest till he establishes Jerusalem and makes her the praise of the earth.

As believers, we assume the name of Christ and serve the God of Abraham, Isaac, and Jacob and find strength. We heed the warnings of the prophets Isaiah, Jeremiah, Ezekiel, Daniel,

Hosea, and Joel and find direction. We sing the Psalms of King David and find hope.

The mention of Jerusalem, our spiritual city, quickens our hearts. We stand with our Jewish brothers and sisters in the battle against antisemitism and the threat of terrorism and reap the blessings of God.

4. God's Word says we are to comfort the House of Israel (Isaiah 40:1-2).

As Christians, we are not engaged in terrorist attacks against our enemies; we are intent upon doing God's work on Earth for Him. We are strong advocates for the State of Israel—defenders of God's Word and His children, supporting programs to provide food, clothing, housing, and more for Jews who have returned to Israel.

5. Jesus' final message to His disciples in Matthew 25:40 calls us to serve those in need, including those in Israel.

> *The King will reply, "Truly I tell you, whatever you did for one of the least of these brothers and sisters of mine, you did for me."*

Not once did Jesus deny His Jewish heritage. The Bible tells us that Mary and Joseph observed the ordinances for the birth of a baby—He was circumcised on the eighth day; He observed the feasts of the Jews; He wore the tallit, the prayer shawl, when He prayed.

He honored His brethren, and you and I are to do the same. For centuries, the Jewish people have seen only the harshness of those who profess to be Christians yet practice antisemitism. The time has come for you and me to practice loving acts of humanity toward the descendants of Abraham, Isaac, and Jacob.

> *Then the King will say to those on his right, "Come, you who are blessed by my Father; take your inheritance, the kingdom prepared for you since the creation of the world. For I was hungry, and you gave me something to eat; I was thirsty, and you gave me something to drink; I was a stranger, and you invited me in; I needed clothes, and you clothed me; I was sick, and you looked after me, I was in prison, and you came to visit me"* (Matthew 25:34-36, NIV).

APPENDIX:

PRAYERS AND BLESSINGS FOR ISRAEL

1 Samuel 12:22, NIV

For the sake of his great name the Lord will not reject his people, because the Lord was pleased to make you his own.

Psalm 17:6-9, NIV

I call on you, my God, for you will answer me;
   turn your ear to me and hear my prayer.
Show me the wonders of your great love,
   you who save by your right hand
   those who take refuge in you from their foes.
Keep me as the apple of your eye;
   hide me in the shadow of your wings
from the wicked who are out to destroy me,
   from my mortal enemies who surround me.

Psalm 17:16-19, NIV
As for me, I call to God,
   and the Lord saves me.
Evening, morning and noon
   I cry out in distress,
   and he hears my voice.
He rescues me unharmed
   from the battle waged against me,
   even though many oppose me.
God, who is enthroned from of old,
   who does not change—
he will hear them and humble them,
   because they have no fear of God.

Psalm 25:22, NIV
Deliver Israel, O God,
   from all their troubles!

Psalm 100, NIV
Shout for joy to the Lord, all the earth.
Worship the Lord with gladness;
   come before him with joyful songs.
Know that the Lord is God.
   It is he who made us, and we are his;
   we are his people, the sheep of his pasture.

Enter his gates with thanksgiving
and his courts with praise;
give thanks to him and praise his name.
For the Lord is good and his love endures forever;
his faithfulness continues through all generations.

Psalm 102:12-16, NIV
But you, Lord, sit enthroned forever;
your renown endures through all generations.
You will arise and have compassion on Zion,
for it is time to show favor to her;
the appointed time has come.
For her stones are dear to your servants;
her very dust moves them to pity.
The nations will fear the name of the Lord,
all the kings of the earth will revere your glory.
For the Lord will rebuild Zion
and appear in his glory.

Psalm 122:6-8, NIV
Pray for the peace of Jerusalem:
"May those who love you be secure.
May there be peace within your walls
and security within your citadels."
For the sake of my family and friends,
I will say, "Peace be within you."

Proverbs 16:7, NIV
When the Lord takes pleasure in anyone's way,
    he causes their enemies to make peace with them.

Isaiah 45:3-4, NIV
I will give you hidden treasures,
    riches stored in secret places,
so that you may know that I am the Lord,
    the God of Israel, who summons you by name.
For the sake of Jacob my servant,
    of Israel my chosen,
I summon you by name
    and bestow on you a title of honor. . .

Isaiah 45:17-18, NIV
But Israel will be saved by the Lord
    with an everlasting salvation;
you will never be put to shame or disgraced,
    to ages everlasting. For this is what the Lord says—
he who created the heavens,
    he is God;
he who fashioned and made the earth,
    he founded it;
he did not create it to be empty,
    but formed it to be inhabited—
he says:
"I am the Lord,
    and there is no other.

Jeremiah 33:6-11, NIV
"'Nevertheless, I will bring health and healing to it; I will heal my people and will let them enjoy abundant peace and security. I will bring Judah and Israel back from captivity and will rebuild them as they were before. I will cleanse them from all the sin they have committed against me and will forgive all their sins of rebellion against me. Then this city will bring me renown, joy, praise and honor before all nations on earth that hear of all the good things I do for it; and they will be in awe and will tremble at the abundant prosperity and peace I provide for it.' "This is what the Lord says: 'You say about this place, "It is a desolate waste, without people or animals." Yet in the towns of Judah and the streets of Jerusalem that are deserted, inhabited by neither people nor animals, there will be heard once more the sounds of joy and gladness, the voices of bride and bridegroom, and the voices of those who bring thank offerings to the house of the Lord, saying, "Give thanks to the Lord Almighty, for the Lord is good; his love endures forever." For I will restore the fortunes of the land as they were before,' says the Lord.

Ezekiel 34:11-15, NIV
"'For this is what the Sovereign Lord says: I myself will search for my sheep and look after them. As a shepherd looks after his scattered flock when he is with them, so will I look after my sheep. I will rescue them from all the places where they were scattered on a day of clouds and darkness. I will bring them out from the nations and gather them from the countries, and I will bring them

into their own land. I will pasture them on the mountains of Israel, in the ravines and in all the settlements in the land. I will tend them in a good pasture, and the mountain heights of Israel will be their grazing land. There they will lie down in good grazing land, and there they will feed in a rich pasture on the mountains of Israel. I myself will tend my sheep and have them lie down, declares the Sovereign Lord.

Ezekiel 34:25-31, NIV
"'I will make a covenant of peace with them and rid the land of savage beasts so that they may live in the wilderness and sleep in the forests in safety. I will make them and the places surrounding my hill a blessing. I will send down showers in season; there will be showers of blessing. The trees will yield their fruit and the ground will yield its crops; the people will be secure in their land. They will know that I am the Lord, when I break the bars of their yoke and rescue them from the hands of those who enslaved them. They will no longer be plundered by the nations, nor will wild animals devour them. They will live in safety, and no one will make them afraid I will provide for them a land renowned for its crops, and they will no longer be victims of famine in the land or bear the scorn of the nations. Then they will know that I, the Lord their God, am with them and that they, the Israelites, are my people, declares the Sovereign Lord. You are my sheep, the sheep of my pasture, and I am your God, declares the Sovereign Lord.'"

Joel 2:19-27, NIV
The Lord replied to them: "I am sending you grain,
   new wine and olive oil,
   enough to satisfy you fully;
never again will I make you
   an object of scorn to the nations.
"I will drive the northern horde far from you,
   pushing it into a parched and barren land;
its eastern ranks will drown in the Dead Sea
   and its western ranks in the Mediterranean Sea.
And its stench will go up;
   its smell will rise." Surely he has done great things!
Do not be afraid, land of Judah;
   be glad and rejoice.
Surely the Lord has done great things!
Do not be afraid, you wild animals,
   for the pastures in the wilderness are becoming green.
The trees are bearing their fruit;
   the fig tree and the vine yield their riches.
Be glad, people of Zion,
   rejoice in the Lord your God,
for he has given you the autumn rains
   because he is faithful.
He sends you abundant showers,
   both autumn and spring rains, as before.
The threshing floors will be filled with grain;
   the vats will overflow with new wine and oil.

"I will repay you for the years the locusts have eaten—
   the great locust and the young locust,
   the other locusts and the locust swarm—
my great army that I sent among you.
You will have plenty to eat, until you are full,
   and you will praise the name of the Lord your God,
   who has worked wonders for you;
never again will my people be shamed.
Then you will know that I am in Israel,
   that I am the Lord your God,
   and that there is no other;
never again will my people be shamed.

Joel 3:16, NIV
The Lord will roar from Zion
   and thunder from Jerusalem;
   the earth and the heavens will tremble.
But the Lord will be a refuge for his people,
   a stronghold for the people of Israel.

ENDNOTES

1. Dennis Prager, "Yes, Anti-Zionism Is Antisemitism," Townhall, Dec. 12, 2023. Accessed at townhall.com/columnists/dennisprager/2023/12/12/yes-anti-zionism-is-antisemitism-n2632292.

2. Adapted from my op-ed "Real Christians Are Zionists and Friends of the Jewish People," Charisma News, October 29, 2018. Accessed at charismanews.com/opinion/standing-with-israel/73805-real-christians-are-zionists-and-friends-of-the-jewish-people.

3. Adapted from my article "The Beth Israel Congregation attack and antisemitism," January 18, 2022. Accessed at israelhayom.com/opinions/the-beth-israel-congregation-attack-and-antisemitism.

4. Robert Solomon Wistrich, *Who's Who in Nazi Germany* (Hove, East Sussex, UK: Psychology Press, 2002), p. 118.

5. John Toland, *Adolf Hitler* (London: Book Club Associates, 1977), p. 116.

6. Houston Stewart Chamberlain, *Letters* (1882-1924 and correspondence with Emperor Wilhelm II) (Munich: F. Bruckmann, 1928), p. 124. (Translated from the German by Alexander Jacob.)

7. "Adolf Hitler," *Deutsche Presse*, April 20-21, 1944, p. 1.

8. Deborah E. Lipstadt, *Beyond Belief: The American Press and the Coming of the Holocaust, 1933-1945* (New York: Simon and Schuster, 1993), pp. 79-80.

9. "Wannsee Conference, Jewish Virtual Library; http://www.jewishvirtuallibrary.org/jsource/judaica/ejud_0002_0020_0_20606.html; accessed March 2012.

10. Ibid. p. 44

11. Ibid. pp. 47-48

12. "*SS Exodus*"; http://en.wikipedia.org/wiki/SS_Exodus; accessed October 2011.

13. Norman Bentwich, *For Zion's Sake: A Biography of Judah L. Magnes* (Philadelphia: Jewish Publication Society, 1954), p. 267.

14. Ibid. p. 90

15. "The Little Known Story of a Christian Minister who helped make Israel Possible," *The Jewish Magazine*, June 2008, http://www.jewishmag.com/134mag/exodus_grauel/exodus_grauel.htm; accessed May 2103.

16. mideastweb.org/trusteeship.htm; United States Proposal for Temporary United Nations Trusteeship for Palestine Source: Department of State Bulletin, vol. 18, No. 457, 4 April 1948, p. 451; accessed December 2013.

17. Ibid.

18. Arab League Declaration on the Intervention in Palestine, 15 May 1948, wikisource.org/wiki/Cablegram_from_the_Secretary-General_of_the_League_of_Arab_States_to_the_Secretary-General_of_the_United_Nations; accessed December 2913; accessed December 2013.

19. The Palestine National Charter, July 17, 1968, Article 22, jewishvirtuallibrary.org/jsource/Peace/PLO_Covenant.html; accessed December 2013.

20. "Oslo II Agreement," December 28, 1995, acpr.org.il/resources/oslo2.html; accessed December 2013.

21. Charles Krauthammer, *The Weekly Standard*, May 11, 1998, eternaltreeofpeace.com/; accessed October 2013.

22. Rockwell Lazarus, "Who Are the Palestinians? What and Where is Palestine?" newswithviews.com/Israel/israel14.htm/; accessed October 2013.

23. Christian Assemblies International; cai.org/bible-studies/bible-prophecy-0; accessed May 2012.

24. "*Lawrence of Arabia*" was a 1962 British-American film based on the life of T. E. Lawrence. The film starred Peter O'Toole in the title role. O'Toole died in December 2013.

25 Colonel C. G. Powles, "The History of the Canterbury Mounted Rifles, 1914–1919," New Zealand Electronic Text Center, p. 195; nzetc.org/tm/scholarly/tei-WH1CMRi-t1-body-d14.html; accessed June 2010.

26 Elli Wohlgelernteri, "One Day that Shook the World," *The Jerusalem Post*, 30 April 1998; accessed October 2013.

27 George Gilder, *The Israel Test* (Minneapolis, MN: Richard Vigilante Books, 2009), pp. 234-235.

28 David Naggar, "The Case for a Larger Israel," http://alargerisrael.blogspot.com/; accessed October 2013.

29 Israel Matzav, "I will bless those who bless you, and I will curse him that curses you," Thursday, April 22, 2010, israelmatzav.blogspot.com/search?q=I+will+bless+them+that+bless+you; accessed June 2013.

30 Daniel 4

31 Martin Gilbert, *Churchill and the Jews* (Toronto: McClelland & Steward, 2007), pp. 160-161.

32 Alfred Lord Tennyson, thinkexist.com/quotation/more_things_are_wrought_by_prayer_than_this_world/12679.html; accessed October 2013.

33 Carino Casas, "Why the Church Should Stand with Israel," roamingchile.com/2013/06/why-the-church-should-stand-with-israel/; accessed October 2013.

34 George Bakalav, "10 Reasons Why Christians Should Support Israel—whether it's Popular or Not," January 20, 2009, voices.yahoo.com/10-reasons-why-christians-support-israel-whether-2498811.html; accessed November 2013.

35 Senator James Inhofe (R-OK), "Seven Reasons Why Israel has the Right to Her Land," senate.gov/~Inhofe/fl030402.html; accessed September 2013.

36 Fuel for Truth; fuelfortruth.org/thetruth/truth_10.asp; accessed April 2010.

37 Michael D. Evans, *Save Jerusalem* (Euless, TX: Bedford Books, 1995), p. 94.

38 Moshe Dayan, Address in the General Assembly by Foreign Minister Dayan, September 27, 1979; mfa.gov.il/MFA/Foreign%20Relations/Israels%20Foreign%20Relations%20since%201947/1979-1980/46%20Address%20in%20the%20General%20Assembly%20by%20Foreign%20Mini; accessed April 2010.

39 Christopher Wise, *Derrida, Africa and the Middle East* (New York, NY: St. Martin's Press, 2009), p. 59.

40 Phillip Misselwitz and Tim Rieniets, *City of Collision: Jerusalem and the Principles of Conflict Urbanism*; (Germany: Die Deutsche Bibliothek, 2006), p. 49.

41 "The Mists of Antiquity 2000-1000 BC, Teddy Kollek and Moshe Pearlman, *Jerusalem: Sacred City of Mankind*, Steimatzky Ltd., Jerusalem, 1991, http://cojs.org/cojswiki/The_Mists_of_Antiquity_2000-1000_BC%2C_Teddy_Kollek_and_Moshe_Pearlman%2C_Jerusalem:_Sacred_City_of_Mankind%2C_Steimatzky_Ltd.%2C_Jerusalem%2C_1991; accessed November 2013.

42 Amikam Elad, "Why did 'Abd al-Malik Build the Dome of the Rock?" Bayt-al-Maqdis: 'Abd al-Malik's Jerusalem, ed. Julian Raby and Jeremy Johns (Oxford: Oxford University Press, 1992), vol. 1, p. 48.

43 Walter Brueggemann, *Isaiah 40-66* (Louisville, KY: Westminster John Knox Press, 1998), p18.

44 Corrie ten Boom, with John and Elizabeth Sherrill, *The Hiding Place* (Old Tappan, NJ: Spire Books, 1971), p. 61.

45 Ibid. p. 63

46 Ibid. p. 101

47 Ibid. p. 196

48 Msgr. John Oesterreicher, "Auschwitz, the Christian, and the Council," *CatholicCulture.org*; catholicculture.org/culture/library/view.cfm?id=609&repos=1&subrepos=0&searchid=527089; accessed June 2010.

49 Corrie ten Boom with John and Elizabeth Sherrill, *The Hiding Place*, p. 212.

50   Corrie ten Boom with John and Elizabeth Sherrill, *The Hiding Place*, p. 238.

51   Quoted by George Gilder in *The Israel Test* (Minneapolis, MN: Richard Vigilante Books, 2009), p. 22.

52   Arthur W. Pink, "The Death of the Firstborn," Old Testament Study: Exodus 11:1-10, scripturestudies.com/Vol11/K10/ot.html; accessed November 2013.

53   William L. Shirer, *The Rise and Fall of the Third Reich*, pp. 10–11.

54   "Lloyd George and Hitler ... Comments on His Visit to Germany and Meeting with Hitler in 1936," *Daily Express*, September 17, 1936; ww2hc.org/articles/lloyd_george_and_hitler.htm; accessed August 2011.

55   "Letter to an Anti-Zionist Friend," Rev. Martin Luther King, Jr., *The Saturday Review*, XVLII, (August 1967) 76

56   Abdulhak Adnan, *La Science chez les Turcs ottoman* (Paris: 1939), 87, 98-99 in Bernard Lewis, *What Went Wrong?: The Clash Between Islam and Modernity in the Middle East* (New York: Perennial, 2002), 7.

57   Lewis, *What Went Wrong?*, 9.

58   Albert Hourani, *Arabic Thought in the Liberal Age, 1798-1939* (Oxford: Oxford University Press, 1970), 37 in Dore Gold, *Hatred's Kingdom: How Saudi Arabia Supports the New Global Terrorism* (Washington DC: Regnery Publishing, Inc., 2003), 19.

59   Gold, *Hatred's Kingdom*, 26-27.

60   Gold, *Hatred's Kingdom*, 13.

61   Mark 12:17.

62   Nadav Safran, *Saudi Arabia: The Ceaseless Quest for Security* (Cambridge: Harvard University Press, 1985), 58 in Gold, *Hatred's Kingdom*, 60.

63   John Loftus and Mark Aarons, *The Secret War Against the Jews: How Western Espionage Betrayed the Jewish People* (New York: St. Martin's Griffin, 1994), 71.

64   Sources: Fonzi, Gaeton. *The Last Investigation*. Thunder's Mouth Press, 1994; Lebor, Adam. *Hitler's Secret Bankers*. Birch Lane Press, 1997; Loftus, John & Aarons, Mark. *The Secret War Against The Jews*. St. Martins Press, 1994; Simpson, Christopher. *Blowback*. Weidenfeld & Nicholson, 1988; Simpson, Christopher. *The Splendid Blond Beast*. Grove Press, 1993.

65   Secretary of State John Foster Dulles in Feb. 1957 quoted on p. 99 of Donald Neff, Fallen Pillars.

66   Nawaf E. Obaid, "Improving U.S. Intelligence Analysis on the Saudi Arabian Decision-Making Process," (Master's Thesis, John F. Kennedy School of Government, Harvard University, 1998), 13 in Gold, *Hatred's Kingdom*, 60.

67   Safran, *Saudi Arabia*), 221 in Gold, *Hatred's Kingdom*, 87. Safran's source was the Saudi Arabian Ministry of Petroleum and Natural Resources.

68   The State Department's U.S. Commission on International Religious Freedom was the first government agency to step forward publicly and finger Saudi Wahhabism as a "strategic threat" to the United States. See Tom Carter's article, "Saudis' Strict Islam called a 'Threat,'" *The Washington Times* (November 19, 2003). Online at washtimes.com/world/20031118-113127-4259r.htm. Accessed: 26 November 2003.

69   Timmerman, *Preachers of Hate*, 66.

70   Safran, *Saudi Arabia*), 221 in Gold, *Hatred's Kingdom*, 119. Safran's source was the Saudi Arabian Ministry of Petroleum and Natural Resources.

71   Gold, *Hatred's Kingdom*, 126.

72   Blaine Hardin, "Saudis Seek U.S. Muslims for their Sect," *New York Times*, October 20, 2001 in Gold, *Hatred's Kingdom*, 126.

73   Reza F. Safa, *Inside Islam* (Orlando, FL: Creation House, 1997)

74   Cockburn, *Dangerous Liaison*, 194.

75   Gold, *Hatred's Kingdom*, 127.

76   Tom Carter, "Saudis; Strict Islam called a 'Threat,'" *The Washington Times* (November 19, 2003). Online at washtimes.com/world/20031118-113127-4259r.htm. Accessed: 24 November 2003.

77   IslamOnline.net, "Sudanese Islamist Group To Look For Office Abroad." Online at islam-online.net/iol-english/dowalia/news-14-2-2000/topnews5.asp. Created: 14 February 2000. Accessed: 26 November 2003.

78   Tom Robbins, "The Lesson: Incident at the Towers, 1993," *New York Daily News*, December 9, 1998 in Richard Miniter, *Losing bin Laden: How Bill Clinton's Failure Unleashed Global Terror* (Washington, D.C.: Regnery Publishing, Inc., 2003), 19.

79   Miniter, *Losing bin Laden*, xvi, xix. (Insert added.)

80   White House Report, "Clinton on Life, Career, Decisions" (Friday, August 11, 2000). Online at: usembassy-australia.state.gov/hyper/2000/0811/epf501.htm. Accessed: 26 November 2003.

81   See Luke 2.

82   Simon Tisdall, "Symbolic gesture seals hopes to end blood and tears" *Guardian Unlimited* (September 14, 1993). Online at: guardiancentury.co.uk/1990-1999/Story/0,6051,112648,00.html. Accessed: 30 November 2003.

83   Ambassador Dore Gold, an interview with Amnon Lord, October 2003.

84   Elliot Engel, address during the Jerusalem Summit: Building Peace on Truth, October 12-14, 2003.

85   Alan M. Dershowitz, *Why Terrorism Works: Understanding the Threat, Responding to the Challenge* (New Haven and London: Yale University Press, 2002), 2.

86   Yoram Etinger, an interview with Amnon Lord, Oct. 25, 2003.

87   Tal Silberstein, an interview with Amnon Lord, Nov.2, 2003.

88   Yossef Bodansky, *The High Cost of Peace: How Washington's Middle East Policy Left America Vulnerable to Terrorism*. (Roseville, CA: Forum, 2002), 223.

89   Tal Silberstein, an interview with Amnon Lord, Nov.2, 2003.

90   *The New Yorker* (March 24, 2003).

91   Ibid.

92   lyrics.com/lyric/3403160/John%20Lennon/Imagine/accessed 5/25

93   Joel Mowbray, *Dangerous Diplomacy: How the State Department Threatens America's Security* (Washington DC: Regnery Publishing, Inc., 2003), 9-10.

94   Mortimer B. Zuckerman, "Graffiti on History's Walls," *U.S. News & World Report* vol. 135, no. 15 (November 3, 2003), 47-48.

95   Mark Gaffney, *Dimona, The Third Temple: The Story Behind the Vanunu Revelation* (Beltsville, MD: Amana, 1989).

96   2 Chronicles 33:7 [insert added].

97   2 Chronicles 7:14.

98   See Appendix C for more information on sales to these countries.

99   See Appendices A and B for more information on U.S. aid and sales to Israel.

100 Hersh, *The Samson Option*, 20.

101 Ibid., 119.

102 Ibid., 121.

103 Ibid.

104 Judges 16:28.

105 Judges 16:30.

106 Hersh, *The Samson Option*, 9.

107 Bodansky, 568.

108 George Santayana, *The Life of Reason*, Volume 1, 1905

109 Thomas Jefferson, "Commerce between Master and Slave," 1782. Available online at http://douglassarchives.org/jeff_a51.htm. (Emphasis added.)

110 Abraham Lincoln, "Second Inauguration Address." Available online at: law.ou.edu/hist/lincoln2.html. Accessed 22 December 2003.

111 "Speech by Prime Minister Mahathir Mohamad of Malaysia to the Tenth Islamic Summit Conference, Putrajaya, Malaysia," (October 16, 2003). Complete text of the speech available online at: adl.org/Anti-semitism/malaysian.asp. Accessed: 22 December 2003.

112 [183] *Der Parteitag der Arheit vom 6 bis 13 September 1937: Offizieller Bericht uber den Verlauf des Reichsparteitages mit samtlichen Kongressreden* (Munich, 1938), p. 157, in Friedlander, *Nazi Germany and the Jews*, 184-185.

113 Ibid., 177

114 [184] Gerald Fleming, *Hitler and the Final Solution* (Berkley: University of California Press, 1984), 17, in George Victor, *Hitler: The Pathology of Evil* (Dulles, VA: Brassey's, 1998), 123.

115 Phyllis Chesler, *The New Anti-Semitism: The Current Crisis and What We Must Do About It* (San Francisco, CA: Jossey-Bass, 2003), 218-223.

116 *The Palestine Times* No.114 (December 2000).

117 Associated Press (March 25, 2000).

118 Ahmad Abu Halabiya, "Friday sermon in Gaza mosque on October 13, 2000," broadcast live on Palestinian Authority TV.

119 Manley Philips, February 20, 2002.

120 *Courierra de la Sera* (April 12, 2002).

121 Genesis 12:3 NKJV.

JERUSALEM PRAYER TEAM
INTERNATIONAL

THE JERUSALEM PRAYER TEAM'S mission is to build Friends of Zion to guard, defend, and protect the Jewish people and to pray for the peace of Jerusalem. Our goal is to enlist, inform, and encourage 100 million people worldwide to pray for the peace of Jerusalem as directed in Psalm 122:6. The Jerusalem Prayer Team also raises funds to meet the humanitarian needs of the Jewish people in Israel, providing coats, blankets, and shelter for those in need. The ministry has a website at JerusalemPrayerTeam.com and more than 30 million followers on Facebook at Facebook.com/JerusalemPrayerTeam

JerusalemPrayerTeam.org